Does Democracy Matter?

Does Democracy Matter?

The United States and Global Democracy Support

Edited by Amb. Adrian A. Basora, Agnieszka Marczyk, and Maia Otarashvili

ROWMAN & LITTLEFIELD
Lanham • Boulder • New York • London

Published by Rowman & Littlefield
A wholly owned subsidiary of The Rowman & Littlefield Publishing Group, Inc.
4501 Forbes Boulevard, Suite 200, Lanham, Maryland 20706
www.rowman.com

Unit A, Whitacre Mews, 26-34 Stannary Street, London SE11 4AB

British Library Cataloguing in Publication Information Available

Library of Congress Cataloging-in-Publication Data

Names: Basora, Adrian (Adrian Anthony), 1938- editor. | Marczyk, Agnieszka, editor. | Otarashvili,
Maia, editor.
Title: Does democracy matter? : the United States and global democracy support / edited by Adrian
Basora, Agnieszka Marczyk and Maia Otarashvili.
Description: Lanham, Maryland : Rowman & Littlefield, 2017. | Includes bibliographical references
and index.
Identifiers: LCCN 2017006667 (print) | LCCN 2017010063 (ebook) | ISBN 9781538101841 (cloth :
alk. paper) | ISBN 9781538101858 (pbk. : alk. paper) | ISBN 9781538101865 (electronic)
Subjects: LCSH: Democracy—Government policy—United States. | United States—Foreign rela-
tions—21st century.
Classification: LCC JZ1480 .D64 2017 (print) | LCC JZ1480 (ebook) | DDC 327.1—dc23
LC record available at https://lccn.loc.gov/2017006667

♾ ™ The paper used in this publication meets the minimum requirements of American
National Standard for Information Sciences Permanence of Paper for Printed Library
Materials, ANSI/NISO Z39.48-1992.

Printed in the United States of America

Contents

Acknowledgments

This book is the result of a highly fruitful collaboration between many bright, passionate, and dedicated individuals who care deeply about the future of democracy. It is a culminating product of the Project on Democratic Transitions (PDT), based at the Foreign Policy Research Institute (FPRI) in Philadelphia, where scholars, policy practitioners, and other leaders are brought together by their belief that "a nation must think before it acts."

The editorial team would like to thank each and every scholar, research assistant, and intern who is or has been part of the PDT. We are particularly grateful to PDT Steering Group members Valerie Bunce, Tom Carothers, Pavol Demes, Bela Greskovits, Ivan Krastev, Katarina Mathernova, Alina Mungiu-Pippidi, Gabriel Petrescu, Jacques Rupnik, and Sharon Wolchik, and Ambassadors Avis Bohlen, Martin Butora, Tom Simons, and Kenneth Yalowitz, as well as our research coordinator Dr. Jean Boone. Their conceptual and experiential perspectives were essential in laying out the foundations for this project a decade ago.

We are deeply grateful to our chapter authors for participating in this stimulating year-long analytical and policy endeavor, which included numerous study groups and multiple chapter reviews. We appreciated the chance to work with them, hope to do so again, and wish them continued success in all their future endeavors.

We are also grateful for the invaluable support of the FPRI staff, especially Alan Luxenberg, Tally Helfont, Eli Gilman, and Michael Noonan. We benefited immensely from working with our fellow FPRI scholars John Haines, Chris Miller, Mitchell Orenstein, Christine Philippe-Blumauer, and Alexandra Sarlo, who participated in our study groups and provided valuable comments in reviewing the chapters in this volume. We also thank Allen Model, Bob Arsenault, Ryan Crow, and Thomas Melia for their participation in these study groups and providing valuable insights from their practitioner perspectives. We are deeply grateful to Christian Caryl of *Foreign Policy*'s Democracy Lab, who provided valuable assistance in organizing and moderating our October 2014 democracy conference.

We give very special thanks to FPRI Research Assistant Otto Kienitz for his essential and tireless work at every stage of researching, footnoting, proofreading, and otherwise contributing to the production of this book.

This entire endeavor would not have been possible without the financial support of the Leo Model Foundation and the Cotswold Foundation, and we are deeply grateful for the backing that they have so generously provided.

Finally, we would like to thank the staff of the Wilson Center and the leaders of its Kennan Institute, Matthew Rojansky and Will Pomerantz, for cosponsoring and hosting the October 2014 democracy conference that served as the driving force behind the production of this book.

Adrian A. Basora
Agnieszka Marczyk
Maia Otarashvili

Introduction

Adrian A. Basora and Kenneth Yalowitz

Does democracy matter? Is democracy on the defensive globally? If so, what can or should be done to support democracy throughout the world?

The present book arose from a conference dedicated to the following three related questions:

Should fostering democracy be a major goal of US foreign policy?
If so, how can its effectiveness be improved?
If not, what are the alternatives?

To be clear from the start, however, we have focused only on "soft power" and peaceful democracy support, and not on democracy imposition by military action.

One of our fellow authors lays out important "realist" arguments and cautions us about the limits and potential pitfalls of democracy promotion. Furthermore, all of the participants in this project are well aware of the many competing goals and priorities that must be weighed in developing an effective national security strategy. Nevertheless, we believe that the United States should provide *some* degree of support for the spread of democracy globally, even though several of our authors are critical of some of our current methods. Their individual chapters examine where and how democracy assistance might be delivered more effectively.

Our book also explores available knowledge and necessary new research agendas that could help us better understand both democratization efforts and authoritarian pushback in today's difficult context. For example, our authors examine the sharp contrast between the 1990s and the recent decade. They also explore whether authoritarian regimes can successfully impede democratization, what role external actors can play, how to streamline and improve existing mechanisms of US democracy assistance, and how to balance the need to reform and restore democracy in its transatlantic heartland with the promotion of democratic values and institutions in other areas of the world. Our goal is to assist the policy community in making sound decisions as to when and how to assist the growth of democracy abroad, and to participate in the ongoing academic, think tank, and public debates about the future of democracy relative to authoritarianism—arguably one of the most portentous debates facing the world today.

ORIGINS AND GOALS OF THE BOOK

This volume represents the culmination of over a decade of research and policy dialogue organized by the Project on Democratic Transitions (PDT), based at the Foreign Policy Research Institute (FPRI) in Philadelphia. The project began in 2005 as an attempt to better understand the dynamics of the postcommunist transitions of Eastern Europe. Our initial goal was to draw salient analytical and policy lessons from the dramatic political changes in the formerly Soviet-dominated countries of Eastern Europe following the fall of the Berlin Wall.

With the dissolution of the Soviet Union, however, our project expanded in geographic scope not only to the former constituent republics of the USSR but also to other selected postauthoritarian transitions. Our inquiry was driven by the wider implications of the postcommunist transitions, and by the unique opportunity they presented for comparative analysis. To lay the conceptual and historical groundwork for this study, the PDT team undertook an extensive review of the wider academic literature on postauthoritarian transitions, with a focus on those factors that seem to correlate most strongly with the success or failure of democratization.[1]

The authors of this introduction have participated in the FPRI PDT since its inception, the first as project director and the second as a member of the PDT's Transatlantic Steering Group, which has provided invaluable advice and perspective.

The former created the project based on his long-term analytical interest in comparative political and economic systems, combined with an operational and policy perspective based on thirty-plus years as an American diplomat involved in sequential phases of US democracy promotion. His career included assignments in Latin America during the "Alliance for Progress," in Spain during the early post-Franco years, at the National Security Council during and after the fall of the Berlin Wall, and as US ambassador to Czechoslovakia and then to the Czech Republic in the mid-1990s—a period of intense US support for Central European democratization.

The introduction's second author is also a former US diplomat, with numerous assignments in Moscow and Washington focused on Soviet affairs, followed by ambassadorships in Belarus and Georgia after the dissolution of the USSR. Democracy promotion was an integral component of US policy in both countries but the outcomes were quite different, with Georgia making progress in its transition but Belarus quickly moving to authoritarianism under President Lukashenko.

HISTORICAL CONTEXT

Democratization and Authoritarianism since 1989

Starting in 1989, the communist dictatorships of Eastern Europe crumbled with remarkable speed, as did the USSR two years later. Initially, Eastern Europe, the Baltics, and even the Russian Federation moved in a reformist, democratizing direction. By the end of the decade, several additional former Soviet republics and much of the former Yugoslavia seemed to be following suit. The momentum was driven in part by popular pro-democracy movements, such as those that culminated in Georgia's Rose Revolution in 2003 and Ukraine's Orange Revolution in 2004.

During this period, many commentators in both the academic and policy worlds came to see these liberalizing trends as the wave of the future and as powerful harbingers of further democratization, not only in postcommunist Europe/Eurasia but also in other regions of the world. By the early 2000s, the US government and many American nongovernmental organizations (NGOs) had begun to provide strong political encouragement and substantial financial and technical assistance for building democracy, not only in the postcommunist countries but also worldwide. The European Union (EU) quickly followed suit, with focus on its own "backyard," the postcommunist region. The fostering of democracy thus became a dominant theme in the eastward expansion of the EU, as well as in the foreign policies of individual European governments. Partly as a result of strong inducements and operational assistance from Brussels, by 2007, ten former communist countries had become members of the EU, all of them deemed to be either emerging or consolidated democracies.

However, the period from 2006 forward presents a striking contrast with the euphoric first fifteen years of postcommunist change. Despite notable success stories in Central Europe and the Baltic region during the past decennium, earlier hopes of definitive democratic consolidation have been disappointed in numerous postcommunist European countries, most notably in post-2010 Hungary, in certain Balkan states, and even in Poland. Farther east, in Russia and a majority of the post-Soviet states, the story has been largely one of autocratic consolidation, with even the halting democratic gains in Ukraine and Moldova currently under threat. Furthermore, in the Middle East, despite the initial euphoria of the Arab Spring, the reversals have been even starker, with a hardening of most of the region's authoritarian regimes in reaction to the initial breakthroughs of popular movements seeking liberalization.

One goal of the present study is thus to further explore the questions raised by the sharp contrast between the fifteen years of rapid democratization after the fall of the Berlin Wall, versus the subsequent decade of far more mixed results.

From its inception in 2005, the PDT has been enriched by a variety of external collaborations with outstanding scholars and experienced practitioners from both the United States and Europe. The most ambitious and recent of these collaborative efforts involved a partnership with the Woodrow Wilson Center and its Kennan Institute. This resulted in a major conference in Washington, D.C., in October 2014, the goals of which were to assess the extent of democratic stagnation and regression during the prior decade; to better understand the causes underlying these setbacks; and to stimulate fresh thinking as to whether the United States and its European and other allies should continue their longstanding policies of support for the spread of democracy abroad.[2]

The conference was designed to serve as the foundation for an extended, in-depth inquiry into these issues, rather than to be a standard, one-time event. The initial conference presentations were thus expanded into draft chapters, and then further refined through a series of study groups and other exchanges during the subsequent year. The present volume is the result of that year-long process of reflection and dialogue.

The Longer Historical Perspective

One of the important questions addressed in this book is whether authoritarian regimes, by cleverly manipulating nominally democratic institutions, can continue to successfully blunt the democratization trend, resulting in diminished prospects for the spread of democracy during the coming decade and beyond.

Certainly, the global picture is far less rosy today than it was in the 1990s or the early 2000s. But, viewed in the longer sweep of history, the postcommunist transitions so far still represent a significant net progression beyond the Cold War status quo. The picture beyond the postcommunist region is more mixed, with progress in some regions but predominantly negative results in others, particularly the Middle East. However, the full story is not yet in, and there is a wide range of views about what the future may hold.

As the eminent political scientist Samuel Huntington has documented, the history of democracy's progression since the American and French revolutions has involved multidecade waves of democratization, followed by long but less extensive "reverse waves."[3] These periodic pull-backs have undone some—but by no means all—of the earlier progress, thus creating a net positive "ratcheting" effect over the longer term. By Huntington's count, the world had twenty-nine democracies as of 1922, and thirty-six as of 1962. We now have eighty-six democracies, according to Freedom House's latest assessment.[4] And, as Larry Diamond points out in chapter 8, that number has held relatively steady over the past decade despite the discouraging reversals that at times dominate the headlines.

But history also makes it clear that the road from autocracy to democracy is at best a long and tortuous one, with inevitable twists and turns, and difficulty in discerning the route ahead. Furthermore, even if democracy is progressing in a majority of countries, there is nothing at all inevitable about any individual country moving onto the path of democratization or, once on it, continuing on this difficult journey. The same may well hold true for authoritarian regression—although some would argue that once autocracy reaches a certain degree of consolidation it may be harder to reverse than democracy.

A major issue underlying the topics addressed in this book, therefore, is whether we are now in the midst of a Huntington reverse wave, or whether instead the adverse developments in postcommunist Europe/Eurasia since 2006, and in the Arab world since 2012, are of a more localized or transitory nature. And, assuming that the die is not yet cast, we must also ask whether Washington, Brussels, and other democratic capitals can realistically make a significant difference in determining the outcome.

The Role of External Actors

External encouragement and support have at times made important contributions to the post-Soviet wave of democratic diffusion. This was particularly apparent in the American and Western European contributions to the rapid democratization progress of the 1990s in Central Europe and the Baltic countries. Nevertheless, the ultimate tasks of democratic consolidation are mainly internal ones and there are major limits on what the United States and other supportive outsiders can accomplish, even in the best of circumstances. Furthermore, the present global context is certainly much less favorable than it was in the 1990s. And to this we must regretfully add the diminished allure of the Western liberal democratic model as currently presented by the United States and the EU and its member states in view of their own prolonged economic travails, internal political challenges, the disruptive impact of mass migration, and terrorism.

Since at least 2004, Russian president Vladimir Putin has seen events such as the "color revolutions" in Georgia and Ukraine as an imminent existential threat to his regime, fostered by a hostile West. He and his inner circle have thus worked hard to stifle democracy both at home and in Russia's "Near Abroad." Moscow's undeclared war in Ukraine is the most dramatic and forceful manifestation of this counteroffensive, but the Putin regime is also using sophisticated propaganda, covert action, and economic tools to undercut democracy elsewhere in the postcommunist region in Western Europe, and even in the Brexit campaign.

In addition, many of Mr. Putin's techniques and countermeasures have been emulated by other autocrats, not only in postcommunist Europe/Eurasia, but also well beyond. In the Middle East, for example, there has been strong authoritarian pushback by the Gulf monarchies and by the Egyptian military. And, more recently, Moscow has joined in this pushback with its military intervention in Syria to prop up the brutal Assad regime. Such counteroffensives help explain some of the democratic stagnation or regression of the past few years.

Another factor contributing to the rise of autocrats is the West's increased public disillusionment with democracy and capitalism, based on weak leadership, pervasive corruption, and failure to deliver sustained economic betterment for a majority of the population. These and other adverse factors have led to diminished public enthusiasm for democracy in the transitional countries themselves, and to extensive soul-searching among advocates of democracy promotion in the United States and other advanced democracies. In the donor countries, negative developments such as these provide fuel for those who argue that democracy support policies are doomed to fail, or that encouraging democratization can destabilize friendly but undemocratic regimes and thus run counter to more immediate and compelling national security interests.

Thus, as a starting perspective for this book, it seems clear that much of the powerful democratizing momentum (and thus the great optimism) of the 1990s has been lost, at least in the short term. In contrast with the 1990s, the spread of democracy clearly no longer enjoys "the best of times." But the question remains: Are we now unavoidably in "the worst of times"?

THE CORE ISSUES

In keeping with the main themes of the October 2014 Wilson Center conference, this book seeks to address the following central policy questions: Should the fostering of democratization abroad remain a major goal of US foreign policy and those of its allies? If we do choose to actively foster democracy in a given country or region, what relative priority should we accord to the task when this goal competes with our other national interests? In the light of today's changed circumstances, should these efforts be targeted more narrowly than in the 1990s? For example, should we limit our efforts mainly to certain selected countries in postcommunist Europe/Eurasia and perhaps a few other special cases such as Tunisia or Myanmar?

If we should not continue to provide broad encouragement and operational support to democratization abroad, what should be the alternative to our present policies? For example, should the United States still work to promote abroad certain traditional American values such as basic human rights and freedoms and the rule of law (which are, after all, key foundations for democracy)? Or should we instead drop these longstanding themes of US foreign policy entirely, and instead move to what some would call total *realpolitik*? If we do continue to pursue the values-promotion path, what can we do to make this a more effective antidote to authoritarianism, given our own diminished image?

If we should continue active support for democracy abroad, what should we do differently so as to make this policy work more effectively in today's adverse environment? In which countries or regions should the United States focus its democracy support over the coming decades, based on what selection criteria? What should future democracy assistance programs look like, in contrast with those of recent years? What "triage" mechanisms are needed to adjudicate among countries—and among competing policy goals—when these democracy-support policies and programs conflict with other foreign policy priorities? And how should American efforts relate to the policies and programs of our European and other democratic allies?

SOME KEY DEFINITIONS

Democracy Promotion versus Democracy Imposition

Disagreements surrounding the issues of support for democracy abroad often revolve around advocates talking past each other based on differing definitions of the concepts central to the debate. It is thus essential to start with a definition of three key concepts that will be used throughout this book to avoid this trap: *democracy assistance*, *democracy support*, and *democracy imposition*.

The term *democracy assistance* will be used narrowly to describe those technical and financial aid and other programmatic activities that the United States and allied democracies undertake to support attempted transitions from autocracy to democracy. In the case of the United States, such aid is provided primarily through the State Department, USAID, and the National Endowment for Democracy.

The term *democracy support* will be used to refer to the much broader range of tools that the United States uses to encourage foreign governments and their citizenry to embrace democratic practices. These include the exercise of traditional forms of diplomacy; rhetorical advocacy by US presidents and other officials; use of the press and other media; and the work of international governmental organizations and NGOs.

Excluded from either of these two definitions is the concept of *democracy imposition*, which we define as the use of overt military action or major covert intervention to overthrow an autocratic regime or to impose democracy by force. In other words, our discussion of *democracy support* does *not* include analysis of issues surrounding the use of force or other external imposition to install democracy. Such were the cases of Iraq and Afghanistan, and of postwar Germany and Japan. The debate surrounding this set of issues lies beyond the scope of this book.

Our focus in this volume will thus be on the pros and cons of encouraging the spread of democratic ideas and institutions through "soft power" and by peaceful means.

Defining and Measuring Democratization

Another frequent cause of confusion and of specialists talking past each other is the lack of consensus as to how democracy should be defined and measured. Many scholars and statesmen have attempted to characterize democracy, leading to a wide variety of competing definitions. For the purposes of this book, we have asked all of our authors to use a single, standardized terminology.

A state will be referred to as *democratic* if it has demonstrated the following minimum characteristics: regular and reasonably fair competitive elections, with near-universal suffrage; political office that is open to most adult citizens; freedom to associate and to assemble; and basic freedoms of speech and press.

This definition covers Freedom House's category of "Free" countries, as reported in their annual *Freedom in the World* survey. In Freedom House's more detailed annual survey of the postcommunist countries, *Nations in Transit*, it is the categories of "Semi-Consolidated Democracy" and "Consolidated Democracy" that coincide with our own use of the term *democratic*.[5] It should be noted, however, that their "Consolidated" category also requires that a country enjoy all the rights and liberties of the Universal Declaration of Human Rights, and well-enforced rule of law, a vibrant civil society, strong free media, freedom of religion, mature political parties, a reasonably free market economy, and a capable, noncorrupt bureaucracy that is accountable to elected representatives.[6]

At the other end of the spectrum lies what we will refer to in this book as *authoritarian regimes*. These will include the categories that Freedom House defines as "Unfree," or "Consolidated Authoritarian" or "Semi-Consolidated Authoritarian."[7] In these cases, many of the democracy characteristics listed previously are absent.

The third category we will discuss includes *hybrid regimes*, or simply countries in transition or "in between" democracy and authoritarianism.[8] This third term defines what is perhaps the most relevant category for the purposes of this book. This is the intermediate category that Freedom House reserves for the large number of countries that have systems somewhere in between democracy and authoritarianism. Some writers also use the terms *transitional regime* or *electoral democracy* to indicate that a given country has some of the trappings of democracy, but not enough of them to assure regular changes of government based on the will of a truly free, well-organized, and properly informed citizenry. Georgia, Ukraine, Moldova, Tunisia, Myanmar, and Venezuela are current examples of this category. Countries regressing from democracy, such as Hungary, also fit this category.

For the purposes of this book, our quantitative measurements of democracy are also based largely on Freedom House data. In the case of postcommunist countries, we have drawn on *Nations in Transit*[9] and, for others, on *Freedom in the World*,[10] which applies an abbreviated version of the methodology used in *Nations in Transit* for its ratings. Our project's work has also been supplemented by other well-respected measures such as the Polity IV scores, the World Bank's "Voice and Accountability" scores, and other analyses such as those of Levitsky and Way in *Competitive Authoritarianism*,[11] which cover a broader range of perspectives than the Freedom House assessments.

ORGANIZATION OF THE PRESENT VOLUME

In this book, one author makes the case that broad support for the spread of democracy cannot realistically be a central goal of US foreign policy in the short term. However, even though most our authors believe that the United States *should* promote the spread of democracy abroad, at least in numerous countries and situations, several have significant reservations about the specifics of current American policies and programs. They believe that new rationales and new approaches are needed if the world is to regain positive democratizing momentum and if we are to deal more effectively with today's resurgent autocrats.

The first chapter, "Democracy Support: Global Challenges and the Importance of US Leadership," is the presentation given by Carl Gershman, president of the National Endowment for Democracy, at our October 2014 conference. We open the volume with his talk because it provides a bird's-eye view of several key issues concerning democracy's global situation and proposes policies to respond to the challenges ahead. Gershman begins by detailing the pushback against the advance of democracy around the globe, and then calls for a commitment to the restoration of American leadership, including the management of political and economic challenges at home. He emphasizes the need for more strategic development plans to counter democratic backsliding, and stresses the importance of supporting independent media and accountability against corruption. According to Gershman, "support needs to be comprehensive, involving grant support, training, networking—like the World Movement for Democracy—research, and political solidarity." He nonetheless reminds us that, ultimately, "democracy must come from within." The best way to rebuild strong international democratic conviction, he concludes, is to connect American citizens with people on the front lines of democratic struggles around the world.

In his chapter, "Realist Counsel on Democracy Promotion," Dr. Nikolas Gvosdev advocates the "American Realist" position. He argues that while the growth of democracy abroad may well enhance the US strategic position *in the long term*, there are too many compelling interests, including stability and security, that must take priority in the short term. While it may be desirable for the United States to promote democratic values as one element in its foreign policy, Americans must come to terms with the fact that "not only can there be clashes between interests and values, but that there can be contradictions between contending values." Helping a country democratize does not necessarily translate into making allies for the United States. Moreover, US democracy promotion efforts have not always been successful. Gvosdev argues that while the vision of a world of peaceful democracies achieved by rapid democratic change in formerly authoritarian states may be enticing for US policymakers, it is a vision that distorts their perception of reality. The real world, according to Gvosdev, is characterized by democratic retreat. Although he does not support either isolationism or a totally values-free version of *realpolitik*, Gvosdev argues for a modest role for democracy promotion in the US foreign policy agenda. He recommends that the US government should develop a system of "democracy triage" that would weigh the risks and trade-offs of democracy promotion in a given country, on a case-by-case basis, arguing that in many cases a push for democracy may undercut other, more important US interests.

In "A Case for Democracy Assistance and Ways to Improve It," Richard Kraemer addresses tensions between the democratic transition paradigm, on the one hand, and the rise of authoritarian regimes, on the other. Kraemer is adamant that the "current democratic recession is temporary and can be remedied as long as the worldwide demand for democracy and human rights continues." He emphasizes values in defending fundamental freedoms and human rights, and frames democracy assistance in terms of political will rather than financial resources. He calls on donors to learn from past democratic transitions and draws attention to the critical role of protesters and opposition parties, and their responsibility to move from protest toward political leadership once a transition takes place. Emphasizing the deleterious influence of kleptocratic regimes and fixed elections, Kraemer advocates conditional assistance programs, support for independent media, and election monitoring as strategies to preserve and advance democratic governance. Kraemer concludes that a return to a policy of engagement must start at home, where Americans must first reaffirm their own democratic commitments and standards.

In her chapter titled "Three Lessons about Democracy Assistance Effectiveness," Dr. Sarah Bush argues that, since authoritarian regimes have learned how to fight democracy promotion in their own backyards, the United States must adopt new strategies to use the resources of democracy assistance by following the "three Ds" of democracy assistance effectiveness. First, the United States and the EU should concentrate their respective efforts in places where democracy assistance can be supported by other measures such as conditionality, a concept she labels as "donor priority." Second, Bush argues that the delivery mechanisms of democracy assistance should be more carefully selected and monitored. Independent analyses show that some existing programs are either ineffectual or, in some cases, counterproductive. Finally, the author concludes that the emphasis of democracy promotion should be political rather than developmental, with more focus on the effective *design* of democracy assistance. With these three strategies in mind (donor priorities, delivery mechanisms, and design), Dr. Bush suggests new ways to approach electoral and other types of assistance in the future, emphasizing that further study of how democracy assistance works on the ground is vital to understanding how to ensure that democracy promotion efforts reach their full promise, and to countering authoritarian pushback.

In "Reforming the Democracy Bureaucracy," Melinda Haring discusses the institutionalization of US democracy assistance in the context of US foreign policy priorities. Arguing that democracies are generally peaceful neighbors, Haring describes the $3 billion democracy assistance "industry" as a safeguard of US national security interests. Haring advocates a substantial revision in the division of labor between field-based programs and independent grant-making organizations that fund democracy-enhancing organizations at one remove. She believes that more emphasis on the latter approach can significantly enhance the effectiveness of US democracy promotion. Her hypothesis is twofold. Independent grant-making donor organizations without field offices, such as the National Endowment for Democracy, are less vulnerable to authoritarian regimes and are therefore better equipped to work in countries that Freedom House ranks as "Not Free." Conversely, field-based organizations, such as the National Democratic Institute, are better suited to working in countries where democratic transitions are in progress or where freer civil and political environments will allow these organizations to extend a positive impact there. Haring also calls for greater transparency, monitoring, and competition when allocating resources for democracy assistance. She concludes that the United States should be promoting democracy in the most targeted and strategic manner possible, not simply injecting funds blindly into places with little hope of improvement.

In her chapter, "The Multiplier Effects of US Democracy Promotion: An Eastern EU Perspective," Dr. Tsveta Petrova argues that US democracy promotion has, in fact, had multiplier effects and offers an Eastern EU perspective to support her argument. Using the example of Poland, the most active Eastern European democracy promoter, Petrova argues that US support for the Eastern EU transitions to democracy has clearly paid off in the period covered by her chapter, as evidenced by the fact that several postcommunist countries have themselves engaged in democracy promotion, thus further enhancing that impact. Eastern EU democracy promotion has been rooted both in these countries' own domestic experience and, to some extent, in the emulation of US democratic norms and practices. In this chapter Dr. Petrova nevertheless offers recommendations for improving the democracy-promotion cooperation between the United States and the emerging democracy promoters of postcommunist Europe. These include (1) moving beyond *ad hoc* to more systematic cooperation in recipient countries in which emerging democracy promoters have a sustained interest for either strategic or moral reasons; (2) respecting such interests as well as treating emerging democracy promoters as equal partners; and (3) stepping up the nurturing of international solidarity among civil society groups across the globe, which Petrova finds have produced some of the most important multiplier effects of US democracy promotion.

Another perspective comes from Dr. Michal Kořan in his chapter, titled "East Central Europe and the Future of Democracy: A Case for a Transatlantic Democratic Reset." Kořan argues that helping democracy flourish in all parts of the world is a quest worth pursuing, but suggests that in order to properly combat the global rise of authoritarianism, the democratic countries should first undergo a thorough and frank introspection of the state of their own democracies at home. "Liberal democracy has become a concept that is under growing pressure from those who see it as a flawed model of government without universal appeal. The elites of the democratic world do not take this push against liberal democracy seriously enough, and democratic societies are becoming increasingly disenchanted by politics in general." Kořan thus voices a call to action, arguing that there is a need for a "transatlantic reset" when it comes to successfully promoting democracy in nondemocratic countries, and this must be done by first engaging in an all-encompassing international debate about democracy.

In "Reviving the Global Democratic Momentum," Dr. Larry Diamond addresses the skeptics of democracy promotion by defending its importance relative to a few different (and, some argue, more pressing) concerns. Diamond acknowledges that there is currently some degree of global democratic recession, and addresses the breakdown of democracy, the implosion of the Arab Spring, the reassertion of authoritarian regimes, and the poor performance of even the most advanced democratic countries around the world. However, he argues, this is not the whole story. Factors such as prominence of societal cleavages, erosion of civic engagement, and lack of accountable governance are contributing to the democratic recession. Dr. Diamond argues that America must first get its own house in order before it can supply democratic assistance to other countries, and even then the United States should focus on helping consolidate democracy in the most promising of cases; upper-middle-income countries are a good place to start. He asserts that ensuring long-term democratic consolidation in new and struggling democracies is the most worthwhile strategy to follow. Diamond calls for more targeted democracy assistance and a respect for liberty and human rights, using all types of diplomacy and trade relations to promote these shared values. Lastly, he invokes the history, philosophy, and culture of democracy, stressing the importance of the spirit of democracy in winning the battle of information and ideas that support freedom, dignity, and self-determination.

In her chapter titled "Academic Conclusions, Working Hypotheses, and Areas for Further Research," Dr. Agnieszka Marczyk examines areas of scholarly consensus and identifies emerging research agendas. Drawing on PDT's working hypotheses, Dr. Marczyk outlines lessons learned from over twenty-five years of postcommunist transitions and suggests that while many of these have been useful in strengthening democracies abroad, there have also been new patterns where nominally democratic practices, like elections, can be used to strengthen authoritarian regimes. As Dr. Marczyk points out: "If there is one thing we know when we take the centuries-long perspective into account, it is that there is no 'historical necessity'—history is patterned but not determined. It remains open to the interplay of individuals and broad economic, social, and political forces; neither success nor demise of democracy is guaranteed and regime change need not be unidirectional." It is therefore crucial to acknowledge that the ongoing authoritarian pushback is drastically changing the rules of the game, and new academic research must be carried out to help advocates of democracy to properly keep up.

With this introduction, we now invite you to read the excellent and varied presentations of our fellow authors.

NOTES

1. In chapter 9, "Academic Conclusions, Working Hypotheses, and Areas for Further Research," Agnieszka Marczyk draws partially upon this work.
2. "Does Democracy Matter," conference cosponsored by the Foreign Policy Research Institute and the Woodrow Wilson Center, Washington, D.C., October 20, 2014, www.fpri.org/multimedia/2014/11/does-democracy-matter/.

3. Samuel P. Huntington, *The Third Wave: Democratization in the Late Twentieth Century* (Norman: University of Oklahoma Press, 1991).

4. *Freedom in the World 2016*, Freedom House, https://freedomhouse.org/sites/default/files/FH_FITW_Report_2016.pdf.

5. Semi-Consolidated Democracies (3.00–3.99), or countries that meet relatively high standards for the selection of national leaders but exhibit some weaknesses in their defense of political rights and civil liberties.

6. "Methodology," in Freedom House, *Nations in Transit, 2015*, https://freedomhouse.org/report/nations-transit-2015/methodology.

7. Consolidated Authoritarian Regimes: countries that are closed societies in which dictators prevent political competition and pluralism and are responsible for widespread violations of basic political, civil, and human rights. Semi-Consolidated Authoritarian Regimes (5.00–5.99), or countries that attempt to mask authoritarianism or rely on external power structures with limited respect for the institutions and practices of democracy. They typically fail to meet even the minimum standards of self-governing, electoral democracy.

8. Transitional or Hybrid Regimes (4.00–4.90), or countries that are typically electoral democracies that meet only minimum standards for the selection of national leaders. Democratic institutions are fragile and substantial challenges to the protection of political rights and civil liberties exist. The potential for sustainable, liberal democracy is unclear.

9. This annual publication scores all twenty-nine postcommunist countries of Europe and Eurasia along a spectrum that is divided into five categories, each associated with a precise range of numerical scores.

10. *Nations in Transit 2015*, Freedom House, Survey 2014, https://freedomhouse.org/report/nations-transit/nations-transit-2015#.VZ7F1vlVliko.

11. Steven Levitsky and Lucan A. Way, *Competitive Authoritarianism: Hybrid Regime after the Cold War* (Cambridge: Cambridge University Press, 2010).

Chapter One

Democracy Support

Global Challenges and the Importance of US Leadership

Carl Gershman[1]

It is a very different period today than it was twenty-five years ago, when the Soviet Union fell, the third wave of democratization crested, communism collapsed, and democracy appeared to be triumphant around the entire world. The gains for democracy back then were real, but there were also many illusions that people had at the time about the prospect for democracy. Its forward progress was thought to be unstoppable. Many democracy specialists embraced what Tom Carothers, in an article in the *Journal of Democracy*, called the "transition paradigm," which was that the transition to democracy in different countries would proceed inexorably in sequential stages. Many also assumed that the welcoming attitude toward US support for democracy in a pro-American country like Poland was typical of attitudes in other countries and regions; and that since aiding democracy was no longer politically sensitive, the function should be taken over by development agencies and other government bureaucracies. Such naïve views were widely held in the aftermath of the Cold War, a period that Charles Krauthammer aptly called "a vacation from history."

We're a lot more realistic today because we have learned from the many obstacles that democracy has faced over the last quarter of a century. We understand better now how difficult it is to build liberal democratic societies, especially in countries that lack strong institutions and a democratic political culture; and we no longer underestimate the capacity of the old establishment to thwart efforts to promote tolerance and the rule of law. This doesn't mean that people don't want democracy—they are fighting for it in China and Russia, from Venezuela to Saudi Arabia, from Pakistan to Azerbaijan. And it also doesn't mean that the difficulties democracy is experiencing result from a failure of "democracy promotion." The problem is far more serious than that, and it has five broad dimensions.

The first is that there is a growing effort by the world's autocracies to push back against the advance of democracy. Their purpose is to contain democracy by controlling civil society and independent media, by projecting their own version of reality around the world through state-run communication initiatives, and by trying to erode the democratic norms embodied in the Universal Declaration of Human Rights and replacing them with counter-norms based on the inviolability of state sovereignty.

The second dimension is the failure of the Arab Spring to produce any significant gains for democracy, save for the very fragile transition that's now underway in Tunisia. These uprisings fostered great hope for democratic progress, and the fact that they have now succumbed to authoritarian backlash and the growth of extremist movements has generated an acute sense of disillusionment among advocates of democracy in the United States and Europe. The savage and growing violence in Syria is also having far-reaching geopolitical consequences, with instability now spreading to other countries in the Middle East.

The third problem involves backsliding in countries that were once considered stable or newly consolidating democracies, but that are now experiencing a surge of populism, extreme nationalism, and threats to independent media and civic institutions. The coup in Thailand, the trend in Hungary toward what Prime Minister Viktor Orbán has called "illiberal democracy," the growing centralization of power in Turkey, and the steady erosion of democracy in Venezuela and other ALBA[2] countries in Latin America are examples of such backsliding.

The weakness of the response of the world's major democracies to the challenges posed by the new authoritarian resurgence is the fourth problem. Vaclav Havel, when he addressed a democracy conference we organized in Ukraine five years ago, said that "a politics where economic interests are put above basic political values are not only immoral, but they are suicidal." More recently, the Ukrainian philosopher Myroslav Marynovich warned that if values are sacrificed for security, we will lose them both. The suicidal tendency to elevate narrow interests above values is stronger today than ever in both Europe and the United States. Havel was speaking about the weakness of Europe, but the United States is also at fault, and the silence in Latin America toward the assault on freedom in Venezuela has been deafening. We live in a time when the words of the poet William Butler Yeats have special resonance: "The best lack all conviction, while the worst are filled with passionate intensity."

The fifth dimension of the problem has been a crisis of political polarization and governmental dysfunction in the United States and other leading democracies. The crisis is economic as well as political since the financial breakdown in 2008 undermined the stature and influence of the United States. The failure to rebuild infrastructure, to adequately renew human capital, or to control entitlement spending further exacerbates the perception of paralysis and dysfunction in the United States. What makes the crisis even more worrisome has been the rise of China, which is seen by many to represent an alternative and potentially dominant model of autocratic capitalism.

As serious as these problems are, though, the situation is not all gloomy. While there has been a democratic "recession," according to Larry Diamond, there has not been evidence of a severe democratic retreat or depression. According to Freedom House, the number of electoral democracies in the world, which peaked at 123 in 2005, has only fallen to 116. There have also been signs of democratic resilience during and immediately following the financial collapse in 2008. Many people feared that the economic crisis would bring about the collapse of democracy in many countries, but thankfully this did not happen. This period also saw a number of democratic uprisings such as the Y'en a Marre movement in Senegal, the Umbrella Revolution in Hong Kong, and the Revolution of Dignity in Ukraine. These uprisings sometimes faced harsh repression, but they nonetheless have demonstrated the continuing appeal of the democratic idea. The fear that authoritarian regimes have of "color revolutions" betrays their lack of confidence, because while they can marshal force to repress democratic movements, they know that they rule without democratic legitimacy.

The fact that authoritarians have their own vulnerabilities does not justify an attitude of complacency by the world's democracies. The American abolitionist Wendell Phillips once said that "eternal vigilance is the price of liberty," and that's as true today as it was in the fight against slavery more than 150 years ago. Of the many things that need to be done to reverse the democratic retreat, none is more important than the restoration of American leadership in the world. As Samuel Huntington wrote more than two decades ago, a world without US primacy would be a world with more violence and disorder, and less democracy and economic growth, than a world where the United States continues to have more influence than any other country in shaping global affairs. This is a fundamental geopolitical reality that President Obama himself acknowledged when he told the United Nations General Assembly that US disengagement posed a danger for the world since it would create a vacuum of leadership that no other nation would be ready to fill. The urgent challenge now is for the United States to exercise that leadership in a credible and responsible way. If it doesn't, hostile powers will fill the resulting vacuum and the world will be a much more dangerous and less democratic place.

The United States needs to return to a policy of real engagement and get over the fear of getting bogged down in distant wars. The danger today is not that the United States will overreach by trying to impose democracy on other countries. It is that the United States will not back up its diplomacy with a credible policy of military deterrence, as a result of which it will have little leverage with unfriendly countries that don't share our values. Why should they negotiate seriously with the United States and its European allies if they feel that the world's democracies will not resist their efforts to expand their influence through bullying and the use of force? This is the lesson that can be drawn from the failure of efforts to negotiate an end to Russia's aggression in Ukraine, which is directly tied to our refusal to provide Ukraine with the military and intelligence wherewithal it needs to defend itself.

The American policy weakness is compounded by domestic problems. The United States will not be able to provide renewed leadership if it cannot bring its spiraling debt under control. Over the last decade the gross federal debt nearly tripled to more than $17 trillion, and it now exceeds the total US gross domestic product. While there are many reasons for the continuing surge in public debt, including the 2008 fiscal crisis and the wars in Iraq and Afghanistan, the principal factor is the growth of entitlement spending, which has gone from less than a third of the federal budget a half a century ago to more than two-thirds today. In the words of Robert Samuelson, the welfare state is taking over government, while other priorities are being squeezed out, from investment in infrastructure and human capital to defense spending and other international programs.

The resurgence of authoritarianism has made it necessary for the United States to revise the way it thinks about providing democracy assistance. According to a recent survey of democracy activists conducted by the World Movement for Democracy, the greatest need today is for the democracies to back up democracy assistance with strong and consistent political support to activists on the frontlines who are the victims of the growing repression. President Obama's statement on defending civil society made last month at a speech to the Clinton Global Initiative is a step in the right direction, but only if there is real follow-through in terms of using American influence to defend human rights and to speak out strongly in defense of frontline activists and civil society organizations that are under attack. The United States must also do much more to counter the information offensive that is being carried out by Russia and other autocracies. Congressmen Ed Royce and Eliot Engel, the chair and ranking member, respectively, of the House Foreign Affairs Committee, have introduced legislation to reform the governance structure of surrogate radios like RFE, Radio Liberty, and Radio Free Asia. This is an important step that could strengthen the US ability to wage the battle of ideas against the opponents of liberal democracy.

Regarding the difficulty of achieving successful democratic transitions, it's important that civil society and protest activists learn some lessons from the failure of the Orange Revolution and of other protest movements such as the more recent failure of the January 25 Revolution in Egypt. Activists need to realize that resistance against autocracy is just the first step in efforts to achieve democracy. They must also prepare to engage in political action and take responsibility for leadership and governance in the event that the protest movements lead to the downfall of autocratic regimes. This means that they need to mature politically and to start thinking strategically. This is happening in Ukraine today, where many protest leaders are taking part in the parliamentary elections that are going to be held next week.

There are also many other things that need to be done to reverse, or retard, democratic backsliding. Corruption has to be fought with real determination. In addition to making greater transparency and anti-corruption efforts a condition of development assistance from the leading democracies, we need to integrate into development strategies efforts to strengthen independent media, which are an essential tool for reducing corruption and achieving higher levels of economic growth. We also have to develop strategies for strengthening democratic culture by supporting indigenous civic groups committed to building tolerant societies. It's also important to strengthen the linkages among these groups so they can learn from each other.

Finally, we must work to rebuild a sense of democratic conviction in the United States and Europe. I'm just back from the Czech Republic, and I was struck by how strongly our friends there share our concern over the growth of cynicism and delusionary thinking about the dangers facing democracy. We will soon be celebrating the twenty-fifth anniversary of the Velvet Revolution, and on this occasion there will be a ceremony in the US Capitol unveiling a bust of Vaclav Havel. This will be an appropriate time to recall how strongly he felt about cynical and suicidal policies that put narrow interests above freedom and human rights.

I think that the best way to rebuild democratic conviction is to connect Americans with people on the frontlines of democratic struggles around the world. People who know firsthand the dangers of dictatorial systems and who are prepared to sacrifice to defend their dignity can be an antidote to the tendency in established democracies to take freedom for granted. There is an obvious moral case that can be made for maintaining a lifeline of support for the work of democracy activists. But the case also needs to be made in terms of self-interest. Since our security depends on the well-being of democracy in the world, it follows that we have a powerful stake in the survival and success of people who share our values and who are fighting to defend them. In aiding them, we are also safeguarding our own future.

NOTES

1. Editor's note: This is the text of Carl Gershman's talk given at "Does Democracy Matter?"—the conference which gave rise to this book and which was cosponsored by FPRI's Project on Democratic Transitions and Woodrow Wilson Center's Kennan Institute on October

20, 2014. Although important new developments have taken place throughout the world since then, we are keeping the talk in its original form here because it lays out the key challenges we are still facing today, and provides crucial insights about supporting democracy.

2. Editor's note: ALBA, formally the Bolivarian Alliance for the Peoples of Our America (Spanish: Alianza Bolivariana para los Pueblos de Nuestra América), is an intergovernmental organization based on the idea of the social, political, and economic integration of the countries of Latin America and the Caribbean.

Chapter Two

Realist Counsel on Democracy Promotion

Nikolas K. Gvosdev

Should the government of the United States—as opposed to American civil society—make the promotion of democracy around the world a top foreign policy priority? (Here, the term *democracy promotion* is understood to mean the use of a variety of instruments of national power short of direct military action to encourage and support changes in another country's domestic political system along liberal-democratic lines.) And to what extent should the promotion of democracy take precedence over other foreign policy priorities?

When asked, the general public tends to respond consistently in the negative, as opinion poll data collected by the Pew Research as part of its quadrennial *America in the World* survey indicates. Whereas only 29 percent of Americans identified democracy promotion as a top priority for the US government in 2001, that number had decreased further to 18 percent in 2013.[1] Certainly, senior policymakers have to be willing to undertake hard decisions that may be highly unpopular in the short term but be absolutely vital for the long-term interests of the country rather than allowing policy to be driven solely by the poll numbers—but the barometer of public opinion serves as an indicator as to whether leaders have been able to craft a narrative that can persuade the general public as to why a particular course of action ought to be chosen. When it comes to the question of democracy promotion, it is clear that proponents of the position that it ought to serve as one of the central organizing principles of US foreign policy are struggling with the reality that many Americans remain unconvinced that it is necessary for the United States to be concerned with the forms of governance other states choose as the basis of their political system—and do not understand why this consideration should enjoy equal billing with other priorities, such as securing the American homeland from attack and ensuring the prosperity and well-being of US citizens.

It is important to recognize how events over the past fifteen years have helped to shape popular attitudes. No matter whether it is fair or accurate, the democracy promotion enterprise has become identified in the minds of many Americans not simply with foreign assistance programs but with a series of armed interventions in the Middle East that were sold to the American public as quick and relatively cost-free liberations. In addition, assessments that predicted rapid and relatively risk-free (in terms of damage to other vital US interests) transitions to democracy once authoritarian governments were dislodged (whether by US military action or by popular protests supported by American assistance) have not been borne out by actual developments.[2] The Arab Spring created a "highly versatile geopolitical situation" where the prospects for quick and stable transitions to democracy are now highly unlikely while the region has been plunged into turmoil.[3]

A series of perceived setbacks for US efforts to foster Western-style liberal democracy, particularly but not limited solely to the states of the Middle East, as well as the negative impacts of the turmoil unleashed by regime change (encompassing both the results of military interventions and the political and economic support for what came to be termed the "color revolutions") have led a majority of Americans, concerned about the potential negative impacts of such developments to their own security and prosperity, to place a greater emphasis for US foreign policy to promote stability, even at the expense of further progress on democratization.[4] In addition, the perception that support for democratic reform in other countries equates to demands for the United States to provide large amounts of economic aid has helped to sour support for the democracy enterprise. Over the last several years, there has been a clear emergence of fatigue when it comes to supporting these types of efforts.[5]

Ironically, guided by the fear that American public opinion would decisively reject strategies that would entail cost and long-term, sustained commitment of American resources, successive presidential administrations have minimized the challenges and difficulties involved with supporting democratic transitions, thus further contributing to popular disillusionment with the whole enterprise once the inevitable setbacks occurred. This now makes it far more difficult to sustain popular support for any concerted effort at democracy promotion or any sort of new "Marshall Plans" fueled by generous amounts of American resources and attention as a way to reshape recalcitrant states into liberal democratic allies of the United States.[6]

This skepticism about the value of embracing democracy promotion as one of the principal US government priorities for foreign policy, in turn, has deep roots in two particular strains of thinking about foreign policy: (1)

noninterventionism and (2) a particular form of American exceptionalism, which maintains that the US political experience with democracy results from specific cultural and historical factors that cannot be easily replicated in other societies.

Noninterventionists, even those whose domestic views might make them sympathetic to the arguments advanced by supporters of democracy promotion, usually seek to apply the criteria of just war theory (specifically, the requirement that action must have a significant chance of achieving more good than harm) to US government democracy promotion activities. In so doing, they have come to the conclusion that, despite the best of intentions, the effort is not justifiable because, in their view, the US government is not particularly effective at democracy promotion. Using such criteria, David Rieff makes an argument in favor of noninterventionism:

> I believe that it is at long last time for us to stand down, and that not to do so is the true existential threat to the American republic. But if we insist on leading, let us lead by example, not by the projection of power, whether hard or soft, just as John Quincy Adams suggested we do in his great Independence Day speech of 1821. In the tradition of Adams, I wish Egyptian, Iranian, Burmese, and, for that matter, Chinese democracy well, but I do not see why the United States has the duty to "promote" it, except, again, by example. It is not so much that I question our good intentions as I do our wisdom. America is a remarkable country in many ways, but I would say that, historically, wisdom has not been our strong suit—and to intervene, above all militarily, without wisdom is a recipe for disaster. [7]

For the exceptionalists, the United States can and should act as a guide, a source of emulation for other nations, but the internal politics of other societies are their own affair and of no concern to the American decision maker. US foreign policy ought only to be concerned with specific external behaviors of other countries to the extent they negatively impact the interests of the United States or its allies. [8]

These two views come together in what Ian Bremmer has described as the "democracy in one country" perspective: abandoning a "vain attempt to micromanage the evolution of global politics" by recognizing "that other societies have other values, and that we can't simply force our faith on others no matter how certain we are that our system is best. The best way to promote our ideas and values around the world is not by bribing or blackmailing other governments to accept them, or by imposing them at gunpoint, but by rededicating ourselves to perfecting democracy at home." [9]

A MODEST ROLE FOR DEMOCRACY PROMOTION

The "democracy in one country" approach, however, remains a minority view within the US foreign policy community. Moreover, a closer perusal of the public opinion data which, at first glance, suggests the American public does not support the democracy promotion enterprise, reveals a more nuanced picture. Most Americans do not support making democracy promotion one of the *central* organizing principles of US foreign policy, but, at the same time, are not indifferent to the proposition that support for democracy and human rights ought to play *some* role in America's engagement with the rest of the world. They agree with the assertion by American political leaders that US action in the world ought to be informed by "our values" and be consistent with core moral principles.[10] A purely *realpolitik* approach to American foreign policy has never resonated with either US political elites or the general public, in part because of a genuine "American missionary impulse"— the desire to intervene in the affairs of others in an effort to improve their quality of life, to "fix the world" (and, in the process, win new friends and partners). This is a driver for US foreign policy that cannot be ignored.[11]

As a result, American realism, as opposed to a pure European-style *realpolitik* approach[12] or the dictates of so-called academic realists,[13] accepts that US foreign policy cannot be divided from value considerations, given the importance they hold in the formulation of American identity and political institutions. Even Henry Kissinger, usually held out as the doyen of the *realpolitik* approach in the conduct of US foreign policy, has blunted stated, "The realist school does not reject the importance of ideals or values."[14]

But Americans want policies that will both advance interests while aligning with core values.[15] In particular, they are insistent that policy not result in dangerous risks or excessive costs to the United States. American realism, as a result, has been grounded in two key observations made last century by Walter Lippmann: that responsible statesmen must hold in equilibrium the "purposes" and "means" and to recognize that "no nation's power is without limits."[16] American policymakers—and the general public—are on the lookout for an approach to world affairs that retains US involvement and leadership in the international system but avoids overstretch; that is true to a moral compass but not draining of American resources and energy.[17] At the same time, as former Australian prime minister Kenneth Rudd has observed, the challenge now facing policymakers is not to transform the world but to "quarantine and manage" critical problems.[18] Thus, as Paul Saunders has observed, laying out the American realist position when it comes to the question of democracy promotion "is not whether—the answer is yes—but when, how, and at what cost, both in absolute terms and relative to our other international priorities."[19] Those who describe themselves as American foreign policy realists will have a different perspective on how democracy promotion fits in to the overall set of US foreign policy priorities and how it ought to be balanced against other interests and values than those who might consider themselves to be liberal internationalists or neoconservatives.

The American realist assessment of the value of democracy promotion accepts the premise that, in the long term, US national security is generally enhanced by the existence of other, well-established, stable democracies—which provide, on average, higher standards of living for their citizens, decrease the root causes of domestic and external conflicts, and generally are predictable, transparent actors in the international system.[20] Realists, however, generally avoid overpromising the benefits that accrue from the spread of democracy. A greater number of stable democracies may reduce—but not eliminate—some of the drivers for international conflict. Yet realists question the expansive claims that have been made as a way to try to generate public support for a foreign policy predicated on democracy promotion—such as the idea that the "promotion of democracy multiplies the number of nations likely to be friendly to the United States."[21] They are also leery of a grandiose vision that says that a shared commitment to democracy

> would knit the nations of the world together into a global community espousing common values and shared interests, backed up by a rising tide that would "lift the boats" of all nations and eliminate the need for zero-sum perspectives in world affairs. . . . [T]his process [would] be accompanied by an alignment of other nations with U.S. values and interests.[22]

Realists are more skeptical. Many will accept the premise that shared values and systems of governance can help to reduce tensions or promote nonmilitary means for dispute resolution—and that democratic states can find it easier to work with each other in setting up workable international institutions. The operative word here is "can"—there are no guarantees. Shared democratic values have not eliminated tensions in the relations between Japan and South Korea or engendered a workable and lasting diplomatic process to resolve their outstanding maritime territorial disputes.

Realists, however, reject the assertions made by the partisans of the most optimistic interpretation of the democratic peace theory—the claims that democracies *never* fight other democracies and that shared democratic values between countries automatically lead to a decreased probability of conflict and increased likelihood of cooperation.[23] Realists raise concerns about the policy implications of the assertion that shared values produce shared interests, as this seems to put the proverbial cart before the horse. Yet the main evidence offered in support of this proposition—the long period of peace that has characterized relations between the states of the North Atlantic basin as well as extended periods of peace between the world's main industrial democracies—raises a critical question of causality. Are the democracies that are used as the basis for this assertion able to avoid conflict and war and experience higher degrees of political integration because they are democracies, or did these states resolve their pressing security issues and settle questions of regional primacy and territorial claims (which often are the basis for wars) *prior* to democracy taking root throughout the industrialized Global North?[24] The evidence is inconclusive. Moreover, if the long interval of peaceful integration that has marked the Euro-Atlantic basin occurred because of a common threat faced by Soviet aggression from 1945 to 1989,[25] then one draws very different policy conclusions: that shared security interests served as the initial basis for effective cooperation. Indeed, nondemocracies were part of the North Atlantic Treaty Organization (NATO) and other Cold War–era regional security alliances created by the United States—and it was only over time that the rationale for such organizations shifted to a conception of strengthening shared liberal values beyond a commitment to collective resistance against Soviet pressure and subversion.[26]

Indeed, the inability to build on the NATO model to create a true global alliance of democracies suggests that, even though Japan, Finland, Colombia, Botswana, Australia, and Poland may share similar political systems, they have very different perceptions of their national interests which preclude the formation of any sort of workable security community, especially if it means taking on major commitments.[27] Moreover, efforts to mobilize disparate groups of countries in various international and regional contexts to support promotion of democracy as a value in and of itself, apart from a connection to an immediate and pressing security need, suggests that shared values are insufficient as a basis for sustained collective action.[28]

Moreover, realists warn against overselling the immediate benefits that may accrue to the United States, particularly the narrative that democratization brings an end to intrastate rivalries and conflicts or guarantees regional stability. Indeed, in the short term, the process of democratization in many states can lead to disruptions and conflict which may work against US security interests—a concern that even supporters of making democracy promotion a major priority have acknowledged. Thus, *how* one navigates the short-term security dilemma toward the longer-term vision of a greater number of stable democracies in the world, therefore, is of critical importance, especially given that the US government will always be torn between focusing on short-term interests versus long-term promotion of values and rarely can effectively focus on both.[29] Indeed, the increasing reactive focus of the US government lends to a predisposition for short-term horizons—either to grasp at the mirage of rapid, no-cost democratization or to face pressures to abandon the enterprise altogether when it appears to become inconvenient.[30]

ASSIGNING AND ACCEPTING RISK: DEMOCRACY TRIAGE

Despite the rhetoric found in President George W. Bush's Second Inaugural Address, proclaiming no contradictions between American interests and values, the reality is that not only can there be clashes between interests and values, but that there can be contradictions between contending values. We have seen, for instance, in the Middle East, where pushing authoritarian regimes to have greater respect for the principle of popular sovereignty in governance can lead to erosions in legal protections for women as well as ethnic and religious minority groups.[31] Successful policymaking requires acceptance of the reality of trade-offs between different clusters of values and interests. Advancing one set of interests and values may very well mean accepting setbacks or retreats on other, equally vital interest and values. President Barack Obama's 2015 National Security Strategy bluntly recognizes that "hard choices" will have to be made from "among competing priorities" reflecting different US interests and value preferences. In so doing, abstract values may very well be subordinated to concrete objectives. As Samantha Power noted in her 2013 confirmation hearings to become the US ambassador to the United Nations, "We must make choices based on the best interests of the American people."[32]

Thus, as we have seen from the events of the Arab Spring, an unelected monarchy may place limits on how much power an elected assembly can wield in the governance of the country but be a better guarantor of civil and political rights. The premature push to depose unelected leaders or to press ahead with elections may bring to power parties which are virulently anti-American or groups that possess no commitment to establishing a liberal democracy. These are all risks that must be assessed when considering what role democracy promotion ought to play in US foreign policy.

At the same time, democracies and democratizing states may be less willing to cooperate with Washington and carry out a US security agenda. A democratic form of government is no guarantee that a state will be more of an ally or partner to the United States than an authoritarian regime. In some parts of the world, democratic governments may have less incentive or leeway to cooperate with Washington. This tendency to diverge, observed in Latin America (especially in the last two decades), in some European states (especially at the time of the Iraq War), and among rising democracies like India and South Africa, can be caused by different perceptions of national interest but also by what happens when the unpopularity of US policies among the general populace does influence government behavior (rather than being ignored or suppressed as authoritarian allies are able to do). The stunning reversal in British Prime Minister David Cameron's willingness to commit the United Kingdom to a military action in Syria alongside the United States after a defeat in Parliament in August 2013 testified to the impact that public opinion in a democracy can have on the ability of even a close ally of the United States to support Washington's preferences when they run up against popular preferences.[33]

A real problem that Washington has often faced is that democratization creates conditions where anti-American parties can contest elections and take power. Sometimes governments that are shielded from popular pressure are freer to cooperate with the United States. A particular dilemma has been how to approach a situation where an authoritarian government may be friendly to the United States but where mass-based political parties may espouse platforms that directly contravene US preferences. Governments that are thus more open and responsive to the popular will may thus reduce their support for the United States. This has been a particular problem in the Middle East, and to a lesser extent in Latin America and Asia, where "shared interests are regime-specific; should allied regimes fall, there is no guarantee that their replacements would share the same objectives."[34] The March 2003 vote in the Turkish parliament which failed to receive the necessary majority to authorize US military action into northern Iraq from Turkish territory was a clear reminder that pursuing democratization (including, in this case, ensuring civilian control over the military), while in line with US values, did not mean that subsequent governments would automatically support US preferences.[35] While this may be a blessing in disguise—where the opposition of democratic states to US policies may prevent Washington from undertaking actions that could end up being disastrous, while authoritarian regimes may end up facilitating US mistakes—it is also true that the British and Turkish decisions, even though democratically arrived at, were harshly criticized by many segments of the US foreign policy community because they negatively impacted America's freedom of action on the global stage.[36] They also produced a degree of cognitive dissonance for those who promoted the view that "democratic" equated "pro-American" while opposition to US preferences was seen as a hallmark of authoritarian governments.[37]

Finally, policymakers cannot ignore what Ian Bremmer has labeled the "J-curve" dilemma: that the process of democratization and liberalization means that a formerly stable, if authoritarian, state must pass through "a transitional period of dangerous instability."[38] In turn, this may cause democratizing states to become more, rather than less, prone to both internal and external conflict—leading, in the short term, not to greater regional and global peace but to its opposite.[39] Nor is there any guarantee that democratization will continue; in fact, faced with the prospect of extended chaos and collapse, a society may elect not to continue with reforms. This imposes on policymakers the need "to measure the pros and cons whether the security of stability or the insecurity of democracy is better" given the political turmoil that can be unleashed in efforts to promote radical and sudden political change, which "decreases the ability of the new regimes to maintain security domestically and consequently the stability of the region."[40] In the overall assessment, the expert consensus is that, in general, "democratization is not a guarantee of improved security."[41] Thus, a critical risk that has to be recognized—and that has unfortunately been proven by recent events in Eurasia and the Middle East—is that there is no guarantee that initial breakthroughs will be followed by more substantive progress toward democracy rather than reversion to authoritarianism. Even those identified as "liberal internationalists" who believe in the long-term applicability of the democratic peace acknowledge this reality; Anne-Marie Slaughter, who headed the Policy Planning staff at the State Department for Secretary Hillary Clinton during the first term of the Obama administration, has observed that "a transitional democracy, a weak democracy, a democratizing country, those countries are often very unstable and often more warlike. . . . Long term, it is in our interests [to see democracies emerge], but short term—and certainly trying to topple a regime to establish a democracy—that's not going to help our security."[42] Realists maintain this tension must be acknowledged—not dismissed or papered over—if consistent, coherent policies are to be developed and executed.

Thomas Risse and Nelli Babayan argue that not recognizing the reality of these risks and trade-offs, or denying their existence on the grounds that values and interests cannot come into conflict, "leads to false hopes and then to accusations of double standards."[43] This is especially true when a US ally falls short of meeting democratic standards and creates what I have termed "pretzel logic" situations where US representatives try to find ways around the dilemma—refusing to call a military coup in Egypt against an elected but illiberal leadership a coup; criticizing partners in human rights reports but then providing assurances that the flow of security assistance and cooperation in other areas will be unhindered; or changing definitions and standards so that a partner can qualify for assistance or avoid sanctions. Real damage can be done to democracy promotion when democratization is conflated with the political success of specific individuals, which can lead to a willingness to overlook deficiencies in the democratic process as long as the preferred outcome is achieved.[44] There can also be pressure to claim progress on behalf of an ally or strategic partner even where none exists.[45]

Thus, it is important neither to oversell the strategic benefits of democracy promotion nor to gloss over the risks and trade-offs inherent in any strategy of democracy promotion. This means subjecting the democracy promotion enterprise to a much more case-by-case analysis, recognizing that in some cases, democracy promotion will occur smoothly and will strengthen the US position in the world, but that in other cases, there is a heightened risk of destabilization or the empowerment of governments less amenable to US interests. Finally, there is the unpleasant reality that, to safeguard both the United States and its allies as well as existing democracies around the world, cooperation with nondemocratic states may be absolutely essential—and where pressing for democratization in the short term may torpedo that collaboration.[46] There must be a calculus in place to allow policymakers to decide when, where, and under what conditions it is worth taking those risks to promote democracy.

What might be termed the maximalist approach is one which argues for taking no risks with US security interests. In this view, the short-term risks with democracy promotion will almost always outweigh any possible long-term gains. Yet we have seen the weakness of the approach with regards to Egypt. Every year since Hosni Mubarak took power upon the assassination of Anwar al-Sadat in 1981 was the wrong year to begin pressing him to take meaningful steps toward real political and economic reform in Egypt—given the risks to the tenuous Arab-Israeli peace process, the ongoing security cooperation between Washington and Cairo, and the likelihood that the main electoral beneficiary of any democratic reform would be the Muslim Brotherhood. Opportunities where US pressure and assistance could have helped to shape the post-Mubarak future toward a sustainable transition to democracy were missed, and Mubarak's overthrow in 2011 then put into jeopardy both US security interests and prospects for democracy.

Yet even the maximalist approach does contain the possibility of modest support for political reform. If the first and preeminent national security goal of the United States government is the pursuit of a more secure and peaceful international order, its focus should be on concentrating its efforts to ensure that states are effective purveyors of internal stability and order and are not exporters of strife and tension. Democracy promotion may need to be a subordinate goal, with the immediate priority to help create conditions for effective (albeit nontyrannical) governance first, creating room and space for an eventual evolution in a more liberal direction. There is some evidence, for instance, that targeted security assistance can work to assist in such evolution. Because the disbursement of US security assistance is governed by legislation, such as the Leahy Amendment, that requires units receiving American aid to be compliant with human rights criteria, there has been some basis for using the self-interest of other governments to undertake action that can create the basis for reform. Some studies have concluded that US military engagement activities are "positively and systematically associated with liberalizing trends" and, in places like South Korea and the Philippines, it has helped to create conditions for democracy to emerge.[47] Under the right conditions, US training and security assistance to partner militaries can assist in the transition process.[48] Thus, programs intended to bolster US national security interests could have secondary impacts in helping to create space for eventual reform.

Yet Egypt again demonstrates possible advantages—and limitations. The close US security relationship with Egypt was cited as one of the reasons for the Egyptian military helping to facilitate the peaceful departure of Hosni Mubarak from power in 2011, but the military's role in aiding the transition to elections in 2012 was much more complicated.[49] And, ultimately, it was the military which snuffed out Egypt's experiment with electoral democracy and restored authoritarian governance.

A more nuanced realist approach not as committed to the maximalist position argues that there are times when the United States will have to accept short-term setbacks in order to take the gamble that longer-term value will be generated, both in terms of securing a successful transition to democracy and preserving or even enhancing US security interests—as the United States did in 1986 when facilitating the removal of the pro-American authoritarian president Ferdinand Marcos to support a newly elected but untried Corazon Aquino, even when faced with the dangers posed by a powerful pro-Soviet Marxist insurgency.

This means subjecting the democracy promotion effort to the cold, steely-eyed gaze of the banker assessing loan proposals. In particular, being able to calculate trade-offs where the United States would be prepared to accept short-term instability and insecurity as a price for pushing ahead with democratic change, but also being willing to assess where the risks of a transition to democracy would outweigh any potential gains—a type of democracy triage. This means that policymakers ought to be able to provide answers to two key questions: (1) Where is the risk of instability justified?; and (2) Where must we recognize that we have little chance of succeeding with the effort to promote democracy, or that efforts will be wasted or even counterproductive?

In turn, assessing risk tolerance also allows for determining where and when critical resources ought to be spent, both on those countries whose democratic transition is critical for US interests and/or where it can be achieved with a minimal amount of time at the bottom of Bremmer's J-curve. Such an effort is needed because there is a clear lack of enthusiasm in the United States for large, massive government programs that can help closed/authoritarian societies get over the J-curve hump to transition quickly to more open and democratic systems.

An attempt to develop such a democracy triage calculus to assess when and where the US government ought to make democracy promotion a priority was done by the Commission on America's National Interests, a bipartisan study group set up to provide options and advice for US foreign policy and cochaired by Robert Ellsworth, Rita Hauser, and Andrew Goodpaster. In a report issued on the eve of the new millennium (whose lead authors were Graham Allison and Robert Blackwill), the commission attempted to provide a hierarchy to guide policy choices: the United States had "vital interests," "extremely important interests," "important interests," and "less important or secondary interests."[50] Rather than embracing an approach of supporting democracy as a top priority everywhere and at every time, the commission divided up the democracy promotion enterprise based on geography and likely success. It concluded that support for democracy promotion in the Western Hemisphere was an "extremely important US national interest" because the consolidation of liberal democracies in America's immediate geographic neighborhood would help to promote stability, economic growth, and further integration. This is where experts had concluded that the possibility of rapid consolidation at low cost could occur, given a set of favorable conditions on the ground—and where the benefits of democracy might lead to more open societies and vibrant economies, which would reduce incentives for their citizens to illegally immigrate to the United States or take part in the drug trade while expanding export markets for American firms.[51] This is where the commission advised a future administration to ensure sufficient resources and follow-through for democracy promotion.

The commission recommended that the promotion of pluralism, freedom, and democracy "in strategically important states" was an important national interest—with the caveat that this should be done "as much as feasible without destabilization"—on the grounds that democratization might increase the chances for their long-term stability and ability to cooperate with the United States, but recognizing that this gamble had to be balanced against other, shorter-term security and economic interests. Finally, "enlarging democracy everywhere for its own sake" was seen as a secondary interest—one that could be trumped by the need to preserve stability, retain security cooperation, or safeguard economic growth.[52]

The criteria employed by the commission were certainly open to debate, particularly in determining which countries constituted "strategically important states." It was left unspoken whether this was based on size, geographic position, importance to the global economy, strength of military establishment, or ability as a keystone country to influence a larger neighborhood of states. After all, Singapore, the People's Republic of China, Venezuela, or Afghanistan could, based on different criteria, all be seen as strategically important. In addition, no guidelines were provided as to how to measure the feasibility of democracy promotion or when such activities would constitute destabilization. Yet the broad strokes of the commission report provided a way to begin assigning priorities to different parts of the democracy promotion enterprise, based both on strategic importance to the United States as well as the likelihood of success.

Alongside the template provided by the commission, there is also the "triple test" that Steven Metz has put forward to assist in making a decision to remove a dictator, which can also serve to inform any such triage calculus.[53] The first is a calculated assessment of the regime in question. That it may be authoritarian is not enough: either the crimes being committed by the dictatorship are so egregious in nature that its removal is justified no matter the consequences, even if the aftermath results in major instability; there is *no* possibility of a peaceful evolution to a more pluralist and responsive form of governance; or there is strong evidence that suggests that the transition can be successfully made with minimal consequences either to regional security or US interests. Given the disruption that can result, especially if an existing authoritarian regime is dislodged by revolutionary action, the second test is whether regional stakeholders, who must live with the consequences of regime change, support immediate removal. The third, and perhaps the most critical, "is that the U.S. must decide in advance whether it is committed enough to see the job through. The ultimate objective should not be simply to get rid of a dictator, but to set that dictator's country on a path to success while bolstering the resiliency of the region. . . . If this price is too high, removing the dictator is a bad idea."[54] Metz's criteria build from the position that, no matter the motive, "interveners do bear some moral responsibility for what happens in an area after they have undertaken action that removes the existing government," and that if an intervention worsens the situation it was meant to improve, it might then not be seen as the most ethical choice.[55]

This is especially important because, despite the rhetorical promises made by supporters of state-sponsored democracy promotion that the United States and its allies will (or ought to) assume shouldering the massive burdens of ensuring security and easing the costs of transition, the reality is that the aid that is often proffered is but a fraction of what is required.[56] Given these realities—particularly, in the early twenty-first century, a growing fatigue in Western countries, given conditions of greater budget austerity, to assume responsibility for transformational projects in other parts of the world[57]—a more prudent course may be to identify where it is possible to "go big" to support a rapid and sustainable transition to democracy; where instead to support evolutionary, sustainable change, accepting a much longer time horizon; and where such efforts will not only fail but be counterproductive to other, competing US interests and values. Triage is rooted in Thomas Melia's observation that

> America cannot actually make other countries democratic; we can only encourage and empower our natural allies and penalize and constrain those working against democracy. The principal impediments to the expansion of democratic freedom in the world reside in other countries—in determined dictators or feckless oppositions, disillusioned publics and entrenched corruption—and so do the possibilities for positive change. Although we may be influential at key moments in some places, the United States is rarely determinative—though it still matters who we help and how.[58]

AN OBJECTION TO TRIAGE: WHAT ABOUT THE EAST CENTRAL EUROPEAN EXPERIENCE?

Critics of a "democracy triage" approach would argue that it is possible to simultaneously promote stability, reconstruction, and democratization anywhere in the world at any time, while avoiding any compromise of fundamental US national security interests—assuming that there is sufficient commitment of resources, will, and effort.[59] The experience of East Central Europe in the immediate years following the opening of the Berlin Wall, the collapse of the Soviet bloc, and the disintegration of the USSR itself is often used to validate such an approach. A democratic opening in one state (Poland), the argument runs, helped to spur other, largely peaceful, revolutions across the region. Focused assistance provided by the United States and the countries of Western Europe helped to start and buttress a process of democratization. The postcommunist governments which came to power pursued liberal democratic and free-market reforms, and also shifted their geopolitical alignments to move closer to the United States in security matters.[60] Particularly in the so-called northern tier, the four countries that formed the Visegrád Group (Poland, Hungary, the Czech Republic, and Slovakia) agreed to work together and support each other's aspirations for membership in Euro-Atlantic institutions (the European Union [EU] and NATO).[61] Indeed, these countries were soon viewed as more reliable American security partners than the long-established European treaty allies, forming a group labeled by then Secretary of Defense Donald Rumsfeld in 2003 as "New Europe," and often described as forming a promising new bloc of US partners.[62] The Eastern European experience was thus assumed to be a template that could be replicated successfully in other parts of the world, and lead to similar results of producing stable liberal democratic governments who would become close security partners of the United States.[63]

Yet this narrative downplays the extent to which post-Soviet East Central Europe turns out to have had a number of factors in place where a rapid and successful transition could occur with some degree of targeted Western assistance. Democratization did not occur "from scratch," and even countries like Bulgaria and Romania had had some pre-1939 experience with parliamentary government, constitutionalism and competitive elections. In responding to assertions that the transition that had occurred in this region after 1989—specifically in Poland—could be applied as a template to other societies around the world, Sebastian Plociennik of the Polish Institute for International Relations responded bluntly:

> The transformation of Poland was not a technocratic exercise, nor universal or applicable everywhere. It was a unique, specific phenomenon reflecting the nature of its time, international environment, and features of the country.[64]

This does not mean that the Eastern European experience can never be relevant in any other part of the world, but Plociennik's warning requires us to identify preconditions and factors where what might be termed the "breakthrough to democracy" model has a reasonable chance of success as it did in Poland. These factors would include some experience with electoral politics, a strong judicial system and long-term foundations for the rule of law, a political culture that facilitates the concept of the loyal opposition, and reasonable levels of social trust where significant cleavages on racial, religious, ethnic, linguistic, or economic lines either do not exist or are tempered by common institutions.

In addition, the post-1989 experience of democracy promotion in East Central Europe was a case where there was clear alignment between advancing democratic values and enhancing US national security. There was little risk that new, democratizing governments would align with Washington's foes, given that pro-Soviet governments had been forced upon them. In addition, these states had real security threats (concerns about the role of Germany, worries about a resurgent Russia) that led them to seek closer security ties with the United States and to support the US global security agenda in return for US security assistance and guarantees. They also realized that reform was the only way to ensure a potential invitation to join the two main organizations of the Euro-Atlantic world: NATO and the EU. In turn, both the EU and NATO could impose standards for membership that encompassed a wide range of political and economic reforms without jeopardizing security cooperation with these countries.

Moreover, the reform process was generally accepted across the political spectrum, and there was support for the general geopolitical reorientation to the West. Anti-Western parties were either discredited or confined to the political fringe. This, in turn, allowed the United States to focus on developing processes rather than worrying about outcomes and avoided temptations to try and pick "winners and losers" in terms of political and business elites. Polish postcommunists who followed Solidarity in power, for instance, did not derail reform or seek to distance themselves from the United States. The West could "relax" about election outcomes in East Central Europe given that all parties were more or less committed to the Euro-Atlantic path— unlike US efforts in Russia in 1996, where the priority was to ensure a reelection victory for Boris Yeltsin because of fears that his communist opponent would alter Russia's domestic and international trajectories away from Western security preferences. Yeltsin won his campaign, but at a cost of compromising fundamental democratic principles—techniques which were later utilized with even greater effectiveness by Yeltsin's successor Vladimir V. Putin to further dismantle the fledgling democratic process. [65]

The prospect of EU and NATO admission was a powerful incentive for East Central European governments to stick to difficult reforms; having the highest levels of the US government reinforce the message that lack of progress on democratization was not an option was also critical to success. There are few such sweeteners elsewhere in the world, since EU and NATO membership is by necessity limited by geographic criteria and there are no such organizations in other parts of the world with the same degree of attractiveness or the same set of democratic requirements.[66] Moreover, there are additional challenges. We have seen the limits of EU and NATO incentives once a candidate country has achieved its initial objectives in being able to push for further democratization or to prevent backsliding.[67] And the rise of non-Western powers also capable of offering aid and assistance detached from any conditions to engage in political reform gives developing countries options to embrace development without having to democratize on a Western-imposed timetable.[68] Finally, in a number of authoritarian states, there is concern that US-government-sponsored democratization, far from being benign, is designed not simply to open the political process but to actively replace (and perhaps even criminalize) existing elites who would have no place in the new system, heightening rather than lessening resistance to pursuing democratization.[69]

At the same time, geopolitical conditions have changed. In conditions of unrivaled US superpower dominance during the 1990s, the United States neither feared "losing" states to other great powers nor felt as much need to accommodate governments resisting reform; it could impose democratic conditionality without as much fear of compromising core security interests. Today, the continued rise of China does create incentives for neighboring states in Asia as well as states further afield (in Latin America and Africa) for closer alignment with the United States, but much depends on whether the United States will insist on adherence to democratic standards as price of support or, as in the case of the Cold War, will accept authoritarian allies to balance the emerging peer challenger. The cases of Vietnam and Myanmar suggest that a certain degree of de-tyrannization and reform is necessary for these governments to be seen as partners and to be eligible to obtain US security and economic assistance, but it is also clear that the United States is willing to accept standards far short of full commitment to liberal political and economic reform as sufficient for closer relations with Washington. On the other hand, particularly in Latin America and in the Middle East, in the absence of existential crises that equally befall a newly democratic regime succeeding a pro-US dictatorship (e.g., North Korea to South Korea), a democratic government that takes over from an authoritarian regime that was supported by the United States is going to distance itself from Washington, at a time when growing geopolitical challenges to US global leadership are on the rise. This again highlights the importance of having criteria for assessing risk: is having a democratic government that moves further from the US agenda in the short term worth the trouble and instability if it creates conditions for longer-term engagement?

As Thomas Carothers has noted, the preferred American "model of transition featuring a decisive breakthrough in which the old regime collapses and the country moves very quickly to open national elections, followed by longer-term processes of state reform and civil society strengthening" is not going to characterize most countries. As he continues, "Only a minority of countries in the past several decades have closely adhered to this model, however, and they have been (as in Central Europe) generally well positioned in terms of facilitative factors."[70] Olaf Osica, director of the Center for Eastern Studies in Warsaw, concurs, pointing out the difficulties of exporting the East Central European model to other areas where automatic commitment to democratic values cannot be taken for granted or where there is no overall societal commitment to undertake the sacrifices needed for a successful transition. In such areas, "the West must first create an environment in which pro-Western tendencies can evolve into a pro-Western course—one where these tendencies constitute the main component of the public's social identity and the ruling elite's political strategy."[71]

Ultimately, the template used in Eastern Europe can only succeed in other areas assuming that there are certain preconditions in place that depend on the legacy left by the previous administration and the nature of that society. Moreover, substantial reform is not possible in states that are at war, undergoing significant conflict, or failed states.[72] This fits in with an observation made both by Amitai Etzioni and by G. John Ikenberry, that the problems of Hobbes (i.e., ensuring basic security both within a society and in its immediate environment and having a government that can meet basic needs) must be solved before the promise of Locke (moving to more representative forms of governance, particularly characterized by electoral competition) can be realized.[73] In other words, the creation of a functioning and orderly government which can ensure security and a modicum of economic well-being must precede efforts to open and liberalize the regime—just as creating a secure world must be the first priority of US policy before promoting liberalization. East Central Europe, particularly its northern tier, possessed reasonably developed economies, existing instruments of governance, and was not subjected to either external invasion or internal unrest. Nor would support of democratization by the United States undermine other critical US foreign policy goals. All of these conditions do not exist in other parts of the world. This further underscores the need for a democracy triage calculus that can give guidance to decision makers forced to make tough choices in allocating scarce resources.

APPRECIATING CONSTRAINTS

In contradistinction to an East Central European paradigm, there is the East Asia model for promoting gradual, evolutionary change. This approach was used by the United States to nudge then-authoritarian allies toward a more liberal path, foregoing pressure for immediate democratization (and drawing criticism from many activists as a result, for apparent abandonment of democratic principles). The gamble was that steady change—combined with economic development—would allow for the eventual succession of truly democratic governments (in part, because elites would feel more secure to begin initiating reforms); in turn, these newly democratic states would be loath to interrupt productive ties with the United States even if they had been forged by autocratic predecessors.

The East Asian experience is one of the bases of Amitai Etzioni's "Security First" paradigm—the assessment that short-term engagement with other states on the basis of shared security concerns, coupled with continuing dialogue about governance, can create conditions for long-term, sustainable evolutionary change in a more liberal direction. In turn, the resources of the American democracy promotion community can be better utilized to take advantage of these internal shifts and to assist a domestic process in favor of change when it is sustainable and supported by the proper preconditions. [74]

Confidence in this approach is buttressed by the assessment that such long-term change did occur in East Asia over several decades—that as regimes enjoyed a greater degree of internal and external security, coupled with the rising prosperity these conditions generated, there was a greater willingness to explore reform and to push for greater openness and pluralism and to anchor governance in adherence to the rule of law. [75] Indeed, some researchers have explicitly cited developments in Southeast Asia over the past several decades as validating the "Security First" approach, arguing that the creation of benign security conditions allowed for more stable governments and thus a greater chance to sustain democratic openings precisely because regimes did not fear that initial reforms would be utilized by internal or external adversaries to press for advantage. [76] Nor were critical US alliances and relationships damaged by the transition from US-supported autocracies to democracies.

The East Asian experience, however, also has its limitations. While the United States may have been reluctant to push too aggressively, the states in question also were not in a position to entirely disregard American suggestions given their dependence on US security and economic assistance or need for access to American markets. The democracy promotion enterprise, however, must also consider two other categories: countries in which the United States government possesses little leverage and where official support for democratization efforts reduces chances for making progress on other vital issues of importance to the United States; and regimes whose cooperation with the United States is viewed to be so vital (and whose likely successors would be even less interested in cooperating with America) that official Washington is loath to engage in anything that would suggest support for a change in governance or governing personnel, for fear of ending up with an even worse alternative.

There is a tradition, going back to the Washington administration, which can be of use in such circumstances: a division of labor where the government maintains diplomatic relations with an existing regime while encouraging civil society to stand for American values. Certainly, US diplomats must be frank in notifying governments when their domestic policies may preclude or hinder partnership or cooperation with the United States, but may find it extremely difficult to assist political change while simultaneously negotiating with a government for immediate considerations. The idea of compartmentalization—that the United States can fence off its immediate engagements with an existing regime from the goals of assisting a democratic opposition to eventually come to power—sounds appealing in theory but rarely works in practice; either the regime accuses the US government of attempting to undermine it by stealth or democracy activists complain that the United States government is only paying lip service to its values.[77] In terms of laying the foundations for a longer-term transition to democracy, private civil society organizations may be in a better position to develop capacity over the long term, rather than working via direct government action, because such groups are not required to balance immediate US government interests and, at the same time, they provide the US government with clear deniability that diplomats are engaging in efforts at regime modification or change. As Melia observes:

> Efforts to promote democracy need not be controlled by the US government to be in the national interest. Part of what we want to convey in many countries, after all, is that the state ought not control all aspects of society. Government needs to organize itself as an opportunity multiplier, as a platform from which private initiatives can be launched, not as a puppeteer of those efforts. . . . Diplomats should concentrate on aid and trade deals, visits by senior administration and congressional officials, and political analysis.[78]

Melia encourages more effort to secure private, nongovernmental sources of funding; advice in 2006 that has been shown to be prescient given the increased propensity of democratic activists around the world to be leery of accepting grants from the US government for fear of being tarred as foreign agents.

Yet it is possible that even this more limited approach—eschewing direct government action to promote liberal democracy with more indirect support for civil society efforts to educate and persuade such societies to undertake reform—may neither be feasible nor seen as desirable by some of the countries in these categories. From Egypt to Russia, US civil society organizations have been expelled and their work proscribed. Yet the United States may not have the luxury of waiting until an odious regime becomes more acceptable before deciding to engage it diplomatically or to work with it on other issues.[79] It is not an option, with the exception of a few minor countries who are neither located in critical regions of the world nor possess needed capabilities or resources, for the United States to take the position, "We're not going to deal with you if you're not a democracy."[80] For the foreseeable future, the United States will still have to work with a variety of nondemocratic and authoritarian states in pursuing its foreign policy objectives. In some cases, the United States may be able to impose some degree of democratic (or at least nontyrannical) conditionality. In others, some states may demand that, as a price for cooperation, Washington throttle back on efforts to promote democratization. Without a clear calculus in place, it will prove difficult for decision makers to decide whether or not to accept such a bargain when it is proffered by an autocracy.

A CONCLUDING THOUGHT

A vision of a world of peaceful (and pro-American, to boot) democracies—brought about via rapid and easy democratic change in formerly authoritarian or failed states—is compelling for US policymakers. Yet it may not entirely reflect reality. Walter Russell Mead has stated "the grim reality is that democracy is in retreat in much of the world"—including backsliding not only in East Asia but in East Central Europe as well. He thus counsels that it is "almost always an error to base policy decisions on the imminence of democratic transformation" and instead to see democracy promotion "as, at best, a long-term proposition."[81]

The challenge facing US foreign policy is how to create conditions for long-term, sustainable evolutionary change around the world in a more liberal direction without compromising the security and well-being of the United States and its allies. Realists and democracy advocates may thus find areas of common ground in helping to develop the criteria whereby the resources of the American democracy promotion enterprise can be best utilized for maximum effect.

NOTES

1. See the research compiled by the Pew Trust, "Public Sees U.S. Power Declining as Support for Global Engagement Slips," Pew Research Center, December 3, 2013, http://www.people-press.org/2013/12/03/section-3-long-range-foreign-policy-goals/.

2. The apparent inability to consolidate initial breakthroughs has been a key part of this popular disillusionment, and, for many, Libya post-2011 has become the poster child for such failures, as outlined in Missy Ryan, "Libyan Force Was Lesson in Limits of U.S. Power," *Washington Post*, August 5, 2015, https://www.washingtonpost.com/world/national-security/a-security-force-for-libya-becomes-a-lesson-in-failure/2015/08/05/70a3ba90-1b76-11e5-bd7f-4611a60dd8e5_story.html.

3. Peter Rada, "Rethinking the 'Democratic Peace Theory': Turbulent Democratization in North Africa and the Middle East and the External Dimension," *Panorama of Global Security Environment 2012*, ed. Marian Majer, Robert Ondrejcsák, and Vladimír Tarasovič (Bratislava: CENAA, 2012), 427.

4. Bruce Drake, "Americans Put Low Priority on Promoting Democracy Abroad," *Fact-Tank*, December 4, 2013, http://www.pewresearch.org/fact-tank/2013/12/04/americans-put-low-priority-on-promoting-democracy-abroad/. See also James Poulos, "The Western Dream of Democracy Promotion Is Back: It's a Trap!" *The Week*, April 9, 2015, http://theweek.com/articles/548669/western-dream-democracy-promotion-back-trap.

5. Stephen Blank and Younkyoo Kim expressed their concern that such fatigue would make it harder to rally public support for new programs for assistance and lead to further setbacks. "'Ukraine Fatigue' and a New U.S. Agenda for Europe and Eurasia," *Orbis* 57, no. 4 (Fall 2013), http://www.fpri.org/articles/2013/10/ukraine-fatigue-and-new-us-agenda-europe-and-eurasia.

6. See, for instance, Jamie Dettmer, "Obama to Cut Middle East Democracy Programs," *The Daily Beast*, January 2, 2014, http://www.thedailybeast.com/articles/2014/01/02/obama-administration-plans-decrease-in-funding-for-middle-east-democracy-promotion.html. See also Amitai Etzioni, *Hot Spots: American Foreign Policy in a Post-Human-Rights World* (New Brunswick: Transaction Publishers, 2012), 157–58, dealing specifically with why proposals for a "Marshall Plan for the Middle East" are not feasible.

7. David Rieff, "First, Do No Harm," *The New Republic*, July 12, 2010, http://www.newrepublic.com/blog/foreign-policy/76197/first-do-no-harm.

8. See, for instance, the position taken by Patrick Buchanan in his debate with Natan Sharansky on NBC's "Face the Nation," February 13, 2005, for an exposition of this position.

9. Ian Bremmer, *Superpower: Three Choices for America's Role in the World* (New York: Portfolio/Penguin, 2015), 73–74.

10. As an example, see President Barack Obama's address to the graduating class at West Point, May 28, 2014, where he notes, "The values of our founding inspire leaders in parliaments and new movements in public squares around the globe." Later, he reiterates that in taking action around the world, "we must uphold standards that reflect our values." A transcript and video of the speech was made available by Catherine Traywick of *Foreign Policy* and is archived at http://foreignpolicy.com/2014/05/28/president-obama-at-west-point-watch-the-speech-read-the-transcript/.

11. Bill Keller, "The Return of America's Missionary Impulse," *New York Times Magazine*, April 15, 2011, http://www.nytimes.com/2011/04/17/magazine/mag-17Lede-t.html?_r=0. See: the observation of an "ascendant United States" believing it ought to "shape the world in its own image," Dominic Tierney, "The Rise of Alien Warfare," *The National Interest* 136 (March/April 2015): 21.

12. The difficulties in fitting the European *realpolitik* approach into the American way of strategy was discussed by Michael Lind, *The American Way of Strategy: U.S. Foreign Policy and the American Way of Life* (Oxford: Oxford University Press, 2006), esp. 250–52.

13. On the distinction between so-called academic realists who focus on assessing the relevance of things like balance-of-power theory as predictive tools for state behavior, versus those who comprise a realist camp within the US national security community, see, for instance, Justin Logan, "Dan Drezner Is (Partly) Wrong about Realism," *National Interest*, January 12, 2012, http://nationalinterest.org/blog/the-skeptics/dan-drezner-partly-wrong-about-realism-6360.

14. "Realists Versus Idealists," *International Herald Tribune*, May 12, 2005, http://www.nytimes.com/2005/05/11/opinion/11iht-edkissinger.html?pagewanted=all&_r=0.

15. See, in particular, the comments of Anne-Marie Slaughter, in "Experts Discuss Global Democracy," *PBS Newshour*, July 4, 2007, http://www.pbs.org/newshour/bb/politics-july-dec07-democracy_07-04/.

16. See the discussion by Owen Harries and Tom Switzer, "Leading from Behind: Third Time a Charm?" *The American Interest* 8, no. 5 (2013), http://www.the-american-interest.com/2013/04/12/leading-from-behind-third-time-a-charm/.

17. Walter A. McDougall, "Can the United States Do Grand Strategy?" *FPRI Telegram*, April 2010, http://www.fpri.org/articles/2010/04/can-united-states-do-grand-strategy.

18. Comments made at a forum, "The West and Russia: A New Cold War?" Sponsored by the Center for International Relations and Sustainable Development, the Harvard Club, New York, February 18, 2015.

19. Paul J. Saunders and Morton H. Halperin, "Democracy Promotion as Policy," *Council on Foreign Relations*, June 2, 2006, http://www.cfr.org/democratization/democracy-promotion-policy/p10784.

20. Nikolas K. Gvosdev and Paul J. Saunders, "On Liberty," *The National Interest* 79 (Spring 2005): 6–7. Some of the empirical research has been summarized in Jose Maria Maravall, "Elections and the Challenge of More Democracy," in *Democracy in a Russian Mirror*, ed. Adam Przeworski (New York: Cambridge University Press, 2015), 165–69.

21. Charles Krauthammer, "The Unipolar Moment Revisited," *The National Interest* 70 (Winter 2002–2003): 15.

22. Derek S. Reveron, Nikolas K. Gvosdev, and Thomas Mackubin Owens, *U.S. Foreign Policy and Defense Strategy: The Evolution of an Incidental Superpower* (Washington, D.C.: Georgetown University Press, 2015), 244.

23. Karen Rasler and William R. Thompson, *Puzzles of the Democratic Peace: Theory, Geopolitics and the Transformation of World Politics* (New York: Palgrave Macmillan, 2005), 3.

24. See, for instance, William R. Thompson, "Democracy and Peace: Putting the Cart before the Horse?" *International Organization* 50, no. 1 (Winter 1996).

25. Joanne Gowa, *Ballots and Bullets* (Princeton, NJ: Princeton University Press, 1999), 113.

26. See, for instance, Marc F. Plattner, "New Challenges to the Free World," *Estoril*, June 25, 2009, http://www.ned.org/about/staff/marc-f-plattner/new-challenges-to-the-free-world.

27. Nikolas K. Gvosdev, "NATO Is Regional for a Reason," *Atlantic Community*, September 21, 2007, http://www.atlantic-community.org/app/index.php/Open_Think_Tank_Article/NATO_Is_Regional_For_A_Reason.

28. Aidan Hehir and Eric A. Heinze, "The Responsibility to Protect: 'Never Again!' for the Twenty-first Century?" in *Human Rights, Human Security, and State Security: The Intersection*, ed. Saul Takahashi (Santa Barbara, CA: ABC-CLIO, 2014), 18; and Arthur A. Stein, "Incentive Compatibility and Global Governance: Existential Multilateralism, a Weakly Confederal World, and Hegemony," in *Can the World Be Governed?: Possibilities for Effective Multilateralism*, ed. Alan S. Alexandroff (Waterloo: Centre for International Government Innovation and Wilfrid Laurier University Press, 2008), 74.

29. This is true especially of the military but is present even in the civilian agencies as well; see Reveron, Gvosdev, and Owens, *U.S. Foreign Policy*, 71, 123.

30. David Rhode and Warren Stroebel discuss these tendencies as they relate to the Obama administration and Syria in "The Micromanager in Chief," *The Atlantic*, October 9, 2014, http://www.theatlantic.com/international/archive/2014/10/obama-micromanager-syria-foreign-policy/381292/.

31. See, for instance, Zainab Salbi, "Why Women Are Less Free 10 Years after the Invasion of Iraq," *CNN*, March 18, 2003, http://www.cnn.com/2013/03/18/opinion/iraq-war-women-salbi/.

32. Hearing of the Senate Foreign Relations Committee chaired by Senator Robert Menendez (D-NJ). Witness: Samantha Power, nominee to be representative of the United States to the United Nations, representative of the United States in the Security Council of the United Nations, and representative of the United States to the Sessions of the General Assembly of the

United Nations, United States Senate, July 17, 2013, archived at http://blog.unwatch.org/index.php/2013/07/19/samantha-powers-nomination-hearing-video-transcript/.

33. Amy Davidson, "The Cameron Trap: Obama's Lesson from the British Vote," *The New Yorker*, August 30, 2013, http://www.newyorker.com/news/amy-davidson/the-cameron-trap-obamas-lesson-from-the-british-vote.

34. Eva Beillin, "Democratization and Its Discontents: Should America Push Political Reform in the Middle East?" *Foreign Affairs* 87, no. 4 (July/August 2008), https://www.foreignaffairs.com/reviews/review-essay/2008-06-01/democratization-and-its-discontents. See also, Ray Takeyh and Nikolas K. Gvosdev, "Democratic Impulses versus Imperial Interests: America's New Mid-East Conundrum," *Orbis* 47, no. 5 (Summer 2003): 415–31.

35. Tulin Daloglu, "Turkey's Path to Real Democracy," *The Globalist*, April 17, 2003, http://www.theglobalist.com/turkeys-path-to-real-democracy/.

36. Charles Blow discussed the "shocking blow" of the British vote to US hopes of constituting a coalition to act in Syria; see his "War Weariness," *New York Times*, August 31, 2013, A19, http://www.nytimes.com/2013/08/31/opinion/blow-war-weariness.html?_r=0.

37. For a discussion of the categorization of governments, see, for instance, Ivan Krastev, "Autocratic Capitalism versus Democracy," *Policy Review*, March 30, 2012, http://www.hoover.org/research/authoritarian-capitalism-versus-democracy.

38. Ian Bremmer, *The J-Curve: A New Way to Understand Why Nations Rise and Fall* (New York: Simon and Schuster, 2006), 4.

39. See, for instance, the analysis of the empirical data as collected by Edward D. Mansfield and Jack Snyder, *Electing to Fight: Why Emerging Democracies Go to War* (Cambridge: Belfer Center for Science and International Affairs, 2005).

40. Rada, "Rethinking the 'Democratic Peace Theory,'" 427.

41. Herbert Wulf, "Security Sector Reform in Developing and Transitional Countries," *Berghof Research Center for Constructive Conflict Management* (July 2014), 2.

42. Slaughter, "Experts Discuss Global Democracy."

43. Thomas Risse and Nelli Babayan, "How (Il)liberal States Promote Democracy and Autocracy," *Washington Post*, April 28, 2015, http://www.washingtonpost.com/blogs/monkey-cage/wp/2015/04/28/how-illiberal-states-promote-democracy-and-autocracy/.

44. Lincoln Mitchell raised these concerns, for instance, with regards to Georgia, and the twin temptations to both overlook democratic deficiencies of a government held forth as a poster child for the "Freedom Agenda" and cooperating with a US security agenda and to identify the success or failure of democratization with the electoral victories of specific parties and individuals, especially when opposition forces were also committed to democratic reform. See his *Uncertain Democracy: U.S. Foreign Policy and Georgia's Rose Revolution* (Philadelphia: University of Pennsylvania Press, 2009), esp. 131–34.

45. On the latter problem, see Melinda Haring, "Reforming the Democracy Bureaucracy," *Foreign Policy*, June 3, 2013, http://foreignpolicy.com/2013/06/03/reforming-the-democracy-bureaucracy/.

46. The classic examples are the accommodation of the Soviet Union in World War II to preserve the alliance against Nazi Germany and the US willingness during the Cold War to accept illiberal systems in the People's Republic of China and Saudi Arabia, among others, to contain the USSR and preserve important benefits for the "Free World."

47. William J. Crowe Jr., who served as commander in chief of Pacific Command during the 1980s, has noted that Asian leaders attributed the stabilizing presence of the US military and military engagement exercises with helping create confidence to undertake democratic transitions. See his "U.S. Pacific Command: A Warrior-Diplomat Speaks," in *America's Viceroys: The Military and U.S. Foreign Policy*, ed. Derek Reveron (New York: Palgrave Macmillan, 2004), 74. On the general linkage between US security activities and liberalization, see Carol Atkinson, "Constructivist Implications of Material Power: Military Engagement and the Socialization of States, 1972–2000," *International Studies Quarterly* 50, no. 3 (2006).

48. Zoltan Barany, "The Role of the Military," *Journal of Democracy* 22, no. 4 (October 2011).

49. On initial optimism that a US trained and equipped military would help transition, see David Sanger, "Obama Presses Egypt's Military on Democracy," *New York Times*, February

12, 2011, A7. On further developments, see Ahmed Hashim, "The Egyptian Military, Part Two: From Mubarak Onward," *Middle East Policy* 18, no. 4 (Winter 2011).

50. Graham T. Allison et al., *America's National Interests* (Washington, D.C.: Commission on America's National Interests, 2000).

51. On conditions in the region, see Scott Mainwaring, "Democratic Survivability in Latin America," *Kellogg Institute Working Paper* 267 (May 1999).

52. Allison et al., *America's National Interests*, 6–8.

53. Steven Metz, "After Libya Failure, New Thinking Needed for Removing Dictators," *World Politics Review*, May 1, 2015, http://www.worldpoliticsreview.com/articles/15664/after-libya-failure-new-thinking-needed-for-removing-dictators.

54. Metz, "After Libya Failure."

55. Nikolas K. Gvosdev, "What Metrics for Assessing the Ethics of Intervention?" *Ethics and International Affairs*, June 24, 2014, http://www.ethicsandinternationalaffairs.org/2014/what-metrics-for-assessing-the-ethics-of-intervention/.

56. The mismatch between rhetorical commitment and actual deliverables in support of lasting change is currently very clear with regards to Ukraine, where the real value of Western assistance is calculated at around $1 billion—far short of what the country needs to survive its J-curve trajectory. Given this reality, the massive assistance program tendered on behalf of Poland a generation earlier—and often held out as the model for how to support other struggling, democratizing states—now increasingly appears to have been an outlier. See "Slipping Away from the West," *The Economist*, May 21, 2015, http://www.economist.com/blogs/freeexchange/2015/05/ukraine.

57. This question of donor fatigue was very noticeable to the author on a May 2015 trip conducted under the auspices of the William Ruger chair of defense economics of the Naval War College to several countries in Europe to assess assistance to Ukraine, in meetings with both national and EU-level officials.

58. Thomas Melia, "The Democracy Bureaucracy," *The American Interest* 1, no. 4 (2006), http://www.the-american-interest.com/2006/06/01/the-democracy-bureaucracy/.

59. See, for instance, the points in Larry Diamond, "Promoting Democracy in Post-Conflict and Failed States: Lessons and Challenges," paper presented at the National Policy Forum on Terrorism, Security, and America's Purpose, New America Foundation, Washington, D.C., September 6–7, 2005, https://web.stanford.edu/~ldiamond/papers/PromotingDemocracy0905.htm.

60. "Push to Export Democracy Produces Surprises," *All Things Considered (National Public Radio)*, January 28, 2006, http://www.npr.org/templates/story/story.php?storyId=5176545.

61. Paul Latawski, *The Security Road to Europe: The Visegrád Four* (London: Royal United Services Institute for Defence Studies, 1994), 15.

62. Justin Paulette, "America's Future in New Europe," *Ashbrook Center*, June 2011, http://ashbrook.org/publications/oped-paulette-11-new-europe/.

63. See the comments of Nikolas K. Gvosdev in the first panel, "Revisiting the Case for Democracy Assistance," at the *Does Democracy Matter* conference cosponsored by the Foreign Policy Research Institute and the Woodrow Wilson Center, Washington, D.C., October 20, 2014, http://www.wilsoncenter.org/event/does-democracy-matter.

64. Sebastian Plociennik, "Can Ukraine Mimic Poland's Transition? The Limits of Its Latest Economic Changes," *PISM Policy Paper* 5, no. 107 (March 2015): 1.

65. For a discussion of what Yeltsin's administration bequeathed to subsequent governments, see Peter Rutland, "Putin's Path to Power," *Post-Soviet Affairs* 16, no. 4 (2000).

66. A point made to the author in 2015 by several Lithuanian and Polish advisors to the Ukrainian government stressed how the lack of any such "European perspective" complicated efforts to promote democratic and economic reform in Ukraine because there was no definitive goal that could help build political will to sustain difficult political decisions. At the same time, in other parts of the world, organizations like ASEAN or the Shanghai Cooperation Organization impose no such conditionality in terms of meeting democratic standards for prospective members.

67. See, for instance, Maia Otarashvili, "Hunger for Power in Hungary? The Alarming Nature of Viktor Orbán's New 'Manifesto,'" *The International Relations and Security Network*, September 10, 2014, http://www.isn.ethz.ch/Digital-Library/Articles/Detail/?id=183448.

68. For example, see Madison Condon, "China in Africa: What the Policy of Nonintervention Adds to the Western Development Dilemma," *Praxis: The Fletcher Journal of Human Security* 27 (2012).

69. The "king of the hill" dilemma is discussed in Boris Makarenko and Andrei Melville, "How Do Transitions to Democracy Get Stuck, and Where?," in *Democracy in a Russian Mirror*, ed. Adam Przeworski (New York: Cambridge University Press, 2015), 276–78.

70. Thomas Carothers, "The 'Sequencing' Fallacy," *Journal of Democracy* 18, no. 1 (January 2007): 25.

71. Olaf Osica, "The Eastern Partnership: Life Begins after Vilnius," *CEPA*, December 13, 2013.

72. Wulf, "Security Sector Reform," 6–7.

73. Amitai Etzioni and G. John Ikenberry, "Point of Order: Is China More Westphalian Than the West?" *Foreign Affairs* 90, no. 6 (November/December 2011), http://www.foreignaffairs.com/articles/136548/amitai-etzioni-g-john-ikenberry/point-of-order.

74. These arguments were laid out in depth in Amitai Etzioni, *Security First: For a Muscular, Moral Foreign Policy* (New Haven, CT: Yale University Press, 2007).

75. See, for instance, Kishore Mahbubani, "ASEAN as a Living, Breathing Modern Miracle," *Horizons* 2 (Winter 2015): 147.

76. Lynn Kuok, "Security First: The Lodestar for U.S. Foreign Policy in Southeast Asia?" *American Behavioral Scientist* 51, no. 9 (May 2008): 1428.

77. The author saw this firsthand in Moscow and St. Petersburg in 2006 during the G8 summit. The US government sent representatives to meetings held by the political opposition (the "Other Russia")—steps which Russian officials saw as counterproductive to cooperative efforts between the United States and Russia, but which were also derided by the opposition as mere window dressing. These efforts complicated US-Russia relations without leading to any progress in terms of moving the democracy agenda forward.

78. Melia, "The Democracy Bureaucracy."

79. For a discussion of these factors, see Nikolas K. Gvosdev, "The Other Iran Timetable," *National Interest*, April 26, 2007, http://nationalinterest.org/commentary/the-other-iran-timetable-1567; and Nikolas K. Gvosdev, "Playing the Clock on Iran's Regime," *World Politics Review*, January 29, 2010, http://www.worldpoliticsreview.com/articles/5018/the-realist-prism-playing-the-clock-on-irans-regime.

80. Comments of Anne-Marie Slaughter, in "Experts Discuss Global Democracy."

81. Walter Russell Mead, "The Paradox of American Democracy Promotion," *The American Interest* 10, no. 5 (2015), http://www.the-american-interest.com/2015/04/09/the-paradox-of-american-democracy-promotion/.

Chapter Three

A Case for Democracy Assistance and Ways to Improve It

Richard Kraemer

Contemporary challenges to democracy worldwide are multiple, often tactically unprecedented, and on the rise in a range of countries. While it would be premature to posit that we are witnessing a third "reverse wave"—to use Samuel Huntington's term—it is nonetheless clear that some of the factors that contributed to previous Huntingtonian democratic reversals have resurfaced.[1] Furthermore, it is apparent that today's environment is very different from that of the 1980s and early 1990s. Contrary to Francis Fukuyama's view during that period, history had no intention of ending.

At the dawn of the twenty-first century, authoritarian regimes became increasingly adept at containing democratic activists, controlling civil society, and imposing limits on political space.[2] Successful postcommunist and other democratic transitions of the 1990s were followed by disappointing outcomes in more recent efforts to democratize many other postauthoritarian regimes, especially in the Arab Spring countries. The ongoing struggle for human rights and democratic values has left many discontented and disillusioned. In many countries, the economic prosperity believed to accompany the establishment of a democratic system has been disappointingly slow to realize, as crony capitalism and corruption in numerous countries supplanted a genuine market economy. In others, initial attempts to build functioning democratic institutions have fostered instability instead of diminishing it. In places like Egypt, Hungary, and many South American states, citizens are questioning the fundamentals of democratic norms, accepting instead more restrictive rule in exchange for what they perceive to be greater physical or economic security. Moreover, the "China Model" and populist economic policies alike carry special appeal. In countries with a socially conservative populace or strong nationalist currents, many of democracy's liberal values are increasingly perceived as foreign, profligate, and immoral.

While disconcerting, the current democratic recession need not be permanent, and it can be remedied as long as the worldwide demand for democracy and human rights continues. The authoritarian backlash would be less intense were it not for people's continued will to live in democratic societies, which preserve the bedrock norms of respect for individual rights, rule of law, equal treatment, and genuinely representative government. Globally, there have been numerous examples of late: in the streets of Tehran, Kiev, Hong Kong, Ouagadougou, Cairo, Moscow, and Tunis, democratic activists and their supporters have braved adversity and state-sanctioned violence in their calls for more representative and accountable government. Recent elections in Afghanistan, Turkey, and Venezuela had high voter turnouts resulting in electoral victories for liberal democratic parties.[3] And while Freedom House's 2015 *Freedom in the World* survey showed worrisome deterioration, the number of democracies worldwide still remains significantly higher than in the early 1980s.[4]

It is my firm conviction that these recent troubles reveal not that democracy is in decline, but that democratic progress will always face difficult and dangerous challenges. Support for democracy requires hard and persistent work, coherent strategic thinking, strong democratic convictions, the courage to stand up against oppression, and international solidarity. With thorough self-examination, analysis of lessons learned from previous failures, and renewed faith in the value of democracy, the United States can and should reinvigorate its fight against the authoritarian pushback. In what follows, I argue that this should be done by fighting corruption through conditionality, restructuring our democracy assistance programs, supporting independent media, and empowering civic movements and indigenous groups fighting for democracy throughout the world.

IS SUPPORT FOR DEMOCRACY ABROAD IN AMERICA'S NATIONAL INTEREST?

Before considering the contemporary challenges to democracy and effective means of countering the new antidemocratic authoritarian tactics, reasons for supporting democracy must be addressed. Why is it in America's national interest to promote the spread of democracy worldwide? Why must America provide democracy assistance to activists and civil society in partly free or unfree societies? Today, there is no shortage of skeptics posing such questions. The global democratic recession, poorly performing governments in Afghanistan and Iraq (despite massive assistance), post–Arab Spring instability throughout the Middle East, and the geopolitical tumult following the fall of the former Ukrainian president Viktor Yanukovych are among the recent events that have fueled skepticism about America role in promoting democracy throughout the world.

Some of the enduring US foreign policy priorities include the physical safety of Americans, border integrity, US influence in global affairs and world order, and the advancement of American economic interests in trade, investment, and natural resources.[5] These can be more easily advanced when there are more democracies in the world. Successful US cooperation is more likely with established, consolidated democracies that enhance global security. Democracies are much less likely to go to war with one another; in fact, no war has been fought between two genuine, liberal democracies.[6] Conversely, America's greatest security threats emanate from autocratic or totalitarian states such as Iran, North Korea, Russia, and, to a lesser extent, China. Importantly, threats also emanate from nonstate actors such as ISIS, whose creation was a result of lack of democracy in the region in the first place. Well-functioning democratic institutions beholden to transparency, rule of law, and the protection of property rights also support stronger domestic economies, which, in turn, boost trade and bolster confidence in investment. Finally, democracies are more capable of responding to conditions leading to famine[7] and preventing genocide[8]—tragedies that can severely strain American leadership and resources.

It is to our long-term advantage to keep the support for human rights and democracy as a component of US foreign policy. Democratic governments that are "open and transparent, subject to scrutiny and criticism, are much more constrained than dictatorial regimes and, in some ways, more predictable."[9] Backing consolidated democracies and those in transition coincides with the consistently increasing demands from people around the world for their basic human rights to be respected. While some societies in unfree states like Russia have been conditioned to think that authoritarian stability is safer than freedom in potential chaos (such as in Syria and Egypt), the overall global trend is toward a desire for greater freedoms. The increase in the number of the world's democracies after the rapid expansion in the 1990s supports this assertion—we went from sixty-five democracies in 2000 to eighty-eight last year. Based on a comparison of four global democracy indices made by the renowned political scientists Steven Levitsky and Lucan Way, this figure has plateaued at roughly one-half of the world's states.[10] In addition, according to Freedom House's *Freedom in the World* survey, the mean democracy score for the world shows only a meagre decline from 0.62 to 0.63 in the years 2005–2013.[11] These figures indicate that the majority of democratic transitions, starting with the 1990s onward, have been sustained, and this reflects people's desire for the freedoms, representation, accountability, and rule of law, which consolidated democracies afford. Simply put, "Democracies do a much better job of protecting human rights."[12]

Since the end of the Cold War, there have been several places where damage was caused by suspended, delayed, or tepid US involvement—including Afghanistan (post-Soviet withdrawal until 2001), Bosnia-Herzegovina, Darfur, and Syria, among others. Recently, our withdrawal from certain regions has created ripe opportunities for authoritarian states such as Russia, Iran, and Venezuela to fill the vacuum with political and proxy cohorts regurgitating their sponsors' distinctly anti-American rhetoric in word and deed. The result is weakened US influence in world affairs.

The US role in helping maintain a more stable world order through multilateral or bilateral relations can be significantly enhanced by our status as the world's longest functioning democracy. America's demonstrated commitment to fundamental rights spans from its Bill of Rights to its backing of the Universal Declaration of Human Rights and beyond. This recognition of fundamental freedoms and the elevation of democratic values in policy making reflect positively on international perceptions of the United States, enhancing our credibility among states and their citizens and, by extension, our international influence. [13]

Accepting democracy and human rights promotion as an enduring and relevant principle is not fundamentally at odds with a *realpolitik* approach to foreign policy. To place this term in context, I cite Henry Kissinger's test of a statesman, which is "his ability to recognize the real relationship of forces and to make this knowledge serve his ends."[14] If we accept ideological forces—nationalistic, religious, liberal democratic, and so on—as real, and having significant impact on events affecting the United States, then these forces cannot be discounted. Accordingly, policymakers should make use of one of the great aspects of America's brand, which is its persistent (albeit imperfect) endeavor to recognize universal human, political, and civil rights—as affirmed by constitutions, treaties, or customary norms. And as our respect for these values is doubted or disbelieved, opportunities to further our interests abroad may fall prey to assertive, antidemocratic adversaries, who are quick to cite our alleged "hypocrisy" and "double standards."

It follows that our pursuit of enhanced international security is bolstered by support for states and peoples who share our democratic values, particularly when threatened by internal or external forces. By way of example, US backing was decisive in the democratization of several countries whose burgeoning or fragile transitions were threatened—including Poland, South Korea, the Philippines, Peru, Taiwan, and certain Central American states in the late 1970s and 1980s. [15] While some have since regressed (e.g., Ecuador and Bolivia), US democracy assistance work in the bulk of these states aided paid off. As Tsveta Petrova argues in this book, not only has US democracy support in Central and Eastern Europe been successful, it has even had multiplier effects. Poland and other postcommunist EU member states are now actively promoting democracy in Europe's east, despite worrying antidemocratic trends in the recently elected government in Warsaw.

With the persistence of democratic values throughout much of the world, adherence to the Cold War paradigm of "my enemy's enemy is my friend" to justify support for authoritarian regimes is not in US long-term interest. Recent history has witnessed instances where the demise of autocrats propped up by the United States has resulted in the rise of anti-American governments (the Shah's Iran and Diem's Vietnam) or a country's descent into civil war (Mobutu's Zaire and the Samoza family's Nicaragua). Democracies function based on acceptance of the peaceful transfer of power as the norm. It can be argued that some of those calamities may have been averted or lessened had the United States pressed for greater respect for human, political, and civil rights for the peoples of our erstwhile allies, as was the case with the countries noted in the preceding paragraph.

Prerevolutionary Iran is a prime case. From President Eisenhower through to President Carter, Washington consistently ignored or overlooked the Shah's increasingly brutal oppression of political opposition and the ever-growing income disparity that had come to characterize Pahlavi rule. Driving Washington's apathy was a persistent fear of communism's spread throughout the country, along with other military and commercial factors. This unwavering support was not lost on ordinary Iranians whose resentment for their ruler was extended to the United States. This history still poisons US-Iranian relations like no other. Had Washington extended its concerns beyond the Shah's interests to those who eventually brought him down, our countries' relations would stand to be very different.[16]

RECOGNIZING LIMITS

These arguments demonstrating the overall benefits of effective democracy assistance are not without certain caveats. The first is that, among other factors, American assistance to a foreign country's democratic transition is more likely to succeed when the wheels have been put in motion by indigenous forces, preferably from the grassroots up and with the support of more liberal members of the ruling elite for a gradual shift. In contrast, swift and direct imposition by military means or coercive force will more likely result in systemic dysfunctionality and instability, if not nearly complete state collapse or the concomitant rise of authoritarian figures. Moreover, for a democratic opening to be effectively seized, it must be with the clear recognition that building legitimate democratic institutions demands assisting the country's affirmed political will, ongoing resource provision, and direct assistance to their own civil society.[17]

In taking such steps, US policymakers should accept that a country's membership in a community of democracies does not inherently provide for a greater likelihood of its alignment with American interests, as Nikolas Gvosdev argues in this book. This fact should be acknowledged and accepted. Democratically elected executives and legislatures of US allies have often opposed our foreign policy agendas in recent years, from support for the 2003 Iraq invasion to debates surrounding Syria's civil war. It is natural that allies' interests will not always align; however, they remain more stable and predictable when compared to the unaccountable authoritarian. Nor are there guarantees that more recently established democracies—particularly those in the southern hemisphere—will in turn encourage the democratization of their neighbors, as has been the case with India, Brazil, and South Africa.

There is also the important reality that democracy assistance and respect for human rights in a given country need to be prioritized among a range of US national interests. However, for the aforementioned reasons, both need to be given their permanent place on the US foreign policy agenda. The variable priorities in which democracy and human rights are to fit may be multiple and complex—they may include regional dynamics and political, geopolitical, security, economic, budgetary, and energy considerations, among others. However, none of these excludes values-informed foreign policy formulation. One successful example of a multitrack approach was taken in the summer of 1986 when President Ronald Reagan met with General Secretary Mikhail Gorbachev at the Reykjavik Summit. Setting the agenda, President Reagan expanded talks beyond arms control (as desired by the Soviets) and succeeded in putting human rights on the table for discussion as well. Reagan further raised the issue of the plight of the USSR's numerous dissidents and the war in Afghanistan. In the months that followed, *glasnost* was underway, the Soviets announced their withdrawal from Afghanistan, and the physicist Andrei Sakharov was permitted to return to Moscow from his state-imposed exile in Gorky. Of course, the factors contributing to these outcomes went beyond one American administration's influence; but given America's superpower status, the denial of a certain causality would be disingenuous. And while the US government was not outright calling for a truly democratic USSR, advocating that another state guarantee fundamental rights for its citizens is a key step toward realizing an open society.

Finally, while assisting transitioning democracies, there needs to be an acknowledgment of America's limited ability to achieve the desired result. As recent experiences in the Middle East have shown, inundating a country with an array of military, financial, and technical resources will not ensure the rapid formation of functioning democratic institutions. Nor will it necessarily shore up state legitimacy, particularly when insecurity is pervasive and citizens' confidence in their government is scarce.[18] Moreover, many transitions will bear a very real likelihood of turbulence and setbacks rooted domestically in political, social, and cultural forces that go well beyond the control or influence of the United States, or any other foreign power.

These are limitations worth accepting given the vast number of benefits to America's greater interests abroad and at home. The separation of US national security interests and democracy assistance is a false dichotomy that even foreign policy realists largely reject, recognizing that a balance needs to be struck between security strategy and the promotion of our democratic values and ideals.[19]

The question, then, is not whether to provide aid to democratic forces, but what kind, how, and in what proportion?

MEANS OF ASSISTING DEMOCRATS

Given America's global stance, the tools that its government may employ for democracy support go well beyond direct democracy assistance.[20] Diplomacy and attendant gestures, such as criticizing an authoritarian government's human rights abuses or calling for a resolution condemning its actions in a multilateral body, send the message that more severe reactions are potentially in store if its course remains unchanged. Other useful tactics include off-camera mediation, on-camera praise, and, of course, official policy statements and situation reports, such as the Department of State's annual assessments of human rights around the world.[21]

Rebukes may be fortified with stiffer measures that impose costs. Economic and trade sanctions are traditional means of pressuring recalcitrant autocratic regimes to uphold citizens' rights and act within the accepted norms of the international community in their interstate relations. While the effectiveness of international or bilateral sanctions remains debated, they do induce varying degrees of economic strain on governments, particularly as they become more targeted. Alternatively, America's use of aid conditionality in efforts to defend human rights and counter social ills such as state-sponsored corruption has also been on the rise in recent years, as attested by the Millennium Challenge Account and the conditional terms of the 2012 Tokyo Conference on Afghanistan.[22]

Finally, there is the provision of direct aid to democratic actors comprising civil society in a transitioning country. Support for a range of civil institutions—including political parties, trade unions, independent chambers of commerce, and media—comes in the forms of technical and financial assistance. Established with and (initially) solely funded by the National Endowment for Democracy (NED),[23] independent nongovernmental organizations (NGOs) such as the International Republican Institute (IRI), the National Democratic Institute (NDI), the Center for International Private Enterprise, and the Solidarity Center share their knowledge and experience with their civil counterparts in emerging democracies abroad. Indigenous NGOs active in the fields of civic education, women's rights, press freedom, conflict resolution, and accountability obtain direct funding from independent donors like the NED or the Open Society Foundation, as well as directly and indirectly from the State Department's USAID and Bureau for Democracy, Human Rights, and Labor. Free and fair elections have also been a priority, as NDI and IRI have led election observation missions worldwide to monitor electoral processes and mediate disputes when possible.

To date, these ways and means comprise the paradigm of US democracy assistance. In view of the current democratic recession, their overall effectiveness demands a reassessment. Of course, the degree of their impact naturally depends on the context of a country's situation and the attendant US foreign policy agenda; however, a reevaluation is presently needed, as new, daunting challenges have arisen, undermining both democratic activists' efforts to achieve greater freedoms and our ability to support them.

THE AUTHORITARIAN PUSHBACK

At the forefront of the causes of the current democratic recession is the pushback by authoritarian regimes throughout the world. These regimes have begun to clamp down on civil society, effectively limiting political and civic space for citizens' activities. In the past few years, many have done so with the adoption of laws or decrees that render civil society organizations' (CSOs) work and acceptance of foreign aid illegal if it is not state "approved" (i.e., under its control). Revamped and ambiguously worded NGO registration, anti-extremist and antiterror, and "foreign agent" laws have been enacted in more than sixty countries in the past three years,[24] some of the most high-profile cases being Russia, Egypt, and Hungary. Russia has gone so far as to begin listing foreign institutions perceived as threatening to its interests. On July 1, 2015, China passed a national security law authorizing "all measures necessary" to protect the country from hostile elements; a draft for its first law regulating foreign NGO activity is en route to adoption.[25] A few states (e.g., Turkey, Ecuador, and Bolivia) have passed laws significantly limiting freedom of assembly as well. Collectively, these laws effectively criminalize public initiatives deemed threatening by autocratic governments, whether they defend citizens' rights or call for greater state accountability.

Stifling freedoms of speech and association through laws is symptomatic of contemporary authoritarians' general manipulation of state institutions to their own ends. Businesses or groups publicly opposed to a ruling party's policies are silenced with castigatory tax levies or trumped up allegations of evasion. By decree or legislation, state intelligence services are given sweeping oversight of social media platforms, from monitoring individuals to access denial. With increasing frequency, at election time, judiciary organs and related electoral commissions are relied upon to restrict potential candidates' entry, validate fraud, or manipulate tallies.

Regimes solidify the effectiveness of their tactics by waging grossly distorting misinformation campaigns via domestic and foreign media outlets. With the slick visual trappings of contemporary Western media coupled with little—if any—commitment to journalistic integrity, major television channels broadcast at the direction of executive offices in Bangkok, Cairo, Caracas, Ankara, and elsewhere. Columnists running critical op-eds or newspaper reporters filing stories unflattering of the government soon find themselves unemployed in such states. Those outlets that function at the state's beckon and call readily craft reportage to reflect the state's messaging. For example, Russia's Kremlin-orchestrated media is categorically biased, misinforming, and keen to sew just enough seeds to point out the alleged hidden hands of conspiratorial, foreign interventionists at home and abroad. The TV has been seized as the most effective medium in this undertaking, and channels like RT (Russia) and Press TV (Iran) are generating distraction and uncertainty, and yet showing disconcerting popularity beyond their borders.

Allegations of menacing foreign elements at work in closed or semiclosed societies are a key part of the new narratives that construct and justify counter-norms to international standards. Authoritarian leaders seek to legitimize their countermeasures against liberal democracy on the bases of security, state sovereignty, and "traditional values."[26] Examples include: new counter-terrorism practices pursued via expanded executive authorities that approve decreasing transparency, greater citizen surveillance, and extraordinary legal procedures;[27] the Shanghai Cooperation Organization's (SCO) guiding "Shanghai Spirit" that elevates the principle of noninterference and a country's sovereignty over universally acknowledged and fundamental human rights;[28] and the curtailing of individual freedoms—typically concerning a person's faith or sexual orientation—in the name of a nation's propagated cultural and religious tenets, an agenda especially pronounced in Putin's Russia.

Along these regressive autocracies, there are countries which were previously consolidating their democracies, and which are now backsliding. Last year, Hungary's Prime Minister Viktor Orbán stated his desire to transform his country into an "illiberal state" to be globally competitive.[29] The mid-2000s signs of Turkey's upward democratic trajectory (free elections, EU negotiations, balanced civil-military relations) have dissipated under the ever-increasingly autocratic rule of President Recep Tayyip Erdoğan. The ill effects of the 2014 military coup in Thailand remain all too severe. These reversals are typically accompanied by populist-nationalist political agendas, media restrictions, the aforementioned anticivil society legal measures, and a fair dose of xenophobia.

Several factors have contributed to the advancement of authoritarian states. First, democratic openings in the past few years have failed to materialize as substantive transitions to functioning democracies. With the important exception of Tunisia, those leading and participating in the Arab Spring uprisings failed to successfully manage the essential shift from protest to politics. The Burmese political reforms of 2011–2012 have yet to provide for genuinely open elections and rights for political prisoners and minority groups, the Royhinga people being a glaring example. Pakistan's emergence from outright military rule in 2008 has not resulted in a recalibration of its civil-military relations, diminished institutionalized corruption, and greater government accountability. Afghans risking their lives to vote in the country's recent presidential elections share similar concerns and disappointments. The sluggishness or stagnancy characterizing these and other stymied transitions erodes faith in democracy's ability to deliver the manifold benefits enjoyed in older, well-established democracies. Correspondingly, it leads to the consideration of other means of governance, such as the "China Model" or the models espoused by extremist Islamic movements. Strengthening the hands of those peddling alternatives to liberal democracy are revenues earned through increased trade (China, Vietnam) or demand for fossil fuels and other natural resources (Saudi Arabia, Qatar, Russia). Meanwhile, in the democracies that provide the financial and technical assistance, the universality of democratic values and human rights is increasingly questioned, given the multiple setbacks in Iraq and Afghanistan, and the unfulfilled hopes of the Arab Spring.

Increasingly deadly violence amid armed conflicts in several states is another obstacle to the establishment of functioning democratic institutions. While activists fighting for enduring change deserve our aid despite extreme civil strife or war, the reality is that without the state's near monopoly on the use of force, the attendant instability will present severe challenges to the successful foundation of democratic institutions. Unfortunately, this condition is not lost on the perpetrators: ISIS leaders and their supporters in the Gulf, the Kremlin in its backing of insurgent forces in Ukraine, and the Taliban together with their Pakistani sponsors.

Violence is not the only prime export of undemocratic governments. As these regimes hone their tactics of oppression, other, smaller autocrats take their cues from them, and develop comparable—if not identical—means in turn. Several former Soviet republics, including Russia, Azerbaijan, Tajikistan, and Kyrgyzstan all share regional norms conducive to repressing CSOs and individual liberties. Citing the principle of state sovereignty to justify diminishment of international norms and fundamental rights is common within the Bolivarian Alliance for the Peoples of Our Americas (ALBA).[30]

SCO and Gulf Cooperation Council (GCC) states also demonstrate a shared affinity for copying peers in their efforts to silence dissenting voices. Moreover, these authoritarian clubs help to facilitate the sharing of techniques of political control, the exchange of "watch lists," which makes travel for democratic activists very risky, and the promotion of agreements for the forcible *refoulment* of dissidents in exile or political asylum seekers labeled as "terrorists."

Domestically, adaptations in governance structures have further served to implement these new tactics of controlling dissent. A number of states already have, or are seeking to, give greater, successfully consolidated powers to the executive, as their governments become increasingly centralized. Whether through military coups (Egypt, Thailand), political strong-arming for pro-presidential constitutional amendments (Kenya, Turkey, Venezuela), or genuine devolution of political authority (Afghanistan, Jordan), the establishment of effective checks and balances in many states is at best not a priority and at worst proactively undermined.

THE NEED FOR A COLLECTIVE RESPONSE

On issue after issue, the opponents of democracy are acting with brazenness and belligerence, while those who should be its main defenders—namely the community of democratic nations led by the United States—appear beset by doubt and a lack of democratic conviction. Economic and energy interests are often disproportionately prioritized over democratic repression and human rights violations in relations between several European Union and BRICS democracies, on the one hand, and with authoritarian China, Russia, Azerbaijan, and GCC states, on the other. South America's free democracies have shown little compunction when, for example, turning a blind eye to compelling allegations of electoral fraud in Venezuela's 2013 presidential elections or the hundreds of political arrests in the wake of the mass protests in the spring of 2014. In the meantime, the US government has demonstrated an inability to balance its various interests abroad, resulting in confused policies that do little to help lead a war-weary American public away from today's prevailing tendency toward isolationism.

When faced with domestic or regional crises, established democracies' concerns with democratic regressions lose priority. The global recession triggered by the 2008 financial crisis dragged European Union economies into a slowdown that shook confidence in markets and the state's ability to maintain effective economic oversight. Greece's seemingly perpetual economic throes have exposed disparate levels of member states' commitment to the breadth of European Union integration, testing its foundations. The 2014 European parliamentary elections provided ample proof of the rise in nationalist, Euro-skeptic elements in several member states including Austria, Denmark, France, the Netherlands, and the United Kingdom. It is likely that they will benefit from Europe's ongoing migrant crisis and recent terrorist attacks. None of these developments bode well for the EU's founders' ambitions to establish a political community of European democracies mutually benefitting from a common, open market.

On this side of the Atlantic, partisanship continues to be the primary motivation guiding members of both congressional chambers. Though there was a gradual trend toward partisan conflicts since the early 1990s, the past several years have witnessed an ever more acrimonious level of divisiveness between the aisles, as demonstrated by an exceptionally virulent conflict over President Barack Obama's efforts to reform health care and the 2013 shutdown of the federal government.

There is no quick fix or magic bullet to overcome these numerous challenges; yet they are not irresolvable. As previously noted, we are facing a democratic recession—not necessarily a reverse wave. This means that the democratic West can counter the authoritarian backlash. A key first step in this is reaffirming America's commitment to its fundamental role as a leader in the international community. In President Obama's remarks to West Point's 2014 graduating class he reiterated this responsibility, adding that "if we don't, no one else will."[31] President Obama further recognized that "America's support for democracy and human rights goes beyond idealism—it's a matter of national security," and that the present "crack down on civil society" abroad demands that we continue to form alliances not with governments, but people as well.[32]

Accordingly, America and its democratic allies must continue and broaden efforts against autocratic repression. Reaffirmations of our commitment to the global expansion of democratic values in America demand the defense of civil society in unfree countries. We need to reiterate this through diplomacy (public diplomacy, in particular), trade relations, and aid; for example, with Azerbaijan, Angola, Egypt, and Vietnam, among others. We need to reiterate that while our interests need to be prioritized, placing persistent pressure on states that sanction human rights abuses and disregard international norms is consistent with our national security interests. Recalling the aforementioned sources of global influence, America must consistently speak out for people's dignity if it is to benefit from a greater degree of moral authority in managing international relations.

SEIZING NEW OPPORTUNITIES

Another vital step in the empowerment of the citizenry is ensuring their access to information by aiding in the development and dissemination of new technologies, while bolstering more traditional forms of media as well. Regarding the former, it is worthwhile to pursue partnerships with private sector firms desiring to strengthen freedom of expression and information. One example is Google's *pro bono* "Project Shield," which has been successful in mitigating distributed denial of service (DDoS) attacks against small news and human rights websites. When it comes to traditional media, continued reforms and concomitant financial support for the singular reporting produced by Radio Free Europe, Radio Liberty, and Radio Free Asia can help counter misleading or false narratives propagated by Russia, Iran, China, and others. News outlets, innovative tech firms, and other institutions supporting dissident communities abroad must help build links between them for the enhancement of democratic messaging in terms of content, delivery, and security.

To generate democratic change, the elevation of the public's greater democratic awareness through the transfer of knowledge and experience requires the mobilization of civil society institutions. Going forward, assistance providers and donors should especially emphasize lessons learned from past democratic transitions elsewhere.[33] Wholly recognizing that each country's transition to democracy is unique, occurring within a specific time, place, and myriad of contexts, certain patterns emerge from which better practices can be adopted. One key current phenomenon is the difficulty activists have in moving from protest to the weighty demands of politics, leadership, and policymaking. Our success in fostering sustained transitions will depend to a large degree on our ability to help civic activists embrace and navigate the move toward effective governance.

To this end, activists-turned-politicians will need to genuinely transform themselves into legitimate leaders. In many dysfunctional states around the world, this requires taking a firm stand against institutionalized corruption. The scourge of kleptocratic systems characteristic of many countries ruled by hybrid or autocratic governments is intensifying. The globalization of finance has provided for the protection and multiplication of state revenues stolen for personal aggrandizement, political domination at home, and international influence purchased abroad. Kleptocracies not only widen their country's democratic deficit, but pose a direct risk to international security; the endemic systemization of corruption can lead to social unrest and insurgence, and facilitate the financing of international terrorist and criminal organizations.[34]

To abate the corrosive effects of state-sponsored thievery, established democracies would be wise to acknowledge the threats emanating from kleptocratic regimes rather than view them as "the cost of doing business." To combat corruption, democratic states should make assistance programs conditional on a government's progress toward citizen accountability and transparent governance. Increased aid should be made available for independent media committed to investigative reporting, as well as CSOs monitoring of government performance and pursuing public anticorruption initiatives.

Election monitoring remains a key undertaking to the global preservation and advancement of democratic governance. As undemocratic governments seek to fabricate a sheen of legitimacy through fixed elections, they employ "zombie" monitors who "try to look like democratic observers, but serve autocratic purposes by pretending that clearly flawed elections deserve clean bills of health."[35] The baseless endorsements of these "zombie" monitors are then publicized by authoritarian-sponsored international broadcasting networks. Ongoing countermeasures in the form of continued observations and public rebuke for states deploying zombie monitors should be taken not only by the Organization for Security and Cooperation in Europe, but also by other regional bodies, which currently have only limited electoral oversight—that is, the Union of South American Nations and the African Union.

In the face of such disruptions to global stability, established democracies should renew their efforts to clearly identify and condemn autocratic governments via unilateral and joint statements, state-issued human rights situation reports, and direct diplomatic dialogue. Additional undertakings should include official meetings with civil society activists and dissidents, advocating for censure within the UN and other international institutions, and restricting trade and investment when warranted. Moreover, established democracies should endeavor to broaden their community to include others with genuinely functioning democratic institutions, which are willing to demonstrate concern about the state of governance and accountability in their regions and with their commercial partners. Doing this would help to fortify international norms that protect civil society through coordinated diplomatic initiatives against laws that curtail or prohibit freedom of the press and assembly, among other basic rights.

Apart from state-to-state relations, democratic governments and international donors must continue their commitment to robust technical and political assistance to indigenous actors such as journalists, lawyers, union leaders, academics, and rights activists, who have helped their people's progress to freedom and democracy—as was the case in Poland, Chile, Yemen, Burma, and elsewhere. To reinforce their efforts, donors must pursue a comprehensive approach involving grant-support training, networking, research, and political solidarity. Entities like the NED and its core institutes, the German Stiftungs, the European Endowment for Democracy, the Community of Democracies, and others, and the publications by the *Journal of Democracy* and Open Democracy are well-positioned to cooperate in this common cause.

TAKING A STAND

America must strive toward rebuilding a firmer global consensus to support countries undergoing democratic transition and those individuals in closed societies advocating for greater freedoms. This will demand an engaged, proactive role of the United States on the world stage.

International reengagement demands that US leaders vocally dispel growing notions that isolationism is an option; they must reinforce the idea that our continued security and prosperity require a robust international American presence. Our interests are best served by working in partnership with democratic states; hence, we should play what affirmative role we can in helping the spread of democracy.

In turn, if the United States is to continue being a source of inspiration for those around the world who believe in the worth of the individual and the inherent rights she or he has in the pursuit of security, well-being, and happiness, Americans need to get their own house in order. The partisan rancor that prevents the cross-aisle compromises needed for our most pressing challenges must be remedied. The problem, however, does not solely reside in Washington. Pew Center research published in 2014 showed an increasing divide of America's homes and communities along partisan lines.[36] Political brinkmanship and the willing closing of the American mind to others' views hardly provide a sustainable standard for a successful democracy.

In sum, the time for consensus building has arrived at home and abroad. While acknowledging the importance of prioritizing foreign policy and national security interests, I maintain that these should not prevent us from supporting other nations and communities who share the democratic values that have served not only the United States, but humankind. Taking a moral position on the defense of fundamental freedoms and human rights empowers our elected leaders with a common guidepost which will help direct American foreign policy in accordance with the character of this nation. Going forward, this is less a matter of financial resources than of consistent political will, which provides the space for innovative responses, reflective of the demands of the civil societies we stand to assist. As indicated by the previous examples of successful transitions, the net gain is that the world's democratic community is better poised to cooperate, despite the competing interests that will inevitably arise. As in any relationship, effectively working together toward mutually beneficial ends is more likely if partners start from a basis of shared values. And if we continue to accept Winston Churchill's often quoted insight that "democracy is the worst form of government, except for all the others," we can rest assured that despite the messiness that this form of government may bring, both time and the right are on our side.

NOTES

1. Specifically, weakness of democratic values among key groups; economic crises; law-and-order breakdown due to terrorism or insurgency; and intervention or conquest by a non-democratic foreign government. See Samuel Huntington, *The Third Wave: Democratization in the Late Twentieth Century* (Norman: University of Oklahoma Press, 1991), 290–91.

2. See Steven Levitsky and Lucan Way, *Competitive Authoritarianism: Hybrid Regimes after the Cold War* (Cambridge: Cambridge University Press, 2010).

3. In Turkey's June 2015 parliamentary election, the liberal and pro-Kurdish People's Democratic Party cleared Turkey's constitutionally mandated 10 percent threshold by 3.1 points.

4. Freedom House, *Freedom in the World 2015*, Survey 2014, https://freedomhoU.S.e.org/report/freedom-world/freedom-world-2015.

5. Larry Diamond, "Promoting Democracy," in *Great Decisions 2012* (New York: Foreign Policy Association, 2012), 81.

6. Diamond, "Promoting Democracy," 81. William R. Thompson also addresses this issue in his 1996 article, "Democracy and Peace: Putting the Cart before the Horse?" *International Organization* 50, no. 1 (Winter 1996); however, his standards for what would constitute a democracy fall short of Diamond's qualifiers.

7. Amartya Sen, "Democracy as a Universal Value," in *Democracy: A Reader*, ed. Larry Diamond and Marc Plattner (Baltimore: Johns Hopkins University Press, 2009), 311–12.

8. NB Since its recognition, no genocide has occurred in an established democracy.

9. Nikolas Gvosdev and Paul Saunders, "On Liberty," *The National Interest* 79 (Spring 2005): 6.

10. Steven Levitsky and Lucan Way, "The Myth of Democratic Recession," *Journal of Democracy* 26, no. 1 (2015): 47.

11. Levitsky and Way, "The Myth of Democratic Recession," 46.

12. Diamond, "Promoting Democracy," 87.

13. Pew Global's 2012 survey of attitudes to American culture and ideas showed an overall ten-point increase in favorable views of American democracy in comparison to the previous survey in 2007, http://www.pewglobal.org/2012/06/13/chapter-2-attitudes-toward-american-culture-and-ideas/#american-democracy.

14. John Bew, *Realpolitik: A History* (New York: Oxford University Press, 2015), 258.

15. Huntington, *The Third Wave*, 98.

16. Diamond, "Promoting Democracy" in re Iran. See Hilton L. Root, *Alliance Curse: How America Lost the Third World* (Washington, D.C.: Brookings Institution, 2008), 122–44.

17. See Alfred Stepan and Juan J. Linz, "Democratization Theory and the 'Arab Spring,'" *Journal of Democracy* 24, no. 2 (2013).

18. Richard Kraemer, "Towards State Legitimacy in Afghanistan," *International Journal* 65 (Summer 2010).

19. See Henry Kissinger, "Meshing Realism and Idealism in Syria; Middle East," *The Washington Post*, August 3, 2012, https://www.washingtonpost.com/opinions/henry-kissinger-meshing-realism-and-idealism-in-syria-middle-east/2012/08/02/gJQAFkyHTX_story.html; Amitai Etzioni, *Security First* (New Haven, CT: Yale University Press, 2007), x–xi; Paul Saunders and Morton Halperin, "Democracy Promotion as a Policy," *Council on Foreign Relations*, June 2, 2006, http://www.cfr.org/democratization/democracy-promotion-policy/p10784; and Gvosdev and Saunders, "On Liberty."

20. For a more in-depth survey of these means, see Diamond, "Promoting Democracy," 88–102.

21. Thomas Carothers, *Democracy Policy under Obama: Revitalization or Retreat?* (Washington, D.C.: Carnegie Endowment for International Peace, 2012), 18.

22. For the latter, see Ministry of Foreign Affairs of Japan, *The Tokyo Declaration*, Tokyo, 2012, http://www.mofa.go.jp/region/middle_e/afghanistan/tokyo_conference_2012/tokyo_declaration_en1.html.

23. In addition to NED support, these organizations have been recipients of significant Department of State and USAID funds since the late 1980s.

24. Harriet Sherwood, "Human Rights Groups Face Global Crackdown 'Not Seen in a Generation,'" *The Guardian*, August 26, 2015, http://www.theguardian.com/law/2015/aug/26/ngos-face-restrictions-laws-human-rights-generation.

25. "Uncivil Society," *The Economist*, August 22, 2015, 37.

26. Alexander Cooley, "Countering Democratic Norms," *Journal of Democracy* 26, no. 3 (2015): 49–53.

27. Kim Lane Scheppele, "Law in a Time of Emergency: States of Exception and the Temptations of 9/11," *University of Pennsylvania Journal of Constitutional Law* 6, no. 5 (2004), http://scholarship.law.upenn.edu/cgi/viewcontent.cgi?article=1365&context=jcl.

28. Cooley, "Countering Democratic Norms," 52.

29. Zoltan Simon, "Orbán Says He Seeks to End Liberal Democracy in Hungary," *Bloomberg Business*, July 28, 2014, http://www.bloomberg.com/news/articles/2014-07-28/orban-says-he-seeks-to-end-liberal-democracy-in-hungary.

30. Christopher Sabatini, "Meaningless Multilateralism: In International Diplomacy, South America Chooses Quantity over Quality," *Foreign Affairs*, August 8, 2014, https://www.foreignaffairs.com/articles/south-america/2014-08-08/meaningless-multilateralism.

31. Catherine Traywick, "President Obama at West Point: Watch the Speech, Read the Transcript," *Foreign Policy* (Online), May 28, 2014, http://foreignpolicy.com/2014/05/28/president-obama-at-west-point-watch-the-speech-read-the-transcript/.

32. Traywick, "President Obama at West Point."

33. For an overview of the scholarly literature on democratization, see Agnieszka Marczyk's chapter in this volume.

34. See Working Group on Corruption and Security and Sarah Chayes, "Corruption—The Unrecognized Threat to International Security," Carnegie International Endowment for Peace, working paper, June 2014.

35. Cooley, "Countering Democratic Norms," 55.

36. "Political Polarization and the American Public: How Increasing Ideological Uniformity and Partisan Apathy Affect Compromise, Politics, and Everyday Life," Pew Research Center Report, June 12, 2014, 42–53, http://www.people-press.org/files/2014/06/6-12-2014-Political-Polarization-Release.pdf.

Chapter Four

Three Lessons about Democracy Assistance Effectiveness

Sarah Sunn Bush

Promoting democracy has never been more difficult. On the one hand, authoritarian rulers have learned how to thwart some of the dimensions of democracy promotion that have been most successful in the past. For example, aiding civil society organizations that are pushing for democratic reform around the world has become more difficult, with at least fifty-one countries—including, most famously, Egypt and Russia—prohibiting or restricting foreign funding of civil society.[1] So, too, has monitoring elections become more difficult, with countries such as Azerbaijan inviting what is known as "zombie" monitoring groups, which endorse flawed elections and counteract the criticisms that might come from more professional or unbiased observers.[2] On the other hand, democracy-promoting countries' commitments to aiding democracy overseas have started to wane. In the United States, which has historically invested the most money of any country in democracy assistance efforts, the public has become skeptical of costly democracy promotion efforts.

These challenging trends force us to think about how best to allocate scarce resources to democracy promotion in an era of new problems. This chapter focuses not on *whether* the United States should promote democracy, but on *how* the United States should promote democracy. The nuts-and-bolts question of *how* the United States should aid democracy in the developing world is vitally important, although it is one that is often overlooked in the big-picture debates about democracy promotion that have been so common in recent years. Yet the devil is in the details.

This chapter tackles the question of how to promote democracy in several ways. I begin by distilling some of the key macro-findings from the scholarly literature on democracy assistance for a broader audience, including practitioners. Then, I identify three lessons about how to promote democracy effectively based on the current state of knowledge. Finally, I conclude that the trend among both scholars and practitioners toward data transparency, experimental analyses, and studying the details of how democracy assistance works on the ground is a promising development—though not a panacea—that can continue to inform effective democracy assistance in the future.

In brief, the three lessons I discuss next are what I refer to as the "three Ds of democracy assistance effectiveness." First, I argue that we should concentrate scarce time, money, and other resources in the countries where the United States and European Union are willing to back up democracy assistance with other tools of democracy promotion, such as conditionality. This lesson reflects the importance of *donor priorities*. Second, I argue that we should prioritize certain channels of aiding democracy—specifically, channels that are relatively independent from the funding of government and channels that are associated with effective monitoring systems. This lesson reflects the importance of *delivery mechanisms*. Finally, I argue that we should shift the emphasis back toward a more "political," rather than "developmental," approach to promoting democracy. This lesson reflects the importance of how democracy assistance is *designed.* Together, these "three Ds" offer important insights into how to promote democracy effectively in an era of authoritarian pushback.

WHAT HAVE WE LEARNED ABOUT HOW TO AID DEMOCRACY?

So what have we learned about how to aid democracy after three decades of active US promotion? Though it was once axiomatic to say that the international sources of democratization had been understudied, this is no longer the case today. There is a very large—and growing—body of research on the topic of democracy promotion, not to mention other international aspects of democratization.

The picture on the effectiveness of democracy assistance is mixed. We can start with the good news. First, American democracy assistance seems to work, on average, at promoting democracy. About ten years ago, the US Agency for International Development (USAID) funded an academic study to examine the efficacy of its democracy and governance funding. This study was conducted by highly respected independent scholars, led by Steven Finkel at the University of Pittsburgh, and published in *World Politics*, a leading peer-reviewed journal based at Princeton University.[3] The commissioned study noted that there are many challenges to identifying the causal effect of democracy aid on democracy. First, the countries that get targeted to receive democratization and governance support are not selected at random, making it difficult to compare the countries where the United States tries to promote democracy with the countries where the United States does not try to promote democracy. Second, it is hard to agree on how to define and measure democracy. Although numerous indicators exist, such as those produced by Freedom House and the Polity project, there are concerns that these indicators capture democratic change at too aggregated a level to effectively demonstrate causality. Third, historical records on some of the US government's programs are poor. Nevertheless, pretty much any way that the scholars analyzed the data, they found that democracy aid was positively correlated with democratization in targeted countries, again, on average.

Readers of the Finkel et al. study might, of course, question its conclusions given that the authors were part of a USAID-funded research project. But other independent scholars, including James Scott and Carie Steele, have replicated this study's overall positive findings about the effects of American democracy assistance.[4] Moreover, Burçu Savun and Daniel Tirone have even shown that US democracy aid can help countries emerging from civil conflict maintain fragile peace by helping reduce uncertainty.[5]

But there is also bad news. Although democracy promotion is correlated with positive outcomes, on average, our understanding of *why* it works, or *where* it works best, is less developed. Studies that identify positive correlations between democracy aid and democratization on average necessarily focus on general tendencies across countries and over time and typically have had a more difficult time identifying the precise mechanism through which aid is most effective. Some of the direct mechanisms through which democracy assistance has been posited to work include supporting civil society organizations, building better political institutions, and improving countries' governance. Aid programs can achieve those goals by encouraging actors and trends that already exist in civil society, whether via the transfer of knowledge or financial resources. Democracy assistance has also been posited to work through indirect mechanisms, such as via signaling the interest of the international community in a particular country or on a particular issue area. The absence of disaggregated data on aid programs as well as on democratization has hampered impact assessments in the past—though, as I discuss next, more disaggregated data are becoming available that should permit these sorts of analyses in the future.

Developing a better understanding of why and where democracy assistance works best is the crucial next step for scholars and practitioners engaged in evaluating democracy promotion, since that knowledge will be vital to designing effective aid programs in the future. Without a full understanding of why democracy promotion works, it is impossible to design programs to be more effective in the future. While a positive correlation between democracy promotion and democratization on average may imply that democracy promotion can be very effective when the conditions are favorable, this intuition should be subject to additional scrutiny in the future so that we know exactly what conditions are most favorable.

Though we still have much more to learn about the mechanisms of democracy assistance's effectiveness, this chapter offers some tentative ideas about the conditions under which it is most likely to succeed. Drawing on lessons learned from scholarly research as well as practitioners' reported experiences, I emphasize what I call the three Ds of democracy assistance effectiveness: donor priorities, delivery mechanisms, and design.

LESSON 1: DONOR PRIORITIES

The first D stands for donor priorities. Here, I am referring to government officials' preferences about how strongly to emphasize democracy in various developing countries as well as about the form that democracy assistance should take in those countries. In other words, government officials worry both about *how much* to aid democracy and *how* to aid democracy. When making decisions about how much and how to prioritize democracy promotion in various countries, government officials consider a number of factors, ranging from their other foreign policy objectives to the prevailing political and economic environment domestically. Thus, donor priorities depend on government officials' *perceptions* of the national interest. As such, donor priorities with regards to democracy assistance vary across donor countries and administrations, and even within the same administration over time.

The donor's priorities matter for the effectiveness of democracy aid. One of the emerging consensus findings among researchers is that democracy assistance works best when it is accompanied by *conditionality*, defined as "the threat or application of punishments, or the promise or implementation of rewards."[6] Examples of negative conditionality include economic sanctions, drops in foreign assistance, suspensions of diplomatic ties, and suspensions of membership in international organizations.

In support of this insight, Daniela Donno, who published an important recent book on democracy promotion and elections, found that it is rarely enough for outside actors to provide aid or criticize flawed elections—leaders with long histories of rigging elections will continue to do so until their incentives change. Instead, countries democratize when the United States and other Western countries bring out the carrots and sticks. To give one example, consider the case of Serbia before and during the country's Bulldozer Revolution in 2000. The international community's assistance to civil society organizations and political parties in the years leading up to the election that led to the overthrow of Slobodan Milosevic has often been applauded.[7] But it was only when the United States and the European Union made it clear to opposition supporters that the country's international standing depended on opposition parties uniting and governing Serbia that they did so. Serbia's future in the European Union, Council of Europe, and Organization for Security and Cooperation in Europe now hung in the balance—and the opposition parties listened.[8]

That example suggests that democracy assistance is unlikely to work in countries where the donors' preferences are not genuinely aligned with wanting democracy. In her book, Donno also provides a more negative example of international efforts to promote democracy in Cambodia that illustrates how failure can result when conditionality is not invoked. There, the international community has consistently criticized Prime Minister Hun Sen and the ruling Cambodian People's Party for holding unfree elections, but it has failed to combine those critiques with reductions in aid. Moreover, and in contrast to the aforementioned European institutions, ASEAN does not have a history of strongly supporting democracy in Asian countries, and Cambodia is no exception. Given that Cambodia depends heavily on other countries for support via foreign aid, there is a ready path through which conditionality could be invoked in favor of democracy—but it has not been.

American democracy promotion in the Arab world has frequently—and justifiably—been criticized for being ineffective due in part to some of these same failures to invoke conditionality.[9] Although some of the problems faced by democracy assistance in this region also relate to how the aid programs are designed—a point that I address in more detail—a more fundamental concern is that donors' priorities are simply not aligned with promoting meaningful democratization in the region. In Arab authoritarian countries such as Bahrain, Jordan, and Morocco, donors may be happy to support small improvements in the rule of law or women's rights under the stated goal of supporting "democracy and good governance," but ultimately they prefer to maintain the status quo there because of strategic concerns, whether related to Israel or to counterterrorism and military cooperation. The most important recent example of these dynamics is Egypt, where the US government refrained from calling the events of July 2013 a coup d'état in spite of all evidence to the contrary so as to avoid having to suspend aid to its important strategic ally.

Given the significance of donor priorities for the effectiveness of supporting freedom overseas, it makes sense to concentrate scarce time, money, and other democracy-promotion resources in the countries where the United States and European countries are willing to back up democracy assistance with other tools of democracy promotion, such as economic conditionality and diplomatic pressure. Invoking such tools does not require the international community to resort to the type of cookie-cutter economic programs that were pursued in the post-Soviet region in the 1990s and then later criticized (e.g., conditioning loans from the International Monetary Fund on economic reforms). Rather, invoking these tools consistently simply means that if countries pledge that they will, for example, suspend foreign assistance or membership in international organizations if countries flagrantly abuse human rights and democracy then they will actually do so. Without this sort of commitment on the part of democracy promoters, democracy assistance is unlikely to succeed—and, in the worst cases, it can end up playing into the hands of undemocratic leaders, as Melinda Haring also argues in her chapter.

It is worth noting that advocates of democracy promotion may hope to instead change donor priorities so that they are better aligned with aiding democracy and invoking conditionality, regardless of the other foreign policy issues that may be at stake. But the road toward changing donors' priorities is likely a long and winding one. As noted earlier, in the United States, at least, democracy promotion is a foreign policy that enjoys only modest public support—and the public is much more supportive of naming and shaming nondemocracies than it is of using more costly strategies to support democracy in them, such as sending aid or using military force.[10] Especially in the wake of costly military interventions in Afghanistan and Iraq, Americans are skeptical about promoting democracy, at least via such aggressive and often counterproductive means. Given those public attitudes, realigning policymakers' priorities is unlikely, at least right away. Thus, concentrating scarce democracy promotion resources in the countries where donor priorities are truly aligned with democratization is a smart strategy.

LESSON 2: DELIVERY MECHANISMS

The second D stands for delivery mechanisms. Any government that is engaged in aiding democracy abroad has an array of mechanisms to choose from. I focus here on the range of mechanisms through which democracy *aid* can be delivered. The US government, for example, can fund democracy assistance programs through the USAID, the State Department, and the National Endowment for Democracy (NED), among others, and those donors in turn pass aid along to other organizations that are typically responsible for designing and implementing projects overseas. Thomas Melia has referred to this dizzying array of funding mechanisms in the United States as the "democracy bureaucracy."[11] A similar democracy bureaucracy exists in the European Union. For the purposes of this chapter, I focus on the delivery options from which the United States can choose. I argue that two aspects of delivery are particularly important: how *independent* the channel of delivery is from the US government and how *feasible* it is for the US government to observe the impacts of the organizations that are delivering the aid. Although I focus on the United States, the argument could easily be extended to cover the delivery options faced by European or other donor governments.

First, to have a shot at supporting democratic change, initiatives that have some level of insulation from the US government, such as the NED, must be an essential part of the formula. Funding democracy promotion outside of the US government is often the best strategy because doing so ties the US government's hands from interfering in programmatic decisions. Otherwise—and to return to my first D—it is too easy for other donors' competing preferences to swamp democratizing good intentions.

Insulation from the US government is also an important strategy because programs that are closely linked to the government often arouse suspicion in countries that are the targets of democracy assistance. Although any American nongovernmental organization (NGO) that receives government funding to work on democracy in the developing world may be the subject of suspicion or even rejection in some countries, it is important from the perspective of credibility and perception to use strategies that are more independent. Especially in countries where anti-Americanism is high, capable local organizations may not want to accept US government funding—and if they do, they may lose legitimacy in the eyes of their fellow citizens, on whom they likely depend for successful programs.

In the Arab world, the perception of collaborating with the United States has posed a significant challenge for local organizations that receive democracy assistance. For example, my research in Jordan suggests that this is an issue that political activists there have often faced. There, an activist told me, "Ever since I became involved with women's rights issues, there have always been accusations that I'm a foreign agent. You wouldn't want to say publicly that you got support from the United Kingdom or United States."[12] Her experiences suggest that when US support can be given to civil society organizations overseas in an indirect manner, it may be more likely to be welcomed and to advance the cause of democracy.

Second, to create effective democratic change, aid needs to be delivered in such a way that the US government is able to observe and assess the impacts of the programs. This attention to measurement is particularly important when government officials follow this advice and opt to give donor agencies some independence. It is often difficult for individuals working in government agencies to keep track of the results of the many programs they fund overseas. As a number of scholars have documented, these difficulties too often lead donor officials to focus their energy on programs that are most likely to produce quick, quantitative outputs—which may not be the kind of programs that are most likely to democratize countries. It is vital for government officials to design and implement programs in such a way that they can set *meaningful* benchmarks for countries' short-, medium-, and long-term levels of democracy, at both aggregated and disaggregated levels. These benchmarks may be qualitative or quantitative, but in any case they should be designed to assess international aid programs' causal effects on democracy.

For example, a typically used output measure is the number of individuals trained by a rule of law program, whereas a typically used outcome measure is the number of women elected to municipal councils after a program that sought to encourage women to run for political office.[13] But we know that the number of individuals trained or the number of women elected to municipal councils are not the right outcomes to use to determine whether a country is democratizing. In fact, in some countries, programs designed to improve the rule of law or enhance the number of women in political office end up feeding into authoritarian survival strategies. Such has arguably been the case in Jordan, for example, where the monarchy has attempted to give the impression of political reform to local and international audiences via the political inclusion of women without fundamentally changing the political system.

Moreover, it is important for democracy aid to be delivered in ways that can help funders monitor success overseas so that they don't encourage organizations in the democracy bureaucracy to "teach to the test" rather than innovate. In her chapter in this volume, Melinda Haring writes persuasively about the important role that competition can play in helping officials keep track of results overseas. This is an excellent suggestion.

Today, we have organizations that are known as "donor darlings" and "Beltway bandits" that consistently receive large amounts of US foreign aid via grants, cooperative agreements, and contracts—as she argues, giving such organizations a bit less freedom and subjecting them to some competitive pressures could be a positive development. Research on contracting relationships in economics and political science confirms the insight that competition is a good way for quality information about program efficacy to be revealed. Of course, competition can be a double-edged sword—too much competition for funding and other resources can cause organizations to avoid cooperating with each other or to become more concerned with getting future contracts than with promoting democracy.

LESSON 3: DESIGN

The third D stands for design. As noted earlier, one of the most consistent problems that has bedeviled democracy assistance in the Arab world as well as in other regions is that Western donor governments are simply not in a position to support activities that are genuinely likely to promote democracy there. Much of the US democracy assistance efforts in the region are therefore quite tame—they take on issues such as promoting women's political inclusion or enhancing local government capacity. This type of programming is typical of work in countries ranging from Morocco and Egypt to Jordan and Lebanon. Though not without their controversies, such activities tend not to fundamentally challenge the political order in the countries that are the targets of such activities, and sometimes even can reinforce the status quo.

This "taming" of democracy assistance in the Arab world is consistent with more general trends in democracy assistance, which has increasingly come to focus on the promotion of good governance over more overtly political activities, such as aiding civil society and political parties. [14] Thomas Carothers would frame these two approaches to promoting democracy as the "political" and the "developmental" approaches. [15] In Carothers' framework, political approaches to democracy assistance are typified by activities such as electoral support, aid to political parties, and funding for politically active NGOs. Political approaches emphasize such activities due to their guiding assumption that democratization is inherently a "political struggle." In contrast, developmental approaches to democracy assistance include a wider range of activities, including aid that supports improvements to the quality of state institutions. They do so because they view democratization as a "slow, iterative process of change."

Supporting good governance, which is core to a developmental approach to democracy promotion, is undoubtedly an important activity. Support for good governance usually involves programs aimed at reducing corruption, increasing efficiency, improving state capacity, and making the state more accountable and transparent. Yet it is crucial to recognize that promoting good governance and promoting democracy are not the same things, even though it is possible that good governance could enhance the long-term prospects for democracy, and vice versa. Indeed, democracies can be poorly governed (e.g., India), and autocracies can be well governed (e.g., Singapore). As Francis Fukuyama recently noted, "We Americans tend to believe that democracy is an intrinsic part of good governance and that more democracy means better quality government. . . . However, this postulated relationship remains just a theory that remains subject to more empirical testing." [16] As a consequence, it is not clear that relatively tame forms of aid are likely to succeed at helping countries transition to democracy or consolidate previous democratic gains, even though they may be worthwhile for other reasons.

Support for women's political participation offers a good illustration of these dynamics. This issue has been a major area of growth in democracy assistance in the past decade. My research suggests that international support for women's political participation has had some important consequences, such as encouraging countries to adopt laws that require a certain number of seats in parliaments to be set aside for women. [17] In India and other countries, such quotas have had major consequences, including encouraging women's political participation and even altering some of the policies that are pursued by elected officials. They may also be desirable for normative reasons.

Yet the positive impacts of gender quotas—and of women's political participation more generally—in terms of democratization are less clear in authoritarian environments. As Melinda Haring says about women's representation in her chapter, "All well and good, but hardly the stuff of real and meaningful social change." After all, if a parliament is not given real lawmaking authority, then the characteristics of its members are unlikely to substantially alter the quality of representation or democracy in a country. In fact, having more women in parliament can sometimes have deleterious consequences for democracy since this reform can help autocracies mimic the appearance of liberal democracy. Doing so is valuable to them both in terms of international audiences, which might reward liberalizing countries with aid, as well as in terms of domestic audiences, which may be satisfied (at least temporarily) by this type of political reform.

Other types of programs that support authoritarian legislatures without a specific gender focus have faced similar problems. Such efforts typically aim to increase the professionalism and transparency of parliamentary representatives and staff members. An example of such a program was the USAID-supported effort in autocratic Azerbaijan's parliament, the Milli Majlis, between 2007 and 2011. An independent evaluation of the program found that although it was highly successful in terms of short-term deliverables, "For the most part, the program did not change how the [Milli Majlis] functions or how ordinary people in Azerbaijan relate to and understand the parliament."[18] In Azerbaijan, as well as other authoritarian countries, parliamentary-strengthening programs can play into incumbents' survival strategies. Research suggests that authoritarian legislatures can perform useful functions for dictators, such as serving as a way to distribute patronage or divide the opposition.[19]

Of course, in countries that are authoritarian, a more confrontational or political approach to democracy assistance—for example, aiding dissidents or political parties—might not be possible. Moreover, it is indeed possible that having more women in parliament will plant the seeds of democratization down the line. Research by Stephen Brown on democracy assistance in Kenya, Malawi, and Rwanda suggests that these rationales have been common justifications of continued democracy assistance efforts in those countries in the absence of clear breakthroughs. He notes that sometimes donors set the bar very low and set long time horizons. "Cautioning against impatience with the slow pace of democratization in Africa, Western officials often invoke the well-worn cliché that 'it took democracy 500 years to take root in Europe.'"[20] Brown correctly acknowledges that donors may have a point—democratization is often a lengthy and complicated process—but he also notes that they can use this reasoning as an excuse for designing programs that are insufficiently confrontational toward dictators.

Indeed, there is no research that I am aware of that suggests that programs that make incremental improvements in parliamentary capacity or women's participation within fundamentally undemocratic countries are likely to lead to democratization. Though I emphasize again that these programs might be worth pursuing for goals beyond democratization, it is important to be clear about what our goals for them are. In the absence of evidence that these programs will lead to democratization, it may be better to concentrate scarce democracy assistance resources where we know they have a decent shot at succeeding and devote other types of aid resources to other goals. In other words, democracy assistance should be sponsored in countries that have genuine opposition movements that the international community can bolster. Moreover, democracy assistance should be sponsored in countries that have some of the structural characteristics that are typically thought to make democratic transition and consolidation likely, such as geographic proximity to other democracies, previous experience with pluralism, and socioeconomic development. In countries where the conditions for democracy are less propitious, democracy assistance should be reduced or shifted to types of assistance with other goals, such as improved governance or gender equality.

CONCLUSIONS

We can choose to view the core components of US democracy assistance from either a "glass half full" or a "glass half empty" perspective: after all, they have positive effects, and they have negative effects. In addition to some of the macro-level positive correlations identified earlier, another reason for optimism about the future is the push toward aid transparency. There is a major USAID-funded initiative, AidData, which is gathering and geocoding micro-level data on US government aid projects.[21] Meanwhile, the Varieties of Democracy project, cohosted by the University of Gothenberg and the University of Notre Dame, has produced more than three hundred disaggregated indicators of democracy across a wide range of countries and years. Finally, AidData—as well as other initiatives—is sponsoring many exciting new case studies, many of them modeled on award-winning economist Esther Duflo's randomized controlled trials out of the Poverty Action Lab. These types of research designs are ideal for identifying the causal impact of foreign assistance programs on the outcomes that we care about most.

To give an example of how such analyses may improve our understanding of why and under what conditions democracy assistance works, consider the case of electoral assistance. Although elections are an essential part of democracy, most countries in the world today hold elections—including many unfree countries. In authoritarian environments, elections are often associated with negative outcomes such as repression, discrimination, instability, and violence.

Since elections are such important events—though by no means the only aspect of democracy or democratization—international organizations and

Western states have invested considerable resources in support of free and fair elections. According to Judith Kelley, "A multitude of international activities and processes permeate elections . . . and they epitomize the prevalence of international influences on domestic politics."[22] Western governments reported to the Organization for Economic Cooperation and Development that they spent $525 million supporting elections in 2010; the United States, the largest donor government, spent $264 million alone. Though many aspects of electoral assistance have been applauded, many aspects have also been criticized. Election observers, for example, are generally successful at detecting and deterring fraud, but they have also at times refrained from condemning unfair elections out of political considerations. For example, observers were relatively circumspect about the Kenyan general election in 1997, even though it was clearly not free and fair. The reason was that the observers were afraid of fomenting postelection instability and thus violence and repression.[23]

This anecdote highlights the critical role of *perception* in many aspects of democracy promotion—a theme that has pervaded the three Ds. Local perceptions of elections' credibility can determine whether elections promote—or undermine—peace and stable democratic governance. In the midst of ongoing debates about whether the United States should "give up" or "dig in" on the issue of democracy in the Arab world, it is vital to understand what the effects of its electoral assistance are in the Middle East and North Africa. Along with a collaborator, Lauren Prather of the University of California at San Diego, I am currently analyzing data from two surveys of more than a thousand individuals in Tunisia—where we randomly informed selected respondents about the activities of international actors during the elections to see how that information affected peoples' perceptions. Using the type of experimental research design pioneered by the aforementioned Poverty Action Lab, we find that the nationality of the international actors, as well as the content of their involvement, matters for how Tunisians view the integrity of their recent elections.

The movement toward data transparency, experimental analyses, and studying the details of how democracy assistance works on the ground isn't a panacea. But if democracy promotion is here to stay—and I suspect it is— this kind of knowledge is just what we need to build more knowledge about *why* and *under what conditions* democracy assistance works. Until then, the three Ds—donor priorities, delivery mechanisms, and design—offer some important lessons for how democracy assistance can be more successful in the future.

In an era of authoritarian pushback, we need democracy promotion to work. Some strategies have proven effective in the past, whereas others have not. Democracy promoters should concentrate their efforts on the countries where donors will supplement aid with other forms of diplomatic and economic pressure and where aid can be delivered and designed in ways that will create meaningful change. Only then will democracy promotion reach its full promise.

NOTES

1. Darin Christensen and Jeremy M. Weinstein, "Defunding Dissent: Restrictions on Aid to NGOs," *Journal of Democracy* 24, no. 2 (April 2013).

2. Christopher Walker and Alexander Cooley, "Vote of the Living Dead," *Foreign Policy* (Online), October 31, 2013, http://foreignpolicy.com/2013/10/31/vote-of-the-living-dead/.

3. Steven E. Finkel, Aníbal Pérez-Liñan, and Mitchelle A. Seligson, "The Effects of U.S. Foreign Assistance on Democracy Building, 1990–2003," *World Politics* 59, no. 3 (April 2007).

4. James M. Scott and Carie A. Steele, "Sponsoring Democracy: The United States and Democracy Aid to the Developing World, 1988–2001," *International Studies Quarterly* 55, no. 1 (March 2011).

5. Burçu Savun and Daniel C. Tirone, "Foreign Aid, Democratization, and Civil Conflict: How Does Democracy Aid Affect Civil Conflict?" *American Journal of Political Science* 55, no. 2 (April 2011).

6. Daniela Donno, *Defending Democratic Norms: International Actors and the Politics of Electoral Misconduct* (Oxford: Oxford University Press, 2013), 14.

7. Marlene Spoerri, *Engineering Revolution: The Paradox of Democracy Promotion in Serbia* (Philadelphia: University of Pennsylvania Press, 2014), 1–4.

8. Donno, *Defending Democratic Norms*, 133–41.

9. See, for example, Sheila Carapico, *Political Aid and Arab Activism: Democracy Promotion, Justice, and Representation* (Cambridge: Cambridge University Press, 2014).

10. Dawn Brancati, "The Determinants of U.S. Public Opinion Towards Democracy Promotion," *Political Behavior* 36, no. 4 (December 2014): 724–25.

11. Thomas Melia, "The Democracy Bureaucracy," *The American Interest* 1, no. 4 (June 2006).

12. Quoted in Sarah Sunn Bush and Amaney Jamal, "Anti-Americanism, Authoritarian Regimes, and Attitudes about Women in Politics," *International Studies Quarterly* 59, no. 1 (March 2015): 36.

13. The critical literature on the obsession with measurement in democracy assistance is large. Some of the important contributions include: Thomas Carothers, *Aiding Democracy Abroad: The Learning Curve* (Washington, D.C.: Carnegie Endowment for International Peace, December 1999); Keith Brown, ed., *Transacting Transition: The Micropolitics of Democracy Assistance in the Former Yugoslavia* (Bloomfield: Kumarian Press, 2006); and Sarah Sunn Bush, *The Taming of Democracy Assistance: Why Democracy Promotion Does Not Confront Dictators* (Cambridge: Cambridge University Press, 2015).

14. Sarah Sunn Bush, "Changes in American Grant-Making," in *The Taming of Democracy Assistance: Why Democracy Promotion Does Not Confront Dictators* (Cambridge: Cambridge University Press, 2015), 106–30.

15. Thomas Carothers, "Democracy Assistance: Political vs. Developmental?" *Journal of Democracy* 20, no. 1 (January 2009).

16. Francis Fukuyama, "What Is Governance?" *The American Interest*, January 2012, http://www.the-american-interest.com/2012/01/31/what-is-governance/.

17. Sarah Sunn Bush, "International Politics and the Spread of Quotas for Women in Legislatures," *International Organization* 65, no. 1 (Winter 2011).

18. Lincoln Mitchell and Rashad Shirinov, *Parliamentary Program of Azerbaijan Evaluation: Final Report* (Bethesda: Democracy International, July 2011), 7.

19. Jennifer Gandhi and Ellen Lust-Okar, "Elections Under Authoritarianism," *Annual Review of Political Science* 12 (June 2009).

20. Quoted in Stephen Brown, "'Well, What Can You Expect?': Donor Officials' Apologetics for Hybrid Regimes in Africa," *Democratization* 18, no. 2 (March 2011): 521.

21. "Open Data for International Development," *AidData 3.0*, last modified 2016, http://aiddata.org/.

22. Judith G. Kelley, "International Influences on Elections in New Multiparty States," *Annual Review of Political Science* 15 (June 2012): 215.

23. Judith Kelley, "D-Minus Elections: The Politics and Norms of International Election Observation," *International Organization* 63, no. 4 (Fall 2009).

Chapter Five

Reforming the Democracy Bureaucracy

Melinda Haring

This chapter examines how the United States supports democrats and democratic movements and offers recommendations to improve the delivery of US democracy assistance. US democracy assistance, which began in earnest in the 1980s as a means to support democratization in Eastern Europe and encourage liberalization in the Soviet Union, enjoys bipartisan support and has become an institutionalized part of US foreign policy. Today the United States supports democrats on every continent rhetorically and through assistance dollars. US democracy dollars are distributed through the US Agency for International Development (USAID), the Department of State, the National Endowment for Democracy (NED), and several other government agencies. US assistance provides funding for independent newspapers, coaches political parties, trains citizens how to monitor elections, and supports business associations, among many other examples.

Democracy assistance has been a US foreign policy priority—albeit a secondary one, relative to defense, diplomacy, and development—for moral and pragmatic reasons. From Ronald Reagan to Barack Obama, official rhetoric on the importance of democracy has largely remained the same: humans long to be free, and democracy is the system that provides the most freedom for human flourishing. Pragmatically, democratic states make better neighbors. Scholars have posited that democratic countries by and large do not fight with their neighbors; thus, a world dominated by democratic governments would experience less tension and limit the potential for confrontation. For this reason, supporting the growth of democracies contributes directly to safeguarding US national security.

From its modest beginnings in the Reagan administration, the idea that outside actors can encourage democratic change overseas has grown into a $3 billion industry encompassing a vast array of programs.[1] Scholars and practitioners have argued convincingly[2] that the "democracy bureaucracy"[3] remains uncoordinated, is often counterproductive, contains redundancies, "and [is] characterized by scant strategic thinking and a cumbersome management system."[4] A group of prominent scholars and heads of the top democracy organizations in Washington wrote, "If foreign assistance, including democracy assistance, was a company, it would have gone into bankruptcy twenty years ago."[5] Yet supporting democrats is an important plank of US influence and national security that can be improved with three reforms.

First, the US government should leave democracy assistance in authoritarian countries like Uzbekistan and Zimbabwe to the independent grant-making model exemplified by the NED. Second, field-based organizations like the National Democratic Institute (NDI) and International Republican Institute (IRI) should focus on "free" and "partly free" places already on the road to change like Ukraine and Tunisia. Finally, noncompetitive mechanisms for awarding funds to democracy-promotion organizations should end. The first two reforms entail a strategic approach to a natural division of labor within the democracy-promotion community. Field-based organizations implement programs through field offices staffed by expatriates and locals, while the grant-making organization being discussed maintains its headquarters in Washington, D.C., but does not support field offices. The NED is the best-known grant-making organization, while most partners of the USAID, like NDI and IRI, are field-based organizations.

BACKGROUND

It is difficult to measure the effects of a democracy and governance program, unlike in the more traditional subfields of development such as health, where monitoring and evaluation are more straightforward: this program immunized five thousand people or brought five thousand liters of clean drinking water to a village. The results of democracy programming are often imperceptible at first and may take years to become apparent. While acknowledging the difficulties of measuring program efficacy, the United States should not continue to spend $3 billion annually if it cannot demonstrate that its democracy programs are having an impact.

This chapter is the result of graduate school study, and then work as a practitioner focusing on Azerbaijan, Georgia, and Russia. Like many in the field, I arrived with high hopes that smart development specialists with regional knowledge could design effective programs to enable democratically minded individuals to push for reform. What I observed was disheartening: cookie-cutter programs that did not take into account a country's specific circumstances or incentive structure into program design. As a result of formal study and as a practitioner, I offer this report in the hopes that the second generation of democracy specialists will skeptically evaluate the efforts of the last thirty years and reform a field that truly has the potential to better the lives of millions abroad and enhance the security of Americans at home.

MODELS MATTER

The delivery of nonprofit democracy assistance almost always takes one of two basic institutional forms: a field-based organization that carries out programs in-country through offices in-country and local staff, or a grant-making organization with a centralized office that normally does not have field offices. While both models are taxpayer funded, their ability to operate and carry out meaningful programs, especially those in authoritarian and semiauthoritarian countries, varies dramatically.

The US government overwhelmingly distributes its democracy assistance dollars through USAID, which selects field-based organizations to implement its program ideas; these field-based organizations are nonprofit and for-profit.[6] USAID itself does not implement the actual programs, which led Senator Patrick Leahy to memorably (and accurately) describe it as "a check writing agency for a handful of big Washington contractors and NGOs."[7] Examples of nonprofit organizations that implement USAID programs include the IRI, NDI, IREX, Counterpart International, and dozens of others. For-profit contractors that specialize in democracy and governance programs include Chemonics International, Democracy International, Development Alternatives Inc. (DAI) and many others.

These field-based implementers are structurally similar and operate along roughly the same lines: a large office in Washington, D.C., sets the overall strategy, while field offices scattered throughout the world execute the actual programs. In many of the field offices, an American serves as the director and locals provide administrative support. The field-based model provides a continuous US presence on the ground and can provide different kinds of assistance that can be hard to do through externally based grants. Field-based operations can bring technical knowledge, oversight, local information, and access to decision makers.

The field-based model is often inefficient, as a larger footprint leaves fewer assistance dollars to fund actual programs. Overhead costs, including salaries, rent, and expatriate perks in an organization with field offices can reach up to 70 percent, while overhead at an independent grant-making organization like the NED is 16 percent.[8] It is telling that field-based organizations do not make their detailed program budgets publicly available. By contrast, the NED makes its grant recipients and the amounts they receive publicly available in its annual report and on its website, allowing one to calculate what percentage of the organization's budget goes to the upkeep of its own infrastructure and what percentage goes to actual programs.

Field-based organizations often justify their presence in closed societies as a way to help crack open the door to reform, reasoning that this will pave the way to implement real programs and work with genuine political parties once political space becomes available. That argument is shortsighted, however. If and when political change comes, for example, to Uzbekistan, where President Islam Karimov has ruled for over two decades without a whiff of democratization, having had a field office in Tashkent under the Karimov regime is not likely to enable an organization to take better advantage of a hypothetical political opening. If anything, implementing democracy programs with the permission of a clearly authoritarian regime only tarnishes the credentials of the organization. Moreover, when they allow them in, authoritarian regimes often use the presence of democracy-promotion organizations to bolster their own "democratic" credentials. If and when a democratic

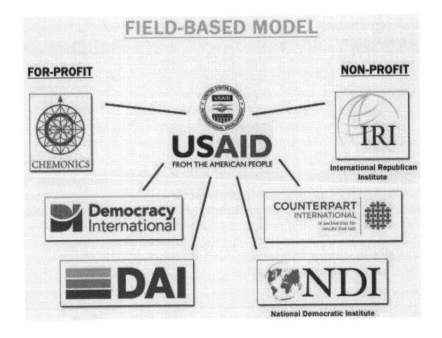

Figure 5.1.   Field-based model: A nonprofit or for-profit organization that delivers programs through local offices; most organizations implementing democracy and governance programs are field-based. *Source: Chemonics International website; USAID website; IRI website; Counterpart International website; NDI website; DAI website; Democracy International website.*

awakening occurs in Uzbekistan, real reformers may even be unwilling to work with an organization that had cooperated with the old regime.

Having relationships with civil society activists, not maintaining field offices, puts organizations in the best position to take advantage of newly opened space.[9] In Tunisia, organizations like NDI and Freedom House, which had built relationships outside of Tunisia with civil society activists during the Ben Ali era, were able to get on the ground and start working immediately after the revolution (NDI is overwhelmingly but not entirely field-based; Tunisia was an exception to its general modus operandi). However, they did not have field offices in Tunisia prior to the Arab Spring.[10]

One scholar suggested that this chapter draw a distinction between in-country work in closed societies with governments versus in-country work that tries to reach the NGO sector in assertive and realistic ways. However, USAID's work with NGOs in semiauthoritarian and authoritarian countries is often not assertive or realistic. USAID's $3.5 million civil society program in Azerbaijan, implemented by the NDI, tried to reach the NGO sector but it was not assertive in the least bit.[11] The program, in part, gave small grants to local NGOs that were intended to empower youth and women, two powerless constituencies in Azerbaijan. The idea that the empowerment of women and youth is a key component in effecting positive change runs through statements by NDI's president and chairwoman, and programmatic documents on the organization's website.[12] They strongly imply that if we empower women and youth, they might convince their friends to pick up trash and start computer centers. All well and good, but hardly the stuff of real and meaningful social change. Even if programs could be implemented in closed countries in ways that tried to reach the NGO sector assertively and realistically, the arbiter would likely be USAID, which is highly problematic. USAID's Democracy and Governance officers often do not know the local environment or language well enough to decide if programs are assertive and realistic.[13] The implementer may have the local knowledge, but it is always in their bureaucratic self-interest to argue that there is sufficient political space to conduct meaningful programs. In addition, there is often a tension within USAID missions between traditional development work and democracy and governance programs, which many aid workers view as threatening the mission's nonpolitical work. In not-free countries, mission directors have little incentive to push aggressively for democratic change because doing so might threaten its health, education, and economic development programs. Thus, this chapter draws a tight distinction between working in not-free countries with NGOs through field-based operations and the independent grant-making model.

As noted, the US government also supports democracy abroad through an independent grant-making approach. In institutional terms, this is the NED. The NED was created to do two things. First, it provides funds to the four "core" institutes: NDI, IRI, Center for International Private Enterprise (CIPE), and the Solidarity Center. Congress established the NED, in part, to fund these institutes, which transfer expertise from business, labor, and politics.

The NED also provides small grants *directly* to domestic civil society organizations overseas. NED staff receive grant applications from small, indigenous organizations and they select and fund the most promising ideas. For example, in 2011 the NED gave the OL! Azerbaijan Youth Movement a small grant to support a biweekly series of seminars and lectures that promote democratic values among young people.[14] The events were videorecorded and made available on the organization's website to any interested party. There is no field office that might worry whether the content of these events will draw regime censure. Azerbaijanis organize the activities, manage the funds, provide progress reports to Washington, design the program from the outset, and decide how far to push the envelope in dealing with their own government. In marked contrast to the field-based model, the NED's grants are conceptualized, overseen, and implemented by locals; they are driven by the needs and interests of local activists, who know their societies far better than any Western development expert. NED program staff who speak relevant local languages visit their grantees often to monitor the projects. Furthermore, NED's grants tend to be very small, thereby reducing the risk that funds might be misused.

Figure 5.2.   Core funding: The NED funds four core institutes: NDI, IRI, CIPE, and the Solidarity Center. *Source: NED website; Solidarity Center website; NDI website; CIPE website; IRI website.*

In not-free countries, the NED's small grants approach is superior because it does not require field offices that depend on the ongoing permission of the government. An organization with a field office in an authoritarian state like Russia, for example, is more vulnerable to strong-arm tactics than a foreign organization that does not seek to maintain a foreign presence. We saw this firsthand in September 2012 when the Russian government ordered USAID to close all of its programs in the Russian Federation.[15] Consequently, all USAID-funded partners with offices in Russia are scrambling to remain active from a neighboring country or are in the process of closing. The crucial point to remember is that field-based organizations in closed societies tend to implement cautious and anodyne programs because their dependence on field offices makes them more vulnerable to pressure from authoritarian regimes.

Congress has acknowledged the superiority of the grant-making model time and time again. Both the House and Senate bills for FY2016 include a large increase in funding for the National Endowment for Democracy to $170 million. Senate appropriators wrote that the NED "is a more appropriate and effective means of conducting democracy programs in closed and transitioning societies than either USAID or the Department of State, as evidenced by the complications arising from programs supported by those agencies in Egypt and Cuba."[16] This position is consistent with previous funding bills. In FY2013, the Senate Committee on Appropriations tried to double the NED's budget from $104 million to $236 million, "recogniz[ing] the NED as a more appropriate and effective mechanism to promote democracy and human rights abroad than either the Department of State or USAID."[17] The Senate Committee on Appropriations "recognizes the comparative advantages of the NED in the promotion of democracy and human rights abroad," citing its "unparalleled experience in promoting freedom during the cold war, and continued ability to conduct programs in the most hostile political environments."[18]

The independent grant-making model acknowledges that outsiders have a limited role to play in democratic transitions. Because of its unique model, the NED is able to operate throughout the world and in some of the most challenging environments. In the Eurasia region, the NED supports civil society organizations in the North Caucasus; no other American organization is able to work in Dagestan or Chechnya. The grant-making model of the NED is unique, and it should be bolstered. A modest 20 percent increase to its current budget, spread over the next ten years in small annual additions intended mainly to keep pace with inflation, would be appropriate. As the NED's budget grows, there should not be an assumption that its funding to the four core institutes will automatically increase, to ensure that the core institutes maintain political creativity and interesting programming.

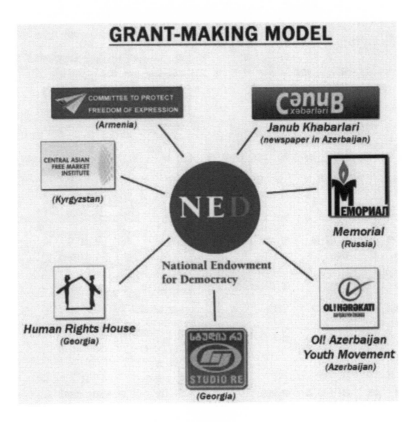

Figure 5.3.   Grant-making model: The NED is an independent grant-making or-
ganization that does not maintain field offices and distributes grants directly to
indigenous NGOs. *Source: NED website; Memorial website; OL! Azerbaijan
Youth Movement website; Studio RE website; Human Rights House website;
Central Asian Free Market Institute website; Committee to Protect Freedom of
Expression website; Janub Khabarlari website.*

There are three downsides to working through indigenous NGOs that
should be acknowledged. First, indigenous NGOs tend to be less professional
and have less capacity. They constantly struggle with retaining talent and
raising sufficient funds, reflect the politics and personality of the NGO's
leader, and are often a single grant-cycle away from insolvency. Second,
domestic NGOs may not have sufficient monitoring and evaluation capabilities. Finally, the grant-making approach offers a much smaller financial
pipeline than the field-office alternative, but this is a virtue. A small country
awash in donor dollars is an invitation to the unscrupulous, as myriad accounts from Afghanistan attest. Societies produce only so many democratic
activists, and too many assistance dollars can create an artificial cottage

industry. The NED cannot pump as much money into a country as USAID, but that is hardly a bad thing.

In sum, the NED has a flexible model that enables it to assist democrats directly in repressive or sensitive political environments where US government support, even if channeled through intermediary institutions, would be diplomatically or politically unfeasible. For example, the NED funds independent print newspapers in Azerbaijan, a country with virtually no independent media and active surveillance of its citizens on the web. USAID would be unlikely to fund such an "aggressive" project. The field-based model, especially the political party institutes, is too cautious in closed societies and too few dollars actually reach the field.[19] Policymakers ought to work exclusively through the United States' most agile organization in not-free countries.

GET SMARTER ABOUT WHERE WE WORK

USAID and its field-office partners should only work in countries where a democratic outcome is likely, or in countries clearly undergoing political transition. The US should curtail current USAID programs in semiauthoritarian and authoritarian regimes like Azerbaijan, Kazakhstan, Jordan, South Sudan, Tajikistan, Turkmenistan, and Uzbekistan. None of these countries has real politics, a viable opposition, a vibrant civil society, an independent press, or free and fair elections, nor are they likely to in the foreseeable future.

USAID should fund programs only in countries that Freedom House ranks as "partly free" according to its annual *Freedom in the World* index. First published in 1973, *Freedom in the World* is a widely referenced index. Its methodology is rigorous, with country-experts providing quantitative evaluations of the state of political rights and civil liberties in countries, along with a qualitative narrative describing major trends over the year the study covers. The index is so highly regarded that the Millennium Challenge Corporation (MCC) uses *Freedom in the World*'s scores as one of its selection indicators to determine country eligibility for MCC assistance.[20]

Triage—the allocation of resources according to strict criteria of priorities—makes sense in a resource-constrained environment. The ten Eastern European members of the European Union have already realized the need to be strategic in their giving priorities. The Eastern EU members do not spread their extremely limited democracy dollars thin—they put most of the money into Georgia, Moldova, Serbia, and Ukraine, all countries where change is either underway or feasible.[21] (Belarus is an admitted exception to this rule; Eastern EU members support change there for historical and geographic reasons.) Eastern EU members do not work in Central Asia, having reasonably concluded that a failure to hold regular and fair elections, high levels of corruption, a closed media environment, murky judiciaries, and elite disinterest in reform make these countries poor investments for scarce democracy dollars.

USAID—which distributes more than 85 percent of US democracy dollars—does not apply the concept of triage to assistance, however.[22] USAID spent $5.6 million through DAI from 2007 to 2011, attempting to "enhance the overall effectiveness" of the Parliament of Azerbaijan—a parliament that has never been freely elected. Every deputy in this parliament is a member of the ruling *Yeni Azərbaycan Partiyası* (New Azerbaijan Party). Yet US taxpayers paid for an orientation program for new members of the Azerbaijani parliament, all of whom were elected in 2010 parliamentary elections that the US Embassy in Baku described as "not meet[ing] international standards."[23] The US Embassy also noted that in the preelection period there was a lack of balanced media coverage, there were continued restrictions on freedoms of assembly and expression, and the candidate registration process was unfair. US Embassy staff spotted ballot box stuffing and other serious election violations.

In other words, the US government found serious fault with the 2010 parliamentary elections and then trained the winners. USAID even paid for a new website to make the illegitimate parliament more efficient. A final assessment carried out by two outside experts found that the parliamentary program "did not change how the [Parliament of Azerbaijan] functions or how ordinary people in Azerbaijan relate to and understand the parliament."[24] After the orientation for members of parliament, they "may be better prepared to do their jobs, [but] there is little debate in the [Parliament of Azerbaijan], indicating that the [Parliamentary Program of Azerbaijan] has not changed the core characteristics of the parliament."[25]

Since Azerbaijan's independence in 1991, USAID has spent more than $55 million on programs to make the country more democratic.[26] Meanwhile, the Aliyev family has governed since 1993, passing the baton from father to son. The regime has jailed young people for making satirical videos, made it increasingly difficult for NGOs to operate, imprisoned hundreds of religious believers it has branded as "extremists," and failed to hold a single election that met international standards.[27]

In spite of the country's obvious negative trajectory and resistance to reform, the US government continues to operate and authorize new multimillion dollar democracy programs in Azerbaijan. In August 2012, USAID issued a $1.5 million call for the Azerbaijan Rights Consortium Project, which would "enable key civil society organizations to better respond to President Aliyev's vision and to calls for more meaningful state and civil society partnerships fulfilling the government's commitments to various international human rights instruments."[28] The idea of US taxpayer dollars going to implement the supposedly democratic "vision" of Azerbaijan's authoritarian president is deeply troubling.

In Turkmenistan, a regular denizen of Freedom House's "Worst of the Worst" list of most repressive countries, USAID through the for-profit QED Group seeks to strengthen governance policies and practices. The program promises to "increase knowledge of effective governance practices, increase the practice of inclusive dialogue and information sharing, and assist the government to better develop and implement legislation and policies."[29] This language might be appropriate for a country with a freely elected parliament that is independent of the executive, but Turkmenistan has never held elections that meet international standards and its leadership does not appear to have any inclination to do so in the foreseeable future.

In Kazakhstan, USAID, working through a contractor, seeks to "increase the capacity" of Kazakhstan's leading civil society organizations so that they might better represent their constituents' interests to the government.[30] The design of the program presumes that Kazakhstan has a parliament that derives its legitimacy from constituents who have an opportunity to "throw the bums out" every few years. Kazakhstan does indeed have a parliament and regular elections, but international bodies such as the Organization for Security and Cooperation in Europe/Office for Democratic Institutions and Human Rights consistently find fault with them.[31] Kazakh election authorities routinely prevent opposition candidates from registering. There are indeed civil society organizations in Kazakhstan, many of whom do commendable work, but what incentive does the government of Kazakhstan or its MPs have to listen to constituents and NGOs if an election can be easily manipulated? Under these circumstances, the concept of a "constituency" in Kazakhstan is highly problematic.

Also in Kazakhstan, USAID recently commissioned the NDI to assess whether the new parliament might play a more important role in the country's political life.[32] USAID commissioned this project *after* Kazakhstan's unsatisfactory parliamentary elections in January 2012, which the US State Department acknowledged as falling "short of the international standards to which Kazakhstan has committed itself."[33] The experience of Kazakhstan's twenty years of independence strongly suggests that the new parliament is unlikely to be given any independence by a president who has ruled with a firm grip and few gestures of reform since the fall of the Soviet Union.

In Uzbekistan, another regular on Freedom House's "Worst of the Worst" list, USAID's political party assistance program, implemented by the NDI, claims to enhance "dialogue and communication between political parties and their constituents."[34] Since independence, Uzbekistan has been governed by a man who crushes dissent, boils his opponents in oil, and has decimated all signs of political life in the country. There are no opposition parties in Uzbekistan. It is difficult to grasp why it would be in the US national interest to promote dialogue between *pro-government* political parties within Uzbekistan. As in case of Kazakhstan, the language of the USAID program misconstrues the political system in Uzbekistan, and an absence of real elections translates into a lack of true "constituents" in the political system.

The NDI program also claims to "contribute to the familiarity of government and election officials with internationally recognized democratic principles and practices." Members of the Uzbek parliament visited Washington, D.C.,[35] and the North Carolina State Legislature in April 2012.[36] Even if this illegitimate parliament were open to learning "internationally recognized democratic principles and practices," what they could learn in North Carolina was not applicable to the Uzbek context. The rules and customs that govern the Parliament of Uzbekistan and the North Carolina General Assembly are so fundamentally different that is hard to imagine what of use could come from comparing the two.

As Thomas Carothers, a leading scholar of democracy assistance, has observed, "Most study tours . . . serve little purpose beyond relationship building. In far too many cases, the wrong participants are selected (because they speak English, or because the party leader owes them a favor), the tour is a grab-bag of superficial meetings in which people in the host country who know little about the visitors' specific context give generic presentations on 'how things work here,' and the participants devote their primary attention to meals and finding opportunities to shop using their travel per diem."[37]

But democracy assistance programs in the former Soviet Union are a drop in the bucket compared to other not-free countries that policymakers prioritize. This means that USAID dumps lots of money into countries that lack any political will to change. These programs are enormously expensive, unsuited for these countries' circumstances, naively constructed, and may do more harm than good.

In Afghanistan, USAID committed $216 million to empower seventy-five thousand women in an attempt to ensure that they will be included in the next generation of Afghan leaders.[38] This is the US government's largest women's empowerment project in history, and its cost exceeds the NED's annual budget. The program is implemented by Chemonics International, DAI, and Tetra Tech Inc. USAID already received a letter from the Special Inspector General for Afghanistan Reconstruction worrying that Afghan women engaged in the program "may be left without any tangible benefit upon completion."[39] The inspector general writes that many of his concerns were echoed by Afghanistan's First Lady, who said, "I do hope that we are not going to fall again into the game of contracting and sub-contracting and the routine of workshops and training sessions generating a lot of certificates on paper and little else."[40] The program wants "women to become leaders alongside their male counterparts, and ensure they have the skills, experience, knowledge, and networks to succeed," which is USAID boilerplate—but largely unrealistic, unattainable, and dangerous to women, given the precarious state of women's rights in the country.[41] As Human Rights Watch noted, 2014 included a series of attacks on and "threats toward, and assassinations of, high-profile women, including police women and activists, to which the government failed to respond with meaningful measures to protect women at risk."[42] In South Sudan, USAID authorized Democracy International to "develop effective, inclusive, and accountable governance" in a country where civil war has displaced an estimated two million people and killed at least fifty thousand. The five-year program, with a $74.7 million price tag, was meant to "promote a peaceful democratic transition by facilitating smooth elections, the establishment of a sustainable constitution, and by promoting the participation of citizens and civil society in the democratic political process."[43] On March 24, 2015, Sudan's national parliament delayed the country's first elections and extended the terms of all elected officials, including President Salva Kiir, by three years. The program was also meant to provide direct assistance to the National Constitutional Review Committee to "support an inclusive constitutional development process."[44] The commission, established in 2012, has failed to produce a draft constitution.

In Jordan, a country where King Abdullah II controls the Senate, approves laws, and can dismiss parliament, the prime minister, and the cabinet at whim, USAID pledged $35.7 million in late 2015 to "support King Abdullah's democratic reforms."[45] King Abdullah has weathered the Arab Spring better than most in his region by sacking a prime minister, passing a new constitution, and holding parliamentary elections. However, his moves to assuage demonstrators are window dressing in the broader context of movement away from autocracy, and they are better understood as a king's ploy to stay in power rather than a genuine desire to embrace democracy.

Why, then, does USAID continue to fund misguided programs in authoritarian and semiauthoritarian countries that display no interest in reform? The reason is as banal as it is galling—bureaucratic self-interest, inertia, and the assumption that more is always better. We can end the waste with a strategic approach to programs and an emphasis on triage, allocating more money where there is a greater chance of real change, not just spending wherever there is a mandate and a mechanism to do so.

The aforementioned USAID programs in Afghanistan, Azerbaijan, Kazakhstan, Jordan, South Sudan, Turkmenistan, and Uzbekistan should have never been approved. If the US government discontinued these and other programs like them in similarly unpromising environments, nothing would change in those countries; the only negative consequence would be for the democracy bureaucracy and its employees. Scarce US dollars to promote democracy should go toward countries where real and genuine progress is possible, such as Georgia, Tunisia, and Ukraine. However, the United States should not give up completely on not-free countries; instead, it should support democrats in not-free countries primarily with modest grants through the NED. The US government can also plant seeds in not-free countries through exchanges and online programs that do not require an in-country presence. In Iran, for example, Tavaana: E-Learning Institute for Iranian Civil Society operates online and offers assertive programs without field offices.

END NONCOMPETITIVE MECHANISMS FOR ASSISTANCE

Democracy is an inherently competitive system, but the democracy bureaucracy has allowed itself to fall into a number of noncompetitive practices that have had negative consequences. All implementers, regardless of their for-profit or nonprofit status, should have to compete, and noncompetitive mechanisms for awarding program funds should be phased out.

USAID is a large, slow bureaucracy that takes months to start programs and allocate funds. Recognizing its own need to respond to changing political circumstances in a more expeditious manner, in 1995 USAID formed the Consortium for Elections and Political Processes Strengthening (CEPPS), which includes the NDI, the IRI, and the International Foundation for Electoral Systems (IFES). The consortium accelerates USAID's response time by circumventing what is normally a competitive application process for each program. While the intent behind the consortium may have been a noble one, these three organizations have not felt sufficient pressure to develop effective and innovative programs because the CEPPS mechanism guarantees them million-dollar awards without real competition for every award.

USAID has internally discussed ending the CEPPS mechanism, according to some development professionals, but the unhealthy lack of competition has already taken its toll. When IRI, NDI, and IFES compete, they often lose to contractors or other nonprofits. In El Salvador, the for-profit contractor Democracy International beat IFES for a program to provide technical assistance to the election commission.[46]

Noncompetitive bidding is also present in the for-profit world. In a noncompetitive bid that many practitioners described as "raising questions," USAID selected Development Alternatives Inc. (DAI), another for-profit implementer, to carry out a parliamentary strengthening program in Kyrgyzstan, a country where DAI had no prior experience.[47]

Transparency is a vital aspect of competition. Congress can encourage the democracy bureaucracy to become more transparent. The NED discloses to whom it gives funds, the amount of the grant, and a general description of the program (except where the information might harm grantees), unlike many USAID implementers. Funded proposals including detailed budgets, quarterly reports, final reports, and evaluations for USAID-funded programs in countries ranked "partly free" or better should be publicly available on a website administered by the Government Accountability Office. Program documents are almost impossible to track down, and ForeignAssistance.gov is missing information and provides only the briefest of descriptions. A separate, more secure protocol should exist for storing and sharing information about programs in repressive regimes, where activists often face reprisals.

CONCLUSIONS AND POLICY RECOMMENDATIONS

To conclude, the promotion of democracy is an important tool for advancing universal values and US interests, but the democracy bureaucracy is in need of reform. In a time of declining budgets, it makes sense to use scarce resources as strategically as possible. The division of labor in the democracy-promotion community between field-office and grant-making institutions points the way to a more effective way of coordinating our efforts.

USAID programs that are executed through field-based institutions like the NDI and IRI should be focused primarily on countries that are already on the road to reform or at least show significant potential for reform. Only grant-making institutions like the NED, which does not maintain field offices and is thus less vulnerable to pressure from authoritarian regimes, should operate in countries ranked by Freedom House as "not free." The field-office approach is better suited to work in "partly free" countries.

The NED is our most flexible tool for working in tough authoritarian regimes. It deserves support, but too great an infusion of funds could have a negative impact on its effectiveness.[48] A modest 20 percent increase to its current budget, spread over the next ten years in small annual additions intended mainly to keep pace with inflation, would be appropriate. To ensure that the NED's four core institutes maintain political creativity, increases in the NED budget should not result in automatic increases to the NED's core institutes, and Congress should not mandate how much of the allocation should go to the core institutes.

Competition and transparency are integral democratic values. USAID should end noncompetitive bidding, including the CEPPS mechanism, and noncompetitive bidding in contracting. Successful proposals including detailed budgets, quarterly reports, final reports, and evaluations for USAID-funded programs in countries ranked "partly free" should be publicly available on a single website that Congress, scholars, and citizens can monitor.

Democracy promotion is a noble endeavor, but it requires more than simply injecting funds into closed societies in the hope that assistance will eventually transform them into robust democracies. Hope and change are fine political slogans, but insufficient if we are, as President Ronald Reagan succinctly put it, to "stand . . . with all those who love freedom and yearn for democracy, wherever they might be."

NOTES

1. In 2016, the US government plans to spend $2.85 billion to support democracy, good governance, and human rights overseas, according to the State Department USAID Foreign Assistance Dashboard, http://beta.foreignassistance.gov/categories/Democracy-Human-Rights-Governance#Funding.

2. Michael A. Cohen and Maria Figueroa Küpçü, *Revitalizing U.S. Democracy Promotion: A Comprehensive Plan for Reform* (Washington, D.C.: New America Foundation, April 2009).

3. Thomas O. Melia, "The Democracy Bureaucracy," *The American Interest* 1 (June 2006), http://www.the-american-interest.com/article.cfm?piece=75.

4. Michael A. Cohen and Maria Figueroa Küpçü call for a "bureaucratic brush clearing" and suggest that the Obama administration working with Congress "make a concerted effort to identify and eliminate the many redundancies in the assistance bureaucracy." See Cohen and Küpçü, *Revitalizing U.S. Democracy Promotion*, 3.

5. "Reorganizing U.S. Government Democracy Promotion Efforts," report of a conference held at Stanford University Center on democracy, development, and the rule of law, May 8–9, 2008, http://fsi.stanford.edu/sites/default/files/res/Reorganizing.pdf.

6. Of the $2.25 billion the US government spent on democracy programs in 2008, 87 percent was allocated to USAID. See *Democracy Assistance: U.S. Agencies Take Steps to Coordinate International Programs but Lack Information on Some U.S.-Funded Activities,* U.S. Government Accountability Office, GAO 09-993, September 2009, 14.

7. "Statement of Senator Patrick Leahy, State Foreign Operations Subcommittee Hearing on Fiscal Year 2009 USAID Budget Request," March 4, 2008.

8. The political party institutes (NDI and IRI) define "overhead" narrowly to keep the number artificially low; if one were to add all the salaries and rent, the figure would be much higher. Officially, overhead at the political party institutes is somewhere between 20 to 25 percent. The political party institutes define overhead as staff salaries for the accountants, technical experts, and executive-level staff as well as rent in the Washington office. Their definition of overhead does not include program staff salaries in Washington, local staff salaries, the expatriate director's salary, the expatriate's apartment, the expatriate's biannual international airfare, private school tuition for the expatriate's children (if applicable), or office rent in an expensive building with Western amenities. Some field offices have more than one expatriate as well. In sum, only a *fraction* of the total grant amount funds programs in a field-based organization.

9. Sarah Sunn Bush, *The Taming of Democracy Assistance* (Cambridge: Cambridge University Press, 2015), 192.

10. Bush, *The Taming of Democracy Assistance*, 192.

11. "USAID Azerbaijan—Our Programs: Democracy and Governance," Strengthening Civic Engagement in Political Processes in Azerbaijan, *USAID Azerbaijan*, http://azerbaijan.usaid.gov/node/9.

12. *Democracy and the Challenge of Change: A Guide to Increasing Women's Political Participation* (Washington, D.C.: National Democratic Institute, 2010), 12, http://www.ndi.org/files/Democracy_and_the_Challenge_of_Change.pdf. See also "Women as Change Agents: Advancing the Role of Women in Politics and Civil Society," statement by Kenneth Wollack, President of the National Democratic Institute, House Committee on Foreign Affairs, June 9, 2010, http://www.ndi.org/files/Women_As_Change_Agents_Testimony_090610_0.pdf. See also http://www.ndi.org/womens-political-participation and http://www.ndi.org/citizen-participation.

13. Cohen and Küpçü, *Revitalizing U.S. Democracy Promotion*, 10.

14. "Azerbaijan," taken from the 2011 Annual Report, *National Endowment for Democracy*, http://www.ned.org/where-we-work/eurasia/azerbaijan.

15. "Russia Expels USAID Development Agency," *BBC World News*, September 19, 2012, http://www.bbc.co.uk/news/world-europe-19644897.

16. "U.S. Senate, Department of State, Foreign Operations, and Related Programs Appropriations Bill, 2016," U.S. Senate Report 114-79, 114th Congress, 1st Session, July 9, 2014, 50, http://www.appropriations.senate.gov/sites/default/files/hearings/

FY2016%20State%20Foreign%20Operations%20Appropriations%20Report%20-%20114-79.
pdf.

17. "U.S. Senate, Department of State, Foreign Operations, and Related Programs Appropriations Bill, 2016."

18. "U.S. Senate, Department of State, Foreign Operations, and Related Programs Appropriations Bill, 2013," US Senate Report 112-172, 112th Congress, 2nd Session, May 24, 2012, 34, http://www.gpo.gov/fdsys/pkg/CRPT-112srpt172/pdf/CRPT-112srpt172.pdf.

19. It should be noted that the IRI wisely closed its offices and programs in Azerbaijan and Kazakhstan after concluding that there wasn't sufficient political space to operate. IRI tends to be far more pragmatic and strategic than NDI. NDI, for instance, is the only Western-funded NGO still on the ground in Uzbekistan. All other US and European NGOs left in 2005 after the Andijion massacre.

20. "Selection Indicators," *Millennium Challenge Corporation*, http://www.mcc.gov/pages/selection/indicators.

21. Tsveta Petrova, *The New Role of Central and Eastern Europe in International Democracy Support* (Washington, D.C.: Carnegie Endowment for International Peace, June 2011), 12, http://carnegieendowment.org/files/east_eur_democracy.pdf.

22. Of the $2.25 billion the US government spent on democracy programs in 2008, 87 percent was allocated to USAID. See *Democracy Assistance: U.S. Agencies Take Steps to Coordinate International Programs but Lack Information on Some U.S.-Funded Activities*, U.S. Government Accountability Office, GAO 09-993, September 2009, 14.

23. "Statement by Philip J. Crowley, Spokesman, Assistant Secretary of State for Public Affairs," Embassy of the United States to Azerbaijan, November 8, 2010, http://azerbaijan.usembassy.gov/pr_110810.html.

24. Lincoln Mitchell and Rashad Shirinov, "Parliamentary Program of Azerbaijan Evaluation: Final Report," *USAID Azerbaijan*, July 2011, 7, http://www.democracyinternational.com/sites/default/files/
Azerbaijan%20Parliamentary%20Programs%20Evaluation%20Final%20Report.pdf.

25. Mitchell and Shirinov, "Parliamentary Program of Azerbaijan Evaluation."

26. "USAID Azerbaijan—Our Programs: Past Projects," *USAID Azerbaijan*, http://azerbaijan.usaid.gov/node/86.

27. Azerbaijan has held one clean election, in 1992, that brought Abulfaz Elchibey to power albeit briefly. Svante Cornell described the 1992 election as "one of the freest elections in the post-Soviet sphere," although the fairness of the 1992 election was partly a result of a law that prevented persons from over the age of sixty-five from running for president. The law was undoubtedly meant to prevent Heydar Aliyev from running again. See Svante E. Cornell, "Democratization Falters in Azerbaijan," *Journal of Democracy* 12, no. 2 (April 2001): 119.

28. "USAID Caucasus Request for Applications (RFA) No. 112-12-000002. Azerbaijan Rights Consortium (ARC) Project," *USAID Caucasus*, June 21, 2012.

29. The project is a $2.5 million one. "Turkmenistan Governance Strengthening Project," *QED Group*, http://www.qedgroupllc.com/project/turkmenistan-governance-strengthening-project.

30. The cost of the program is $1,750,000. "Kazakhstan Civil Society Strengthening Program," *USAID Kazakhstan*, http://centralasia.usaid.gov/kazakhstan/627.

31. "Republic of Kazakhstan: Early Parliamentary Elections 15 January 2012. OSCE/ODIHR Election Observation Mission Final Report," April 3 (Warsaw: OSCE, 2012), http://www.osce.org/odihr/elections/89401; and "Republic of Kazakhstan: Early Presidential Election 3 April 2011. OSCE/ODIHR Election Observation Mission Final Report," June 16 (Warsaw: OSCE, 2011), http://www.osce.org/odihr/elections/78714.

32. The cost of the program is $300,000. "Governance Institutions Initiative," *USAID Kazakhstan*, http://centralasia.usaidallnet.gov/kazakhstan/1164.

33. "Parliamentary Elections in Kazakhstan" US Department of State, Office of the Spokesman, January 16, 2012, http://kazakhstan.usembassy.gov/st-01-17-12.html.

34. This program is a $1.32 million program. "Political and Civil Development," *USAID Uzbekistan*, http://centralasia.usaidallnet.gov/uzbekistan/355.

35. "Current Developments in Uzbekistan's Parliament," conference, April 26 (Washington, D.C.: Carnegie Endowment for International Peace, 2012), http://carnegieendowment.org/2012/04/26/current-developments-in-uzbekistan-s-parliament/acih.

36. "Uzbek Parliamentarians Visit Raleigh," *International Affairs Council*, April 24, 2012, http://iacnc.org/blog/?p=421.

37. Thomas Carothers, *Confronting the Weakest Link: Aiding Political Parties in New Democracies* (Washington, D.C.: Carnegie Endowment for International Peace, 2006), 122.

38. "Promoting Gender Equity in National Priority Programs (Promote)," *USAID*, Fact Sheet, November 2014, https://www.usaid.gov/sites/default/files/documents/1871/Promote%20Fact%20Sheet%20-%20Nov%202014%20(English).pdf.

39. Letter from Special Inspector General for Afghanistan Reconstruction John F. Sopko to The Honorable Alfonso E. Lenhardt, Acting Administrator, US Agency for International Development, March 27, 2015, https://www.sigar.mil/pdf/special%20projects/SIGAR-15-44-SP.pdf.

40. H. E. Rula Ghani, First Lady of the Islamic Republic of Afghanistan, "Keynote Address," *Oslo Symposium on Advancing Women's Rights and Empowerment in Afghanistan*, November 23, 2014, http://www.afghanwomenoslosymposium.org/resourcedocuments1.cfm.

41. "Promoting Gender Equity in National Priority Programs (Promote)," *USAID*, Fact Sheet, November 2014, https://www.usaid.gov/sites/default/files/documents/1871/Promote%20Fact%20Sheet%20-%20Nov%202014%20%28English%29.pdf.

42. "World Report 2015: Afghanistan," *Human Rights Watch*, https://www.hrw.org/world-report/2015/country-chapters/afghanistan.

43. "Systems to Uphold the Credibility and Constitutionality of Elections in South Sudan (SUCCESS)," *Democracy International*, http://democracyinternational.com/projects/systems-uphold-credibility-and-constitutionality-elections-south-sudan-success.

44. "USAID Awards DI Major Program to Support Democratic Elections and Political Processes in South Sudan," *Democracy International*, press release, October 16, 2013, http://democracyinternational.com/news/usaid-awards-di-major-program-support-democratic-elections-and-political-processes-south-sudan.

45. "U.S. Provides $429.7 Million in Grants to Jordan," *USAID*, press release, September 21, 2015, https://www.usaid.gov/jordan/press-releases/sep-21-2015-us-provides-4297-million-grants-jordan.

46. "DI Launches New Elections Program in El Salvador," *Democracy International*, September 26, 2011, http://www.democracyinternational.com/news/di-launches-new-elections-program-el-salvador; and "Technical Assistance to the 2012 El Salvador Legislative and Municipal Elections," *Democracy International*, September 2011, http://www.democracyinternational.com/category/country-region/latin-america-and-carribean/el-salvador.

47. "Kyrgyzstan Parliamentary Strengthening Program," *USAID Kyrgyzstan*, http://centralasia.usaid.gov/kyrgyzstan/328.

48. Thomas Carothers, *Revitalizing Democracy Assistance: The Challenge of USAID* (Washington, D.C.: Carnegie Endowment for International Peace, 2009), 46.

Chapter Six

The Multiplier Effects of US Democracy Promotion

An Eastern EU Perspective

Tsveta Petrova

Since the end of the Cold War, supporting the diffusion of democratic norms and practices around the globe has become an important element of the work of many Western governmental and nongovernmental actors. Although democracy support began to encounter fatigue within these policy circles in the last decade, some of the new democracies in Eastern Europe, Latin America, Africa, and Asia have started engaging in such work. These countries, which were previously recipients of democracy assistance, represent a new generation of international democracy supporters. The US policy community has encouraged and supported their efforts, and made use of their distinctive democracy promotion expertise.

Yet the cooperation between the United States and new democracies in supporting democratization around the globe has not been carefully assessed. This oversight represents a missed opportunity for encouraging better cooperation and possibly more effective democracy promotion. My goal in this chapter is to take on this question by examining the ways in which the United States has supported and cooperated with one group of such emerging democracy promoters, the Eastern European members of the European Union (EU). Some of them, especially Poland, the Czech Republic, and Slovakia, quickly became noteworthy democracy promoters in the former USSR and Yugoslavia.

I argue that US support for the Eastern EU transition to democracy, and later for the democracy promotion activities of states in this region, has made a positive difference. It is not just that American encouragement, institutional backing, and funding for Eastern EU democracy promotion has translated into more pro-democracy activism; much more importantly and sustainably, Washington's initial investment in Eastern EU democratization has had multiplier effects. Some of the main recipients of US democracy assistance are still active not only in supporting democracy at home but also in spreading it abroad.

Consequently, Eastern EU democracy promotion has been rooted both in its own domestic experience and, to some extent, in the emulation of US democratic and democracy promotion practices. Given the resultant complementarity between US and Eastern EU support for the spread of democracy, there are many fruitful opportunities for cooperation between the United States and Eastern EU democracy promoters. I offer some recommendations for improving democracy promotion cooperation between the United States and emerging democracy promoters, such as the Eastern EU states. These suggestions include (1) moving beyond *ad hoc* to more systematic cooperation in recipient countries in which emerging democracy promoters have a sustained interest for either strategic or moral reasons; (2) respecting such interests as well as treating emerging democracy promoters as equal partners; and (3) stepping up the nurturing of international solidarity among civil societies across the globe, which I found to have produced some of the most important multiplier effects of US democracy promotion.

My main focus in this chapter is on Poland as the most active democracy promoter in the Eastern EU group, in the twenty-five years after the country's transition to democracy (1989–2014).[1] Given their limited foreign policy capacity, their democratic "youth," and their uneven democracy promotion records, Eastern EU countries, including Poland, were not democracy promotion heavyweights even at the time of their peak support for the diffusion of democracy abroad (late 1990s to mid-2000s). Since then, Eastern EU democracy promotion has been tempered by external and internal developments, including the evolving US role in democracy promotion and the fact that several Eastern EU countries, most emblematically Hungary and most recently Poland, began questioning their previous commitment to liberalism at home. This has posed dilemmas, not dissimilar to those recently faced by the United States, and consequently restrained and constrained democracy promotion by these states. There nonetheless remains room for some Eastern EU activists to continue exercising their international solidarity with civil societies in other new democracies, and these activists are not only looking to share what worked at home and what did not, but also hoping to learn from the experience of their counterparts abroad.

Still, the fact that the United States has both stimulated and enfeebled the efforts of emerging democracy promoters speaks to the importance of US leadership in democracy promotion. Moreover, to the extent that these Eastern EU countries have had some impact on the democratization of their neighborhood, they demonstrate the potential of emerging democracies to support the diffusion of democracy, and thus the importance of supporting their efforts and cooperating with them. These two issues are therefore the focus of this chapter.

THE UNITED STATES ACTIVELY SUPPORTED THE EASTERN EU TRANSITION FROM RECIPIENTS TO PROVIDERS OF DEMOCRACY SUPPORT

The United States actively supported the Eastern EU transitions to democracy and later to democracy promotion. US assistance for the region's democratization began even before communism collapsed in 1989. In Poland, for example, in the early 1980s under President Reagan, the US government began assisting the underground publication network and launched special programs of the Voice of America and Radio Free Europe/Radio Liberty to provide Polish citizens with independent sources of information. Then, over the course of the 1990s and 2000s, the United States invested considerable political, diplomatic, and financial resources to support democratization in postcommunist states. US democracy assistance to the region amounted to close to $500 million in the 1990s alone.[2] Washington also pursued a strategy of "engagement and enlargement" in the region—it sought to embed these postcommunist countries in various multilateral cooperation networks, which are based on democratic values and principles, and in which the United States is a member, such as the OSCE, the CoE, and perhaps most importantly NATO. In the late 1990s and especially in the early 2000s (when parts of the region were thought to have entered an era of democratic consolidation), the United States also began encouraging and funding the efforts of some of the new Eastern EU democracies to support democratization abroad both indirectly (paragraphs 1 and 2) and directly (paragraphs 3 and 4).

(1) Many US aid programs in Eastern Europe had a regional component, such as the East-East Program of the Open Society Foundation, the Cross-Border Projects of the National Endowment for Democracy (NED), and the Democracy Network (DemNet) programs of the US Agency for International Development (USAID), which facilitated the sharing of transition experiences among countries in the postcommunist region. Also, many of the US-founded international democracy NGOs, such as Partners for Democratic Change, were federations with offices in multiple countries in the postcommunist space (and beyond). In the context of multiple, salient shared experiences and values among postcommunist countries, such transnational contacts created solidarity, reaffirmed it, and mobilized Eastern EU activists working in organizations with the capacity to do transnational work. As some Polish activists explained, "We see that people are interested in freedom and

we have solidarity for them, so we are helping them and encouraging them. We believe in freedom because it ensures respectful treatment of individuals. So we want that not just for Poland but for the region because we feel solidarity for those in the region and those struggling for freedom."[3]

(2) US officers in and behind these transnational networks have sought out best practices and then encouraged and supported sharing these practices within the region by connecting activists perceived to be facing similar democratization challenges. Consider the following typical example from Poland: noting the success of the Polish decentralization reforms in the early 1990s and the importance of restructuring local governance to the democratization process, USAID introduced one of its local grantees, the Foundation in Support of Local Democracy, to a group of local government officials from Kazakhstan. The latter were looking to resist the concentration of power at the center in a relatively nonconfrontational, public service–oriented way, while the former were perceived to be among the most successful US aid recipients in the postcommunist space who worked on democratic decentralization.[4] The introduction and subsequent interactions among many others spurred the foundation to transform its international democracy activism from occasional meetings with postcommunist activists and politicians, aimed at exchanging information and political support, into full-fledged democracy promotion programs in several postcommunist countries.

More broadly, the United States brokered the diffusion of the "electoral breakthrough" (or revolution) model.[5] The United States did not "orchestrate" these revolutions and its democracy promotion efforts were not sufficient to effect regime change.[6] The United States did, however, facilitate the unfolding of this wave of political change by helping to put together the model of electoral breakthrough,[7] and then strategically linking its past adopters to potential future ones. The electoral breakthrough wave began with three overlapping pro-democratic movements in Bulgaria, Romania, and Serbia between November 1996 and March 1997. After the success of the Bulgarian and Romanian breakthroughs, the United States sponsored a delegation of some key Bulgarian and Romanian organizers to Slovakia, which followed with its own breakthrough in 1998. The United States then introduced some Slovak electoral revolutionaries to pro-democratic activists in Serbia, Croatia, Ukraine, Belarus, and Russia, with the first three countries succeeding in organizing breakthroughs on their own. The United States has also been credited with introducing the Serbian activists to the Georgian and Ukrainian opposition movements, among others. The United States thus facilitated the spreading of the wave, within which structurally disadvantaged opposition groups effected successful regime change, at least partly by relying on the influence of the prior example of others.[8]

(3) The United States has also directly encouraged Eastern EU countries to support the democratization of their neighbors to the east and southeast.

Various US democracy promotion institutions working in the postcommunist region not only made funding available for "East-East" work but also subcontracted Eastern EU organizations to implement diverse US democracy assistance programs, and to re-grant US funds allocated for democracy assistance. Returning to Poland, there is a group of NGOs that have been administering the programs of major foreign donors who allocate grant money; for instance, the Education for Democracy Foundation administers the RITA program of the Polish-American Freedom Foundation, the Polish-American-Ukrainian Cooperation Initiative (PAUCI) re-grants NED funding to Ukraine, and the East European Democracy Center awards grants to independent newspapers in Belarus on behalf, or with the financial backing, of some of its US donors who have had a more difficult time supporting the prodemocratic opposition there.

US support and funding has thus allowed many Polish organizations to reach with their programming kindred constituencies abroad. For example, the Polish Civil Society Development Foundation approached their US donors fairly early on about supporting the foundation's fellow activists in Ukraine, and later in Belarus, with civic trainings led in part by the foundation activists. As Eastern EU NGOs were becoming known for their transnational work among more and more donors, many of these NGOs began to increasingly leverage this work to support their domestic projects and expand their presence abroad.

(4) Using diplomatic channels, the United States has also formally and informally conveyed its expectations that Eastern EU states should assist democratization laggards in their region and beyond. In the Obama administration, Vice President Joseph Biden argued, "You've delivered on the promise of your revolution. You are now able to help others do the same."[9] The United States has also supported Eastern EU initiatives in that direction, cofounding the Community of Democracies in 2000, for example. Washington has also worked with and sought the support of Eastern EU states in various initiatives with a democracy promotion dimension, such as NATO's eastern enlargement in the 2000s, or the controversial intervention in Iraq in 2003.

At times, US encouragement resonated not only with moral concerns but also, and primarily, with geostrategic foreign policy challenges confronting Eastern EU diplomats and civic activists. In Poland and the Baltic republics, democracy promotion became primarily an element of a geopolitical strategy to create reliable partners in their eastern neighborhood (especially Ukraine, Belarus, Georgia, and Moldova), bringing these countries closer to Europe and counterbalancing Russian power in the region. In other Central and Southeastern EU countries, democracy promotion became mostly a long-term investment in disempowering nationalist and illiberal rulers on the European fringes, and thus a solution to the political and economic destabilization in the neighboring former Yugoslav and Soviet republics. In Slovakia and the Czech Republic, for instance, democracy promotion became a solution to the political and economic destabilization of Yugoslavia and the arrested political and economic transitions in the neighboring former USSR states (Ukraine, Belarus, and Georgia). Democracy promotion also helped these countries earn their EU and NATO membership by demonstrating that they share the Euro-Atlantic community's values and are not just beneficiaries but also contributors to its security.

US SUPPORT FOR EASTERN EU DEMOCRATIZATION AND DEMOCRACY PROMOTION MATTERED

US support for Eastern EU transitions to democracy and the shift of these states from recipients to democracy promoters has mattered in a positive way—without the support offered by the United States, there would be less Eastern EU democracy promotion today. This impact is the product of two types of US contributions. First, US encouragement, funding, and institutional backing for Eastern EU democracy promotion boosted pro-democracy activism where domestic factors favored its emergence. And second, the initial US support for Eastern EU democratization has had multiplier effects since some of its recipients subsequently became key Eastern EU democracy promoting elites, and since they consequently passed along to others some of the democratic practices that they learned in their cooperation with the United States.

Institutional Support and Funding

The United States has not spurred, compelled, or coerced Eastern EU democracy promotion, but US funding for "East-East" democracy work has been very important in sustaining these efforts by the Eastern EU NGOs. In the 1990s to the mid-2000s, most of them relied largely on various US donors for their programming. For example, a majority of these organizations reported that they had to scale back their democracy promotion work after most US donors began gradually pulling out of Poland in the early 2000s.[10] Moreover, when asked to discuss the counterfactual of what would be different if these US donors had never worked in Poland in the first place, many leaders of these organizations also added that they would not have been able to support much of their more political programming either at home or abroad.[11] For example, a number of internationally active NGOs explained that they can effectively mobilize their domestic constituency to fund traditional humanitarian and development work abroad, but they find collecting funds for democracy work much more challenging. These counterfactuals, as well as reports about the impact of the phasing out of much of US support for such

NGOs, speak to the importance of US funding for democracy promotion by these Eastern EU groups, at least in the early years of the development of such programming. [12]

US institutional support for Eastern EU democracy promotion has been less important than US funding, but it has nonetheless facilitated and legitimized Eastern EU efforts, primarily in the late 1990s and early 2000s. Some of this US support has been specialized—for example, the establishment of the Community of Democracies or the US State Department's program on US-Eastern EU cooperation in providing democracy aid. More broadly, the United States has often sought the support of and joined the Eastern EU initiatives to keep democracy promotion on the agenda of various Euro-Atlantic organizations. Some have even argued that Eastern EU democracy promotion has been in part motivated by the need to earn membership in such organizations and demonstrate commitment to the Euro-Atlantic community's values. [13] In sum, US support and encouragement for Eastern EU democracy promotion, either bilaterally or through various Euro-Atlantic organizations, has, at the very least, created an environment that encourages and rewards democracy promotion by these countries.

Multiplier Effects

In terms of sustainability and the organic growth of Eastern EU democracy promotion, the multiplier effects of US investment in the region's democratization have proved to be more important than the funding itself.

Scope

The importance of the United States in encouraging Eastern EU democracy promotion can be gleaned from local activists' accounts about how they began this work. When asked this question, without being prompted about Western or US contributions, most emphasized their solidarity with other pro-democracy activists abroad, and discussed being a recipient of Western, and especially US, democracy assistance as one of the key factors underlying such solidarity. A majority of Polish civil society groups doing democracy work abroad expressed a strongly felt normative "obligation" to "help others, as . . . [they themselves] were assisted from abroad" in their struggle for democracy. [14] As these activists explained, "there is this feeling in Poland that we're obliged for the strong assistance from abroad during the struggle against communism and so that Poland should help others too." [15] Some even used the language of moral indebtedness: "Poland has received aid for many years and it is now time to pay off this assistance debt."

In other words, by providing democracy assistance to Poland and the rest of the Eastern EU region, the United States, and the various Euro-Atlantic organizations it helped establish, set an example of the importance of defending democracy within the Euro-Atlantic space, and of acting on the sense of solidarity between democratic and democratizing societies.[16] Such socialization, though more weakly, extends to Eastern EU policymakers and some Eastern EU state activities. The promotional materials of PolishAid, Poland's development cooperation agency, for instance, state, "We ourselves received assistance" as one of the reasons why "We provide [development, including democracy,] assistance."[17]

In sum, the United States has primarily facilitated rather than created, compelled, or coerced Eastern EU democracy promotion,[18] but without US support there would be less of this regional democracy promotion today.[19]

Approaches

Similarly, the importance of the United States in encouraging Eastern EU democracy promotion can be gleaned from the activities of Eastern EU countries. Most broadly, both Eastern EU activists and policymakers have been consciously and purposefully passing along lessons they learned about what did and did not work in their own transitions to democracy and Euro-Atlantic integration. Since the United States supported the democratization of Eastern EU countries, some of the US democracy practices "imports" were localized and then "re-exported" as Eastern EU democratization "recipes."

Consider the following example. The Education for Democracy Foundation was established in 1989 at the initiative of Polish opposition activists and educators from the American Federation of Teachers.[20] The foundation's mission has been to initiate, support, and conduct educational activity aimed at propagating the idea of democracy. One of the foundation's first projects involved setting up student-parent-teacher groups in Poland modeled on similar groups in the United States; these were to serve as the backbone of local communities and teach civic values and participation to those involved. By the late 1990s, with the financial support of several of its US donors, the foundation was already supporting the development of similar groups throughout the postcommunist space. The Ukrainian recipients of this Polish support, for example, reported that many (about a third) of these student-parent-teacher groups were still active in 2013.[21]

Similarly, PAUCI was established in 1999 as a tripartite initiative by the Polish, Ukrainian, and US governments, focused on the deepening of contacts among these countries. PAUCI's successor was set up in 2005 to promote the transfer to Ukraine of Poland's "successful experience of transition to a market economy and a democratic civil society." One set of PAUCI's projects focused on setting up apartment building associations, as the building blocks of civil society and a way of representing citizens in their relationships with local governments. According to PAUCI's Ukrainian recipients and partners, more than half of the apartment building associations created with Polish assistance were still active in 2013.[22] Given the success of these projects, PAUCI then encouraged these Ukrainian recipients and partners to consider a similar cooperation initiative between Ukraine and Russia (until the 2014 crisis disrupted such plans).

In other words, both examples are not atypical and illustrate well the multiplier effect of US democracy promotion. In both, initial US support for Poland's democratization has paid off in that some of its recipients have become key Eastern EU democracy-promoting elites, and successfully passed along to their neighbors' practices learned in the course of Poland's cooperation with the United States.[23] Moreover in both, Polish efforts have made some difference, according to the recipients.

The importance of the United States among all Western democracy promoters can also be gleaned from the fact that Eastern EU countries have adopted approaches that are broadly closer to the US approach than to Western European ones. Students of Western democracy promotion have grouped the sectoral priorities of donors into two ideal types: the *political* and *developmental* approaches to democracy promotion. These two types represent the different values donors place on democracy, concepts of democracy and democratization, and methods of supporting democracy.[24] The political approach values democracy as an end in itself, and operates from a core of "elections plus rights" programming. The political approach, moreover, conceptualizes democratization as a process of political struggle in which actors who can be clearly identified as democrats contend with nondemocratic forces. Therefore, the central task of democracy aid is to assist civic and political pro-democratic actors abroad, and to support key political institutions that level the political playing field, such as independent electoral commissions or independent media. The developmental approach values democracy as an element of the larger process of national development, and consequently looks beyond an exclusively political definition of democracy. The developmental approach conceives of democratization as a gradual accumulation of small sequential gains, including an effective state and the rule of law, before political liberalization. Aid is provided to stimulate social and economic development as a way of supporting democracy, building state capacity and good governance, and protecting human rights.

Poland takes a political approach to promoting democracy, focusing on strengthening pro-democratic forces abroad.[25] The emphasis of most Polish democracy promoters has been on strengthening the number and capacity of pro-democratic political and civic actors in its recipient countries. Polish involvement with governing institutions in recipient countries is primarily in the context of creating a reservoir of pro-democratic elites rather than contributing to state capacity development. Therefore, to the extent that the political approach dominates the global profile of US democracy promotion and the developmental approach dominates Western European democracy promotion,[26] the Polish democracy promotion approach is closer to that of the United States than to the approaches of Western European donors. But in contrast to the US political approach, Eastern EU approaches have not paid much attention to the political process.

Consider the following example: In terms of assistance provided to Ukraine, the EU has tied most of its aid to Ukrainian governing institutions; it has focused primarily on legal approximation and, to a much lesser degree, on civil society development. The United States has supported the development of civil society, the strengthening of local and national governing institutions, and the liberalization of the political process in Ukraine. Poland has prioritized targeting civic groups, local and national governing elites, and youth. In sum, except for lack of interest in assisting Ukraine's political process, Polish assistance priorities are much more similar to those of the United States than to those of the EU.[27]

SOME EASTERN EU COUNTRIES EMERGE AS NOTEWORTHY DEMOCRACY PROMOTERS

With certain favorable domestic conditions, and with US and Euro-Atlantic encouragement and support,[28] most Eastern EU countries emerged as democracy promoters. Some of them began this enterprise within the first decade after completing their own transitions, with an initial focus on their neighborhood. Many Eastern EU states have relied on their bilateral diplomatic channels to pressure, persuade, and educate their neighbors to embrace democratic norms as well as to reach out to pro-democratic opposition movements and groups abroad. Eastern EU foreign policymakers have even engaged with political elites in neighboring autocracies, attempting to convince them that "democracy is well worthwhile," and expressing solidarity with dissidents as "brave, responsible and courageous citizens who deserve our highest respect, because they are a conscience of their nation."[29]

Also, most Eastern EU states established and then quickly transformed their development aid frameworks, created as a requirement of their EU or OECD membership, into platforms for democracy assistance Consider that in 2006, for instance, 54 percent of PolishAid project funding for Ukraine and 72 percent of its funding for Belarus went toward democracy assistance programs (compared to about a quarter of USAID's assistance to Ukraine and about two-thirds of USAID's assistance to Belarus that went to democratization projects).[30] While in the same year Eastern EU donors together supplied only about €12 million in democracy assistance, each Eastern EU state usually concentrates on two or three of the following five recipients: Ukraine, Belarus, Moldova, Georgia, and Serbia. Consequently, Poland, for example, gave more democracy assistance to Ukraine than some other generous donors, such as Sweden and the United Kingdom combined.[31]

Finally, as small countries with limited foreign policy capacity and impact, Eastern EU states have also leveraged their membership in various Euro-Atlantic international organizations, showing interest and enjoying some success in securing a greater place for democracy promotion on their agendas. Most consequentially, Eastern EU members have advocated for further EU and NATO expansion to the east and southeast, as well as for enhanced cooperation with these neighborhoods in the meantime.

Bulgaria, Slovenia, and Romania have all supplied little democracy aid and diplomatic support to follow through on their rhetoric of supporting the democratization of their neighbors. Between the early 1990s and mid-2000s, Lithuania, Estonia, Latvia, and Hungary ranked somewhere between the least and most active Eastern EU democracy promoters because they provided limited diplomatic support, without taking much initiative or starting only recently. Also, the institutionalization of democracy aid provision in all four states is relatively weak, and democracy assistance provided by all but Estonia has been either belated or small. Still, even these Eastern EU states have made some distinctive investments in supporting democracy abroad; for instance, Estonia has shared its e-governance expertise (information policy and transparency) with nearby Euro-Atlantic applicants, and Lithuania has been hosting the Belarusian opposition in exile.

The Czech Republic, Poland, and Slovakia, on the other hand, quickly became noteworthy democracy promoters in the former USSR and Yugoslavia. This earned Poland the opportunity to lead EU democracy promotion in its immediate eastern neighborhood and Slovakia—and the chance to become a key agent of European policy in the Western Balkans and Belarus. Poland, for example, has sponsored the Eastern Partnership—an instrument that regulates the EU's relationship with, and democracy promotion to, its immediate eastern neighborhood.

Arguing that "it is in our interest to have as our neighbors countries which share our values and are [thus] stable, democratic, well governed and prosperous,"[32] Poland has also successfully steered the EU's response to democratization crises and windows of opportunity in this neighborhood—from the Russian-Georgian war in 2008 to the Ukrainian regime changes in 2004 and 2013–2014. Similarly, the Czech Republic earned a reputation as a defender of beleaguered oppositions around the globe—not only in Belarus and Cuba but also in Myanmar and Iraq. Czech democracy promotion has built on the beliefs of the former Czech anticommunist opposition activists, who claimed that "the promotion of democracy and human rights in oppressive countries is bound with the struggle for international peace and security" and that all peoples "carry a common responsibility" to come to the aid of the oppressed."[33] Consequently, Czech criticism of the Beijing human rights record and Czech support for the Dalai Lama, for example, persisted in the period covered in this chapter despite costly losses in trade with China. And another example: Prague was successful in supporting Cuba's dissidents by getting the EU to adopt a tougher stance toward Havana. Moreover, while Poland and Slovakia are two of the three countries in the region that began actively promoting democracy within a year of their own democratic breakthroughs, the Czech Republic has the only transition promotion agency in the region. It specializes in "motivating political [democratization] processes leading towards long-term stability and prosperity and helping emancipate human rights defenders, and civil society as key actors in sustainable democratic change."[34] In general, the Czech Republic, Poland, and Slovakia provide the most democracy assistance of all Eastern EU countries, as measured by their share of the overall official development assistance budget. These three Eastern EU countries have also emerged as noteworthy democracy promoters who contributed to the democratic gains in several postcommunist countries that underwent electoral revolutions in the 2000s.[35] In sum, even though they are not democracy promotion heavyweights, these Eastern EU countries demonstrate the potential of emerging democracies to support the diffusion of democracy.

EVOLVING INTERNAL AND INTERNATIONAL ENVIRONMENTS AND US ROLE IN DEMOCRACY PROMOTION

Not only has Eastern EU democracy promotion been uneven (for various domestic reasons[36]), but it has also been tempered over time by several external developments, including the evolving US role in democracy promotion. The fact that the United States has both stimulated and enfeebled the efforts of emerging democracy promoters speaks to the importance of US leadership in democracy promotion.

After the wave of electoral breakthroughs, democracy seemed to be in retreat in a number of countries around the globe, including in some of the key Eastern EU recipients.[37] Moreover, Belarus, Russia, Uzbekistan, Azerbaijan, and Kazakhstan responded to the spread of regime change in their neighborhood by introducing a set of policies and institutions meant to prevent the organization of breakthroughs in their country, and began to more actively label even some Eastern EU democracy promoters as serving foreign interests.[38] Many other recipients were also becoming less receptive to democracy promotion, complaining that it often produces an array of unintended consequences that undermine the democratization of recipient countries.[39] The inclusion of democracy promotion as an objective in the highly controversial war in Iraq since 2003 further discredited democracy promotion and US leadership of this agenda.[40]

In a similar vein, some have been dismissive of Eastern EU democracy promotion because of both the democracy promotion and the democratization records of these countries. Like others in the Euro-Atlantic space, Eastern EU countries have been grappling not only with the often diverging imperatives of democracy promotion as an end in itself and as a means to other foreign policy ends but also with major issues of internal adherence to democratic norms and practices. And as disappointment with postcommunist elites and some transition outcomes began to accumulate after their EU and NATO accession, and as the financial crisis hit Europe in the late 2000s, many Eastern EU countries, most emblematically Hungary, began questioning their previous commitment to liberalism at home, and consequently abroad as well. Moreover, less and less capital, both financial and political, has been devoted to democracy promotion. Finally, when Russia annexed Crimea in 2014, the resultant geopolitical polarization further undermined the democracy promotion commitment of some Eastern EU countries, most notably Slovakia, while also hardening the commitment of others, including Poland and the Baltic republics. At the same time, however, the smoldering conflict in Ukraine made democracy work there and in other former Soviet republics that much more urgent but also sensitive and difficult for the Eastern EU democracy promoters. These Eastern EU countries, moreover, have recently enjoyed limited US support and backing in their democracy promotion efforts in the former Soviet Union, which reportedly made their efforts even more hesitant.[41]

CONCLUSION: A WAY FORWARD FOR US–EASTERN EU COOPERATION ON DEMOCRACY PROMOTION

Given their limited foreign policy capacities as well as their sometimes checkered democratization and democracy promotion records, Eastern EU countries were not democracy promotion heavyweights even at the time of their peak support for the diffusion of democracy abroad (in the late 1990s and early to mid-2000s). Still, to the extent that these countries have had some impact on the democratization of their neighborhood, they demonstrate the potential of emerging democracies to support the diffusion of democracy, and thus the importance of supporting their efforts and cooperating with them. Moreover, the United States has played an important role in encouraging the growth of Eastern EU democracy and the engagement of several of these postcommunist countries in their own democracy promotion efforts. This is not to dispute the problems with US democracy promotion, or its unintended negative consequences, but simply to highlight that, on the whole, these programs and policies have mattered in a positive way.

My focus in this chapter has been the significant positive multiplier effects of US democracy promotion in the Eastern EU countries: many of the main Eastern EU civic groups that received American assistance are still active not only in working on consolidating democracy at home but also in spreading it abroad. Their exposure to US democratic norms and practices has not only stimulated their own pro-democracy activism but also enriched its repertoire.

The multiplier effects of US support for Eastern EU democratization and democracy promotion demonstrate the value of nurturing the international solidarity of civil society in new democracies. Supporting activists interested in supporting their counterparts abroad not only stimulates democracy promotion as an organic bottom-up expression of solidarity between peoples but also legitimizes it as a phenomenon that can be observed around the globe (rather than just in the West). Moreover, such activism could potentially allow the creation of openings in new democracies for state-society conversations about the moral and strategic importance of democracy promotion, with civil society arguing in favor of supporting the spread of democracy abroad.[42] Efforts based on such domestically negotiated commitments are much stronger and more sustainable than those that take their cues from the West.[43]

The United States and other democracy promoters could further strengthen the international solidarity of civil society in new democracies not just by involving interested activists as consultants or subcontractors (as is often done currently) but also by strengthening existing pro-democracy transnational networks and helping to create more regional and cross-border democracy assistance programs. Participating civic activists and their NGOs could also be invited to take part as equal partners to their states in the bilateral and multilateral diplomacy of democracy promotion.

Another important implication of the chapter's findings about the multiplier effects of US support for Eastern EU democratization and democracy promotion is the complementarity of democracy promotion by the US and Eastern EU countries (and possibly by other new democracies). Both the United States and these states tend to embrace political approaches to supporting democracy abroad; this similarity could facilitate their democracy promotion cooperation. This is especially the case since the United States and new democracies, such as Eastern EU countries, also have different strengths and limitations. New democracies have a few limitations related to their capacity and "democratic youth." However, in partnerships between established and new democracies, established democracies can leverage their more developed capacity, reputation as democratic models (or at least their longer experience with democracy), and their expertise (accumulated as a result of their longer experience with democracy promotion), while new democracies can contribute firsthand experience with democratization and local familiarity with recipients (given that their work has tended to focus on countries with which they have significant shared historical experiences). Such partnerships could thus help overcome some of the limitations of both types of democracy promoters.

Yet democracy promotion cooperation between the US and Eastern EU countries (and new democracies in general) at both the civil society and the state levels has been mostly ad hoc. And recent political openings in the Arab world or Asia, for example, have seen little democracy promotion coordination among new and established democracies (even though some Eastern EU countries have expressed interest in supporting the democratization of different countries in these regions). This is unfortunate, because such cooperation could prove much more effective than the sum of the isolated efforts by the United States and other emerging democracy promoters.

In fostering such cooperation, an important caveat is in order. Many US officials are perceived as holding the view that such cooperation is about asking the Eastern EU countries (and new democracies in general) to "sign on to the U.S. agenda."[44] This is counterproductive not only because it devalues and thwarts the possibly valuable contributions of emerging democracy promoters but also because US–Eastern EU democracy promotion cooperation has been successful mostly in recipient countries in which Eastern EU countries have a sustained interest for either principled or strategic reasons.[45] To the extent that such cooperation is both facilitated and constrained by the rationales behind democracy promotion, understanding and respecting the rationales of new democracies could help improve the efficiency of this cooperation and help the United States prioritize its investments in it.

NOTES

1. It should be noted that Poland is not exceptional within the group of Eastern EU states in terms of its democracy promotion or its democracy promotion cooperation with the United States. See Tsveta Petrova, *From Solidarity to Geopolitics: Support for Democracy among Post-Communist States* (Cambridge: Cambridge University Press, 2014). The analysis in this chapter is based on interviews with key civic and political elites involved in Eastern EU democracy promotion, including lead activists managing the international programs of the NGOs supporting democracy abroad and key foreign policy elites.

2. Larry Diamond, "Promoting Democracy in the 1990s: Actors and Instruments, Issues and Imperatives," in *A Report to the Carnegie Commission on Preventing Deadly Conflict* (New York: Carnegie Corporation of New York, December 1995).

3. Interview with O. S., October 28, 2008.

4. Interview with K. M., October 7, 2008.

5. Valerie J. Bunce and Sharon L. Wolchik, *Defeating Authoritarian Leaders in Post-Communist Countries* (Cambridge: Cambridge University Press, 2011).

6. The United States promoted regime change in countries that include both cases of successful (Slovakia, Croatia, and Serbia) and failed (Belarus) electoral breakthroughs. Similarly, the United States also refrained from supporting regime change in countries that succeeded (Georgia and Kyrgyzstan) and failed (Armenia and Azerbaijan) in carrying out electoral breakthroughs. This lack of correlation between US support for regime change and the success

of the electoral breakthrough attempts in East Central Europe and the post-Soviet space speaks to the fact that the United States did not "orchestrate" this democratization wave, as some authoritarians in the region have claimed.

7. As Bunce and Wolchik argue, these revolutions were all centered around campaigns that exposed electoral fraud and used mass protest in defense of existing democratic constitutions to defeat the illiberal incumbent and begin a new democratic chapter in each of the affected countries. See Bunce and Wolchik, *Defeating Authoritarian Leaders in Post-Communist Countries*.

8. A word of caution is in order: the US diffusion-brokerage influence in general should not be overestimated. Consider the limited influence of the United States in steering Eastern EU democracy promotion toward recipients with whom there was little solidarity, illustrated by the example of the US introduction of several Slovak groups to Ukrainian, Belarusian, and Iraqi activists. This US brokerage led to the blossoming of Slovak work in Ukraine and Belarus, but, despite abundant funding made available for work in Iraq, no Slovak group sustained its activities there beyond the end of the occasional project. To take the difference in region between these Slovak beneficiary recipients out of the equation, it should be noted that some of the same Slovak groups have eagerly looked for funding to assist fellow activists in other Third World countries such as Cuba (because of the solidarity developed between Cuba and Czechoslovakia before 1989). In other words, US socialization has not succeeded where other communities and identities have not already formed foundations for solidarity between the Eastern EU countries and potential recipients.

9. Peter Baker, "Biden Asks Eastern Europe to Spread Democracy," *New York Times*, October 22, 2009, A6.

10. The author's assessment based on interviews with representatives of the main NGOs with sustained democracy promotion programs in Poland—a total of twenty-nine organizations.

11. Interview with K. M., October 7, 2008; interview with G. G., October 13, 2008; interview with W. B., October 13, 2008; and interview with M. P., October 8, 2008.

12. After the US exit, most of these NGOs did not die out. Instead, they found alternative sources of funding. This speaks to the sustainability of the US democracy promotion investment in these groups. Still, a word of caution is in order—as in much of the rest of the Euro-Atlantic space, these NGOs continue to perpetually struggle to "keep the lights on." While most Eastern EU governments have begun providing some democracy aid, they are not yet the main sponsors of Eastern EU NGOs doing democracy work abroad. Also, despite the increasing relative importance of funding opportunities offered by various regional international organizations, such as the EU, the OSCE, and the Council of Europe, many of the Eastern EU NGOs report that they often lack the capacity to compete with their Western European counterparts for such opportunities. See Balazs Szent-Iványi, "The EU's Support for Democratic Governance in the Eastern Neighbourhood: The Role of Transition Experience from the New Member States," *Europe-Asia Studies* 66, no. 7 (2014). The Eastern EU NGOs have had a better track record with attracting the support of various Western European government agencies (see footnotes 11 and 12).

13. Laurynas Jonavicius, *The Democracy Promotion Policies of Central and Eastern European States* (Madrid: FRIDE, 2008).

14. Interview with M. P., October 10, 2008.

15. Interview with M. M., October 8, 2008.

16. The UN Development Program and a few other Western development agencies have also offered their help in building the capacity of the Polish state to provide development, including democracy assistance, while platforms of European development organizations, such as Trialogue and to a lesser degree Concord, have done similar work at the nonstate level. Both the EU and the OECD have contributed by setting soft requirements for development aid.

17. "Supporting Democracy," *PolishAid*, https://www.polskapomoc.gov.pl/Supporting,democracy,201.html; and "Why We Provide Assistance," *Embassy of the Republic of Poland in Yerevan*, http://www.yerevan.mfa.gov.pl/en/bilateral_cooperation/polish-aid/.

18. The importance of socialization into Eastern EU democracy promotion through such Western efforts should not be overstated. For example, some have reported that there are

significant differences in the perceived indebtedness to external actors among the most active Eastern EU democracy promoters—Poland, the Czech Republic, and Slovakia. See Zora Butorova and Olga Gyarfasova, "Return to Europe: New Freedoms Embraced, but Weak Public Support for Assisting Democracy Further Afield," in *Policy Brief No. 3* (Prague: Policy Association for an Open Society, 2009). And another example: the activists around whom the Polish movement eventually developed began working on democracy and human rights issues at home and abroad in the early 1980s, before there was any external/US support for their efforts.

19. Such support for the development and strengthening of the transnational solidarity among activists in democratizing countries seems to have been much more consequential than US pressure on certain Eastern EU states to engage in democracy promotion. Consider the contrast between the acknowledged importance of being the recipient of US democracy assistance by Eastern EU NGOs doing democracy work abroad and the lack of similar investment by some of the Eastern EU states that the United States sought to involve in this agenda. For example, like their Polish counterparts, the few Bulgarian NGOs that provide democracy support abroad emphasize the normative obligation they feel to assist others on the road to democracy given the Western and US aid they themselves received. On the other hand, the Bulgarian state has aligned with the United States on many important occasions and even actively lobbied (in the early 2000s) to host a US military base. At about that time, various US diplomats began conveying to Sofia their belief in the value of the Bulgarian democratization model. Washington also offered Bulgaria support for initiatives meant to facilitate the sharing of this experience with neighboring countries and proposed to make Bulgaria a regional hub for a few US democracy promotion programs. The Bulgarian state, however, did not take advantage of this opportunity and remained largely uninterested in promoting democracy.

20. *Education for Democracy Foundation*, http://www.edudemo.org.pl/.

21. Interview with T. K., Ukrainian activist who evaluated this initiative, 2012.

22. Interview with O. G., Ukrainian activist in charge of such cooperation, 2012.

23. These postcommunist democracy promoters have usually modified practices "imported from the United States" by adapting them to their domestic political reality and have then most frequently exported the modified practices in the form of democratization recipes. In the PAU-CI example, the US emphasis in Poland was on the regulatory framework facilitating the establishment and functioning of these associations. The Polish focus in Ukraine has been on leveraging these associations for various policy and political purposes.

24. Thomas Carothers, "Democracy Assistance: The Question of Strategy," *Democratization* 4, no. 3 (1997).

25. Tsveta Petrova, "International, National or Local? Explaining the Substance of Democracy Promotion: The Case of Eastern European Democracy Promotion," *Cambridge Review of International Affairs* 28, no. 1 (July 2015).

26. It should be noted that some authors find that the US and EU approaches to democracy promotion are not that different and are, in fact, converging. See Michael A. McFaul, Amichai Magen, and Thomas Risse, eds., *Promoting Democracy and the Rule of Law: American and European Strategies* (New York: Palgrave Macmillan, 2009); and Sarah Sunn Bush, *The Taming of Democracy Assistance: Why Democracy Promotion Does Not Confront Dictators* (Cambridge: Cambridge University Press, 2012).

27. Tsveta Petrova, "International, National or Local?"

28. Petrova, *From Solidarity to Geopolitics.*

29. Wlodzimierz Cimoszewicz, Foreign Minister of the Republic of Poland, "The Eastern Policy of the European Union," speech, Institute of Political Science, Paris, April 22, 2004; and Pavol Hrusovsky about the Cuban opposition, "Presentation of the Chairman of the National Council of the Slovak Republic," in *Yearbook of Foreign Policy of the Slovak Republic 2003* (Bratislava: Slovak Institute for International Studies, 2003).

30. Petrova, *From Solidarity to Geopolitics.*

31. Jacek Kucharczyk and Jeff Lovitt, eds., *Democracy's New Champions: European Democracy Assistance after EU Enlargement* (Prague: Policy Association for an Open Society, 2008), 21.

32. Adam Daniel Rotfeld, Foreign Minister of the Republic of Poland, "On Poland's Foreign Policy," presentation at a Sejm meeting, Warsaw, January 21, 2005.

33. John Galante and Andres Schipani-Aduriz, "Exporting Dissent: Made in the Czech Republic," *Transitions* (Online), January 10, 2006.

34. Czech Republic Ministry of Foreign Affairs, *Report on the Foreign Policy of the Czech Republic 2003* (Prague: Ministry of Foreign Affairs, 2004).

35. Bunce and Wolchik, *Defeating Authoritarian Leaders in Post-Communist Countries*; Joerg Forbrig and Pavol Demes, *Reclaiming Democracy: Civil Society and Electoral Change in Central and Eastern Europe* (Washington, D.C.: German Marshall Fund of the United States, 2007); and Petrova, *From Solidarity to Geopolitics*.

36. See Petrova, *From Solidarity to Geopolitics*.

37. Michael W. Doyle, "After the Freedom Agenda," *Dissent* 56, no. 3 (Summer 2009): 107–11; discusses this perception and argues that it is erroneous.

38. Karrie Koesel and Valerie Bunce, "Diffusion-Proofing: Russian and Chinese Responses to Waves of Popular Mobilizations against Authoritarian Rulers," *Perspectives on Politics* 11, no. 3 (September 2013): 753.

39. Some have pointed out that democracy assistance, for example, has often made political and civic elites in democratizing countries opportunistic as well as dependent on and account-able to external actors rather than to the publics they are to serve. See, for example, Janine R. Wedel, *Collision and Collusion: The Strange Case of Western Aid to Eastern Europe, 1989–1998* (New York: St. Martin's Press, 1998); Nicolas Van de Walle, *African Economies and the Politics of Permanent Crisis, 1979–1999* (Cambridge: Cambridge University Press, 2001); and Thomas Carothers, "Democracy Assistance: Political vs. Developmental?" *Journal of Democracy* 20, no. 1 (January 2009).

40. Thomas Carothers, "The Backlash against Democracy Promotion," *Foreign Affairs* 85, no. 2 (March–April 2006); and Thomas Carothers, "How Democracies Emerge: The 'Sequenc-ing' Fallacy," *Journal of Democracy* 18, no. 1 (January 2007). For a critique of the US efforts in Afghanistan and Iraq, see Larry Goodson, "Afghanistan's Long Road to Reconstruction," *Journal of Democracy* 14, no. 1 (January 2003); and Larry Diamond, "What Went Wrong in Iraq," *Foreign Affairs* 83, no. 5 (September–October 2004).

41. Interview with R. S., Polish foreign policymaker, March 2014; interview with W. W., Polish foreign policy analyst, October 2014; interview with J. S. W., March 2014; interview with J. R., Polish foreign policymaker, April 2015.

42. This was indeed the case in the Eastern EU countries most active in promoting democra-cy abroad. See Petrova, *From Solidarity to Geopolitics*.

43. Petrova, *From Solidarity to Geopolitics*.

44. Thomas Carothers and Richard Youngs, *Looking for Help: Will Rising Democracies Become International Democracy Supporters?* (Washington, D.C.: Carnegie Endowment for International Peace, July 2011).

45. Consider the limited influence of the United States in steering Eastern EU democracy promotion toward recipients with whom no solidarity developed, as discussed previously.

Chapter Seven

East Central Europe and the Future of Democracy

A Case for a Transatlantic Democratic Reset

Michal Kořan

As several authors in this volume make clear, in today's global environment effective democracy support needs to have two dimensions: external and internal. The United States, Western Europe, and other established democracies—including the East Central European states—need to tackle two interrelated challenges: provide global leadership in supporting democracy in the face of the current authoritarian resurgence, and improve the quality of democracy at home by way of overcoming disillusionment, undue influence of money in politics, and other systemic problems. As Larry Diamond and others suggest—"physician, heal thyself"—improving democracy's functioning at home is an indispensable aspect of making it attractive abroad. This chapter supplements the general argument of the book by engaging critically in a discussion about the state of democracy in East Central Europe in the context of debates on democracy transformation in general.

Second, the chapter examines recent democratic erosion and backsliding in the Visegrád Group (V4) countries: Hungary, Poland, Slovakia, and the Czech Republic. It identifies important sources of idealism and civic engagement in East Central Europe that motivated and provided a solid framework for the region's democratic transitions after 1989. A quarter century ago, the Visegrád countries were celebrated as champions of the "third wave" of democratization, and they became significant democracy promoters in southeastern Europe and Eurasia. However, over the course of the last decade, especially since 2010, all four have experienced significant setbacks to their democracy. This should be cause for concern.

According to the Freedom House *Nations in Transit* report, Hungary leads in terms of democratic backsliding in East Central Europe. In 2015, after seven years of continuous decline in Freedom House scores, Hungary was demoted from "Consolidated" democracy to a "Semi-Consolidated" one. Slovakia's Freedom House rankings have also been gradually declining, especially when it comes to local and national democratic governance, judicial framework, and media independence.[1] In fact, in the 2013 regional elections a far-right party succeeded in central Slovakia and its leader became the governor of the region. Poland's parliamentary election in October 2015 and the immediate aftermath stirred many concerns after the winning conservative party launched a campaign aimed at weakening the Constitutional Court and strengthening the government's grip over public media. In the Czech Republic, popular support for extremist nationalist movements and leaders is also rising while even more worrisome media-ownership issues jeopardize the independence of the press.

Third, the chapter aims to situate these developments in the broader context of recent democratic dysfunction in the EU and the US. Liberal democracy[2] has become a concept that is under growing pressure from those who see it as a flawed model of government without universal appeal. The elites of the democratic world do not take this push against liberal democracy seriously enough, and democratic societies are becoming increasingly disenchanted by politics in general. Although this chapter focuses on East Central Europe, it is important to note that the risk of losing the struggle for democracy is by no means exclusive to this region. Aggressively nationalist, xenophobic, and populist movements are on the rise throughout Europe.[3] Wolfgang H. Reinicke recently depicted liberal democracy as shrinking to a "crisis of governance and increasingly a crisis of identity."[4] A growing number of thinkers contest the belief that Western polities and systems of governance really adhere to liberal democracy.[5] Under these conditions, liberal democracy as a model can hardly be credible or attractive enough for democracy assistance to truly work.

Fourth, the chapter argues that it is possible for East Central Europe, Western Europe, and the United States to act jointly to prevent global democracy decline, provided it will be a two-pronged process: working to improve democratic practices at home while supporting democracy abroad. The only way to safeguard the spread of freedom and democracy begins with engaging in a mutual and candid dialogue together with the entire family of democratic countries. This dialogue needs to be high profile and politically visible to have impact.

Finally, one of the problems with democracy in East Central Europe—and perhaps in the wider transatlantic context—lies in the fact that the term seems to have lost its practical and political meaning. Instead, it is now used more either as a political cliché or a technical tool to measure transformation progress in transitional countries. Efforts to restore political meaning, credibility, and practical sense to democracy need to be carried out on a transatlantic scale. The United States emerged from World War II as the sponsor of the global pro-democracy movement. East Central Europe still owes much to the United States for its democratic hopes and inspiration. Yet, in the past decade or more the United States has also exhibited a worrying number of setbacks in terms of its own democratic governance. Repeated political gridlock resulting from sharpening partisanship has severely damaged the government's functionality. American democracy assistance has at times been abused as a means of legitimizing military intervention, reducing its credibility. Yet, especially in the eyes of East Central Europeans, the United States still serves as a role model of democracy and it remains a natural point of reference for their own democratization efforts. In essence, before engaging credibly in democratic assistance abroad, democratic countries must ensure that their own understanding of and commitment to democracy stands on a firm foundation.

FREEDOM, IDEALISM, AND EAST CENTRAL EUROPE

Before examining the recent erosion of democracy throughout the region, it is worth remembering that a tradition of idealism and courage runs through East Central European history—and this tradition can serve as a source of possible democratic renewal in the region.

In East Central Europe, individual, political, economic, social, cultural, ethnic, and later national freedoms were fundamentally limited well into the twentieth century. Often the only thing people of this region could hold on to was a combination of hope and idealism. At the same time, the underlying values inherent in these freedoms conflicted with one another, and thus some inevitably had to be sacrificed: "Freedom had a price which had to be paid by somebody: a nation, a class or an individual."[6]

What I term here as "East Central European idealism" took various forms in different contexts. Consequently, idealism had different policy implications under the Hapsburg domination over the region, and under communist oppression. Idealism carried different meanings under more recent conditions of rising nationalism, extremism and populism, and distrust in liberal democracy. However, the fundamental principles of "idealism" remained the same throughout the decades. This idealism can be described as adherence to the idea that individual freedom, emancipatory politics, intranational solidarity, and humanism can and should be universally applied and can be universally achieved—without confining oneself to the narrow confines of nationally or ethnically defined communities.

The idea of emancipatory politics and universal humanism emerged into the world of modern East Central European politics with, among others, the first president of Czechoslovakia, Tomáš Garrigue Masaryk. He tirelessly rejected the "archaic rule that the states should not meddle into the interior affairs of other states: if democracy is really human, if internationalism is more than a catchphrase, then state frontiers cannot be shields of absolutism within."[7] It is important to note that his call was made under the specific conditions of "Austro-Hungarian oppression"—that is, during the fight for national self-determination. As such, it was a call for universal freedom and internationalism—but one that stemmed from the particular existential conditions of an oppressed nation. This is what T. G. Masaryk meant when he wrote that the "Czech question is a global question. Whenever we strive to fulfill ideas of humanism, democracy or social justice—that is, whenever we strive for issues that transcend the international and all-human spheres—our national perspectives are hopeful. We always fail when we retreat with our ideals into national or personal privacy."[8]

In the 1970s and 1980s, similar voices could be heard from East Central Europe.[9] Those who defined ideas of internationalism and universal humanism in the region throughout the final twenty years of communism did so mostly out of sheer desperation and for existential reasons. Banned thinkers and writers had little to lose and could express their ideas in very clear ways. In their eyes, the Western world had traded pan-European democracy for European stability throughout the communist era, and this pragmatic approach had helped cement the division of Europe. As particularism kept winning over universalism, as long as advocating stability kept winning over advocating democracy and emancipation, the division of Europe denied East Central European countries their freedom. That is why in 1986, amidst the so-called normalization, Jiří Dienstbier, a dissident and first Czechoslovak minister of foreign affairs after the fall of communism, wrote:

> Maintaining the status quo [bipolarity and division of Europe] protects us from a massacre. But such a status quo is a violence in itself. It protects us from a development which would . . . head towards liberalization of man and of his community . . . it prevents us from fulfilling aspirations of all groups of European people . . . including those who are (or feel themselves to be) oppressed within a group into which they were incorporated.[10]

The essay was called *Dreaming of Europe*, but it was a dream that stemmed from a very real nightmare of the frozen and paralyzed political development in Europe in the mid-1980s. It was a desperate call from those who had nothing but universal values to hold on to when the world refused to listen. It was a call of distress made by those who were direct victims of the fact that the West deemed "stability" and "peace" to be much dear than the individual aspirations of people or nations of the "East."

Universalist aspirations were thus one of the most important aspects of East Central European history during the twentieth century. Let us finally recall the words of one of the region's most emblematic figures, the president-playwright Václav Havel, who appealed to Europe with these words in March 1986:

> It seems that the Western Europeans begin to realize that their own problems will never be solved if the problems of Eastern Europeans remain unresolved. As if it is becoming clear to them that they will hurt themselves if they shield their sight to the East and convince themselves that what is happening in the East does not relate to them. As if they understand more and more strongly how equivocal would their Western happiness be if it was forever redeemed by Eastern unhappiness and how inevitably would their happiness turn to misfortune. . . . Thousands of Western Europeans begin to realize the troubled nature of their consumerist happiness traded for indifference to the fate of humans only hundreds kilometers further to the East, they begin to take an interest, they begin to perceive them as their brothers, as someone, whose fate is essentially tied with their own fate. [11]

This is to illustrate two fundamental points. First, that the universalistic calls for pan-European democracy, for universal humanism, for Europe undivided and perhaps united, stemmed from the very particular experience of politically and individually deprived people, who had lost all other possible ways of changing their destiny and the destiny of their respective countries. We can term these cries as *idealism* in the sense that it tried to transcend and to disrupt the particular oppressive reality by appealing to sets of ideals that were rather unthinkable at the time. In the 1970s and 1980s, Havel's idealism had very practical meaning: if this notion of humanism and emancipation takes hold in the minds of the "Western people" who would otherwise not contest the division of Europe, there might be hope for more freedom in the East.

A second fundamental point is that this was a time when East Central Europeans introduced more than a small dose of their idealism into Western mainstream thinking. Albeit slowly, arguments similar to those presented previously managed to permeate the political speeches of Helmut Kohl, Margaret Thatcher, and others. While after the fall of communism East Central Europeans focused on adopting norms and principles transferred from the West, in the 1980s East Central European thinkers served as pioneers wielding the torch of universal freedom in the face of those who were deemed to be pragmatic and too comfortable "Westerners."

In the dissidents' "dreaming," the idea of overcoming a divided Europe meant the spread of democracy regardless of national borders or superpower divisions. The terms "Europe" and "democracy," while acknowledging all the political shortcomings of Western Europe in the late twentieth century, were in fact very close to each other. This belief stemmed from the universalist, or at least Pan-European, understanding of democracy and human rights.

WHY AND WHEN IDEALISM ABANDONED EAST CENTRAL EUROPE

Today, East Central Europe shows little resemblance to its idealistic dreams of the 1980s. It was no coincidence that Dienstbier's second major book (published in 1999) was called *From Dreams to Reality.*[12] It was as if to become part of Europe, East Central Europeans had to submit to precisely the same comfortable pragmatism they once disapproved.

The dream of reuniting Europe "whole and free" (democratic) quickly gave way to a more egoistic goal of "returning to Europe." This change of expression was not only semantic in nature. East Central Europeans were no longer dreaming of Europe undivided and united. As soon as they saw the doors of the European Union open, they adopted the same sense of "realism" that they once disliked. "Return to Europe" meant to do whatever it took to get into the European Union (and NATO), which was, ultimately, a narrower understanding of the European future than that of "Europe undivided."

The "return to Europe" policy and rhetoric was more selfish and narrow because the dreams from the 1980s worked with a broader understanding of the future of Europe. This understanding was perhaps best embodied in the famous speech by President George H. W. Bush in May 1989, in which he called Europe "whole and free." This concept of undivided Europe, however, referred to formerly communist East Central Europe. Yet, it is easy to demonstrate that already in 1992 the Czech Republic, Hungary, and Slovakia started to be concerned only with their own European fortunes and quickly lost their appetite for engaging in helping to pursue the "European" dream of the countries farther to the east. While Poland retained its Eastern policy mostly due to its geographic location, similar disinterest characterized Polish stance toward the Balkans.

Additionally, the new East Central European EU members far too quickly switched from democracy "seekers" to democracy "providers" (or from "pupils" to "teachers"). After their EU accession, the new member countries quickly joined the old ones in the daily business of promoting EU enlargement and of democracy in the EU's vicinity. Many studies and analyses attempted to answer various questions related to the strategies, capacities, differences, and effectiveness of the policies of democracy promotion of the various postcommunist EU members.[13] But the most important question was seldom—if ever—asked: whether the "new democracies" showcased around the globe as frontrunners of democratization were in fact mature enough to export democracy to other postcommunist states.

Prior to joining the EU, applicant countries were subject to an annual screening by the European Commission which, among other things, accounted for various aspects of the state of democratic governance. However, after they joined the EU, the commission and other member states quite naturally lost virtually all their leverage, and thus the ability to monitor and continue to foster the development of democracy in new member states.[14] Because the necessary political reforms in East Central European countries were largely conditioned from the outside, rather than resulting from an internal demand for change, it was not surprising that there should be extensive backsliding in the pro-democracy reform implementation efforts.[15] Already in 2007 Jacques Rupnik argued that "the populist backlash in East Central Europe . . . shows the return of dormant strands in the region's political culture and . . . vulnerability to the authoritarian temptation."[16] Similarly, Charles Gati warned in 2007 that "the region is drifting away from the ambitious goals set in 1989 and in the years that followed."[17] But these—and other[18]—voices of concern were not taken seriously, or were hastily dismissed, perhaps partly because they would harm the shining story of successful democratization trumpeted mostly by the EU and the United States. And, true, in the years immediately following EU enlargement, nothing dramatic happened to democracy in East Central Europe. The erosion was slow, and some observers reported that there was "no systemic evidence of post-accession backsliding among new member states."[19]

However, less visible trends were evolving underneath the surface. Most important of these was the ever more intense political polarization and widespread corruption that led to growing disenchantment of the public with the East Central European political elites. Worse still, this estrangement and disillusionment did not inspire increased civic involvement but rather growing political apathy and introversion. In the meantime, the diplomatic, societal, and political elites enjoyed the status of being democracy providers to the outside world (namely the Balkans and countries farther to the east), while blithely ignoring worrying signs at home. Looking at the democratic deficits in the countries to the east and southeast of the EU was in fact comforting, and allowed them to downplay their own deficiencies. By becoming "teachers of democracy," East Central Europeans failed to engage in thorough and critical introspection at home. Today, these trends have led to a significant weakening of democracy in East Central Europe.

The first sign of this weakening can be found in the feeble response of East Central European political leaders to the global crisis of liberal democracy. The very concept of liberal democracy as the best plausible system of government is challenged by other ideological alternatives around the world, and the actual number of governments adhering to democratic principles has been shrinking both globally and in the European vicinity.[20] East Central Europeans are reacting with the same indifference that affected them negatively not even thirty years ago, when the West preferred stability to engagement. Nothing exemplifies this better than the political avoidance of difficult questions about the future relationship of Ukraine, Moldova, and Georgia with the EU, or the narrow-minded hypocrisy that drives current policies concerning the recently growing waves of migration from conflict zones in the Middle East and Africa. As a result, East Central European governments have lost their reputation as beloved champions of democratic transitions, and now frequently receive scathing criticism.

Prime Minister Viktor Orbán's antiliberal rhetoric (with strong anti-EU, anti-United States, and anti-Western connotations), accompanied by his tightening grip on power, is particularly alarming. According to Freedom House, media freedom, national democratic governance, and the fairness of the electoral process in Hungary have declined rapidly over the past five years.[21] Worse still, his pandering to the extremist, nationalist, and populist instincts in Hungary does not prevent Mr. Orbán from losing ground against a far more sinister political force—the Jobbik party.[22] There are segments of Hungarian society that do not appreciate the path the Hungarian government has taken. On several occasions, the streets of Budapest filled with protesters. However, the political opposition to illiberal tendencies is very weak and fragmented. Moreover, the potential political opposition carries the weight of its own wrongdoing from the time when the postcommunist social democrats discredited themselves while in power.

In the case of Slovakia, the continuous decline of media independence (both public and private), the rise of popularity of xenophobic, antiminority parties, and widespread intermingling of economic and political structures are also worrying signs for the future. The single party government of the SMER leader Robert Fico has used the current migration crisis as a tool to further strengthen the power of government by introducing a new antiterrorism law, among other things.[23] The overwhelming popular support for the ruling SMER party indicates no change is likely in the parliamentary elections in the spring of 2016. However, the Slovak civil society and nongovernmental organizations (NGOs) are stronger than in Hungary, and the society is more differentiated. As a result, in 2014, the Slovaks elected Andrej Kiska president, an important counter-balancing actor who firmly defends the ideals of liberal democracy.

The Czech Republic is becoming notorious for the instability of its government, widespread corruption, and a slow and ineffective justice system. Furthermore, the unprecedented accumulation of political, economic, and media power in the hands of a single person, billionaire Andrej Babis, has raised many eyebrows (although large portions of Czech society actually welcome his "strong-handed" postures). Opaque financial moguls and capital and investment groups (like PPF, J&T Bank, or Penta) have reportedly loomed behind many big political decisions in the Czech Republic and Slovakia for the past two decades. Despite growing apathy, dissatisfaction, and defensive indifference among the majority of the Czech population—which translates into a weakening sense of political trust and civic responsibility—civil society is showing signs of energetic awakening. There is vital political activity coming from the grassroots level, aimed at critical assessment of the state of democracy in the Czech Republic as well as at safeguarding the basic principles of liberal democracy for the future. More important, some of the top political leaders note the need to speak up for democracy, as was, for example, the case of Prime Minister Bohuslav Sobotka criticizing Czech President Milos Zeman for his endorsements of extreme and xenophobic attitudes within the Czech society.

Poland has been widely referred to as to an exception in its economic and political stability. Yet structural problems in its society and politics make it prone to the same challenges as the three other smaller countries. Let us not forget that Poland exemplified democratic backsliding in 2006 and 2007, during the Kaczynski era. The social and cultural divisions that led to this have not disappeared. The structural political and social divisions became once again clearly visible in the parliamentary elections in 2015, and in the actions of the new government of Prime Minister Beata Szydlo (of the Law and Justice party). The new government took advantage of an unexpectedly heavy victory over the center-liberal party Civic Platform. In what could be first seen as an attempt to shift executive balance after long years of Civic Platform rule, the government took a series of quick steps aimed at seizing control over important state institutions (the Constitutional Court, intelligence services, and media, among others). Some now see this latest development as an attempt to launch a "conservative revolution," not unlike that carried out by Prime Minister Orbán in Hungary. These voices have their merit. However, as in the case of the Czech Republic, civil society in Poland is much stronger than in Hungary, society at large is more diverse, and there are important leaders who amplify the concerns of those dissatisfied with the antiliberal developments in Poland.

All in all, East Central European countries, once shining examples of democratic transition, have unleashed various types of a counterliberal, nationalist, and autocratic offensive, using arguments echoing the words uttered by Mr. Orbán in the summer of 2014.[24] In his view, the West is failing normatively and morally, as well as economically, and the appropriate answer to these failings is a strong, illiberal, nationalistic Hungarian state. Mr. Orbán thus chose to paint a caricature portrait of liberalism to support his own position. In his rendition, the sins of liberalism bring together all the sins of predatory economic globalization, democracy's limited ability to protect the weak, the insufficiency of liberalism to create a strong state (which is a contradiction in itself), decaying values, sex, corruption, and violence. In other words, Prime Minister Orbán links together economic (neo)liberalism, democratic deficits, financial difficulties, and the decaying West, and proposes his own version of "nationalist liberalism" as an alternative. The goal of his speech was clearly to lend normative legitimacy to his efforts to strengthen his grip on power.

The heated recent exchanges between the conservative Polish government and the EU and some European politicians, the vituperative election campaign in Slovakia, and the generally unchecked behavior of the first directly elected Czech president, Milos Zeman, show that Hungary might turn out to be a pioneer, showing a way toward a more general illiberal path in East Central Europe. Europe is now facing the threat that its east central part will once again become a group of largely antagonized states—within each society, against one another, and against anything that they individually and arbitrarily choose to define as "other." This might be an epilogue to the dream of Europe "whole and free." The Euro-Atlantic community runs the risk of losing the single biggest achievement of East Central Europe in centuries: a peaceful, nonantagonist, and even cooperative way of living with each other and within a larger international entity. [25]

HOW AND WHY TO REVITALIZE DEMOCRACY

The difficult part is that liberal democracy, as practiced throughout the world, shows real signs of failing. There are individuals and political movements all over Europe eager to escalate frustration with economic problems and politics and to transform it into political power. As Wolfgang H. Reinicke put it, "Disillusioned by the growing failure to provide economic security and other public goods, civil society is turning away from the traditional transmission belts of politics, as political parties and unions rapidly lose stature." [26] As a result, there is a rising tendency for politicians to resort to populism on the one hand, and on the other, for the public to believe in simple solutions to complex problems. Admittedly, there are many citizens who have found themselves on the losing side of economic transformations and globalization, and their number has risen due to the global financial crisis of 2008. But there are also many who are keen to blame Europe's current difficulties on liberal democracy or on the slowness and ineffectiveness of the democratic process.

There is no magic-bullet formula to tackle this potentially devastating conundrum. Calls for more political responsibility, more political leadership, more unity, and more civic engagement will not have an impact because they underestimate the nature of politics today. As implied earlier, what we might hope for is that the current crisis will help to resurface those positive, idealistic elements that aided the rebuilding of Europe after World War II and the recreating of Europe after 1989. We can maintain optimism about such circumstances creating potential for candid retrospection into what went wrong with the transformations of East Central European societies.[27]

The first step toward revitalizing democracy should consist in thinking hard about *why* liberal democracy is losing its attractiveness. We appear to be looking for reasons for the crisis of liberal democracy somewhere (anywhere) in the outside world, instead of looking at home first. Let me list a few examples. A special 2014 report in *The Economist* blamed the decline of democracy's attractiveness on both the economic crisis of 2008 and the rise of China.[28] Many authors and politicians also blame Russia. For example, Pavol Demeš, former Slovak minister for international affairs, wrote in 2010:

> Once the pre-accession conditionality regime of the EU was over, Russia, rich in energy resources, rediscovered its power and the ambition to use it in the international arena, and populist and nationalist tendencies emerged in some new member states, adding to the voices questioning the EU's character and its further growth.[29]

In a similar vein, in 2009, a group of renowned East Central European political leaders blamed the rising difficulties of the region on the Obama administration's new policy toward Russia, which they saw as leaving the postcommunist space vulnerable to negative Russian influence.[30] Conversely, reflecting on the situation from France, Jacque Rupnik chose to blame the East Central Europeans:

> If current trends [of populism and nationalism] continue, with new members backsliding on democratic practice while pursuing a strident defense of "national interests," we could see internal EU ties loosen to the point where the Union becomes little more than an enhanced free-trade zone, [as] these developments are contributing to widespread estrangement from the post-enlargement EU in the older member states.[31]

Instead of trying to locate blame elsewhere, the Euro-Atlantic community should realize that the challenges and problems are shared and not exclusive to any one region or nation. If there is less political will and responsibility in East Central Europe to withstand populist trends, it might be due to the lack of experience with democracy throughout these societies—not because of some inherent wickedness of the people or its leaders. But it is the general tendency of the European public to become increasingly introverted and ready to blame anyone or anything else for one's own difficulties. Populism, extremism, and nationalism are on the rise in every country of the EU. Avoidance of hard political questions regarding the future of democratic transitions in East Central Europe has become the rule, not the exception. Intra-EU solidarity is weakening while general distrust of politics and politicians is rising. As Nicole Scicluna wrote in 2014:

Economic pain combined with political disenfranchisement has fed anti-European sentiment across the Union, as populist parties sought to capitalize on citizens' frustrations. The rise of the extreme Golden Dawn party in Greece . . . is one of the most notable examples, but there are others. In Finland, the populist True Finns party was able to tap into widespread public dissatisfaction over European bailout policies in the April 2011 parliamentary elections. Longstanding populist figures, such as Marine Le Pen in France and Geert Wilders in the Netherlands, have also recalibrated their rhetoric, making the EU and Eurozone policies much more prominent targets. More worryingly, the crisis has also brought ugly and divisive national stereotypes to the fore.[32]

In a similar vein, John Peet and Anton La Guardia point to the rise of leftist extremists across Europe:

Greece has seen the rise not just of Golden Dawn, an explicitly extreme-right party, but also of Syriza, an anti-austerity left-wing party. Spain has . . . the extreme United Left party and support for the two mainstream center-right and center-left parties has collapsed. Italy has seen the spectacular rise of Beppe Grillo's Five Star movement, which took almost 25% of the vote in the election of February 2013, forcing the center-left and center-right parties into an uneasy coalition.[33]

This account of the state of politics in Europe does not show it as a particularly attractive model for the outside world, and that is why the second step toward revitalizing democracy needs to consist in critical introspection within the Euro-Atlantic family of democratic countries themselves.

WHY THE UNITED STATES MATTERS

The third step toward revitalizing democracy is candid and, above all, political dialogue about the future of liberal democracy, about its shortcomings in the past, and about the West's commitment to it. It is essential for this dialogue to include the United States. From the East Central European point of view, the United States served as the first and most natural point of reference for all who strove for freedom under communist rule in East Central Europe. In 1989, the US Congress passed the Support for East European Democracy Act, and thus Americans were among the first to assist East Central European countries on their path to democracy. Even though the quantity of US funding was quickly and by far exceeded by the European Union's means for democracy assistance, American political commitment and support greatly contributed to the necessary transformation processes. Expanding these collaborative efforts ultimately led many to feel a special kinship over the years.

Nevertheless, after President Barack Obama took office in 2009, significant strains in the relationship between the United States and East Central Europe began to appear. East Central Europeans started to feel abandoned by the new president. As Thomas Carothers writes in his assessment of democratization policy under President Obama, in an attempt to signal distance from the previous administration, whose policies of military interventionism disguised as democracy promotion left the US reputation badly damaged, President Obama's administration softened the American rhetoric on promoting Western-style liberal democracy abroad.

After some contemplation, the United States articulated a "new approach" to East Central Europe's new democracies: they now fully belonged to the family of mature democratic countries, and instead of being the "protégés" of the United States they should develop into equal partners in democracy promotion. This basically meant that the United States largely attempted to outsource its democracy promotion agenda in Southeastern Europe and parts of the former Soviet Union to these new democracies. This approach was announced during Vice President Joe Biden's trip to Eastern Europe in October 2009. The purpose of the trip was to reassure America's allies of continued US attention to this region. However, the main message was best exemplified by statements like: "You've delivered on the promise of your revolution," "You are now in a position to help others do the same," and "Exercise your leadership."[34]

Encouraging words aside, in reality the administration hoped to refocus US attention on what it saw as more pressing global issues, while leaving responsibility of extending democracy further to the eastern and southern flanks of Europe to the Europeans themselves. In principle, there is nothing wrong with this idea—the EU aspires to be a normative power and it has moral responsibility for, immediate interest in, as well as material means to promote democracy in its neighborhood. The East Central European governments—especially through the platform of the Visegrád group—took up Vice President Biden's challenge and invested enormous political and material capital in the cause of democracy advancement to their eastern and southern neighbors. Yet reality showed that without continuous US political commitment and active engagement, the enthusiasm and commitment of East Central European governments began to wane.

Paradoxically, at the same time, the Euro-Atlantic democracies never quite left the comforting view that liberal democracy does not have any serious contenders on the global market of ideologies, and we can thus afford to focus only on technical assistance. As a consequence, democracy promotion has increasingly become limited to technical and essentially nonsensitive (i.e., nonpolitical) projects, as mentioned previously. These projects—in a simplistic and general way—go a long way toward bolstering civil societies, NGOs, institutional capacity, media quality, and so on. But these projects—

because they are nonpolitical by definition—do not address the crucial issue: that is, democratic thinking at the political level. A working democracy first requires a democratic mindset among practicing and aspiring politicians. As a result, there is a growing gap between thriving pro-democracy support on the part of civil society and deteriorating political determination on the other. Without narrowing this gap, pro-democracy support and policies will be ineffective because they do not translate into the actions of political leaders, who are primarily responsible for and will bear the costs of the hard choices that come with the support for democratization.

This brings me to my final point: how to utilize the elements of idealism in East Central Europe, which were discussed earlier in this chapter. During communist oppression and terror, there was nothing but idealism left to fall back on. Despite spreading dissatisfaction with contemporary politics (which some would like to confuse with dissatisfaction with democracy itself), there are many throughout the region who are seriously concerned with the future of democracy. It is important to actively re-engage in dialogue with these potential leaders of East Central European societies, and to benefit from their enthusiasm. Another sector of society that will be supportive and helpful consists of owners of small and medium enterprises. These are the people whose fate is most closely linked with thriving liberal democracy, these are the people who are most endangered by excessive strengthening of the state and by jeopardizing liberal democratic principles. Also, East Central European countries can make effective use of local NGOs and institutions in distributing grants and projects focused on democratic transformation assistance to countries farther to the east. Problems with the distribution of means are chronic and well known: an ever larger share of money being used for institutional (core) financing, crippling administration (mostly in the case of EU money), corruption, government-organized NGOs,[35] and so on. Over the years, organizations from East Central Europe have developed both credibility and local knowledge, and they are generally better equipped to relatively fair and effective distribution of the means than large donor organizations.

CONCLUSIONS AND POLICY RECOMMENDATIONS

East Central Europe is a region that deserves much credit for transforming itself from autocratic and totalitarian rule to functioning democracy. It also deserves credit for standing as a model and inspiration for other democracy-aspiring countries, and for working to help them democratize. Similarly, the United States and the EU deserve their share of praise for enabling and helping East Central Europeans to achieve their dreams that arose during the tragic times of communist oppression. All of this constitutes a healthy and credible foundation upon which the revival of democracy and democratization can take place. For this revival to take place, however, several key steps need to be taken.

The family of democratic countries needs to make sure that liberal democracy reflects the changing social, economic, and political conditions locally, nationally, and globally, and thus demonstrates that liberal democracy is worthy of loyalty. The liberal democratic world has to first reflect on itself, and on its own political understanding of democracy. Functioning democracies have to decide whether they see freedom (and democracy as a way of facilitating the relationship between freedom and the need to govern) as a potentially universal idea that can penetrate the hearts and minds of people and subsequently inform political practices. A deeply sincere reflection on our own democratic deficiencies should accompany any attempt to re-energize democracy promotion in other countries. This kind of initiative must be multinational and comprehensive.

We also have to acknowledge that the idea of democracy is essentially a political, emotional and normative one. There can be no universally accepted empirical proof that liberal democracy is the best way to govern. Therefore, any response to the global democracy crisis must be a political one. Political leaders cannot hide behind administrative tools, projects, and institutions when it comes to democracy promotion. No increase in money, no quantity of well-crafted and thoughtful expert strategies and analyses, can substitute for a lack of confidence and political leadership.

Europe and the United States have shown many times in the past that they are able to engage in undertakings which, in the end, bring positive change. I already recalled the rebuilding of Europe after World War II, but I should also stress the Helsinki process, the peaceful management of the fall of the Berlin Wall, the reunification of Germany, and the ideas and practices of European integration—these are some of the most compelling examples of success. The world has become a more peaceful and more law-abiding place since the Second World War because of the internationalist adherence to the rule of law and universalist approaches to human rights and human freedoms, all of which stand as cornerstones of liberal democracy. The Euro-Atlantic community can and must live up to its potential to once again engage internationally and multilaterally in order to make the world safer for democracy. Should such an international debate take place, it is important to:

1. Engage in the transatlantic dialogue outlined above at the highest political levels.
2. Ensure that this discussion includes a wide variety of actors, groups, and NGOs (not only national governments).
3. Ensure that this discussion includes all countries that share a basic commitment to democracy.

4. Ensure that it is a truly interactive and egalitarian dialogue rather than a series of monologues.
5. This dialogue should not be conceived as a "teacher to pupil" affair but as a "partner to partner" conversation, because the difficulties are the same for everyone.

While these suggestions might sound like a tall order to some, there are institutions and platforms where such a political and normative debate might take place. Let us put aside for a moment the disputes over the functionality and purpose of the OSCE (especially after the events in Eastern Ukraine and democratic regression of many of the OSCE countries). The legacy of the Helsinki process suggests that despite unfavorable international conditions, breakthrough can occur. The OSCE must either be reformed to return to its original purposes or be replaced by a new process, modeled on the OSCE of the 1970s and 1980s.

A lot of criticism has been directed toward Europe recently. However, a closer look at what is happening reveals not only disillusionment with democracy and rising populism but also thriving movements that are energetic and passionate about the ideals of humanism, democracy, and openness to a degree not seen for a long time in Europe. Perhaps the multiple crises that have hit the world in recent years could give back to humanism and democracy the features that were lost over the past two decades. To see such an outcome, the national governments, the EU, and European political elites have to tap this energy instead of giving in to populism; they need to use it to help initiate broad political dialogue about democracy.

Politics is always a matter of compromise. But too many compromises in the field of democracy promotion lead to hypocrisy—and hypocrisy gives the strongest reasons for criticizing democracy promotion and democracy as such. That is why we first have to have a broadly gaged understanding of what the concept of liberal democracy really means to us. By seeking this understanding, I believe, democracy will get reenergized as a cause worth pursuing. Several elements, properly blended, can create powerful new momentum to propel a much-needed democracy revival both at home and around the world: the symbolic and real power of the United States; the unique mix of past experience, idealism, and caution of the East Central Europeans; and the economic, normative, and institutional power of the EU.

NOTES

1. Freedom House, *Nations in Transit 2015*, Survey 2014, https://freedomhouse.org/report/nations-transit/nations-transit-2015#.VoqFFLbhAo7.
2. Throughout the chapter, "liberal democracy" refers to the conceptualization of the term as discussed in this chapter. When the term "democracy" or "Western democracy" is used, it also refers to this concept of liberal democracy.

3. Nicole Scicluna, *European Union Constitutionalism in Crisis* (Abingdon: Routledge, 2014), 131–32; John Peet and Anton La Guardia, *Unhappy Union: How the Euro Crisis—and Europe—Can Be Fixed* (London: Profile Books, 2014), 123–24.

4. Wolfgang H. Reinicke, "Purpose Beyond Power," *Brookings Institute* (Fall 2013).

5. See Walden Bello, "The Global Crisis of Legitimacy of Liberal Democracy," in *Globalization and the Washington Consensus: Its Influence on Democracy and Development in the South*, ed. Gladys Lechini (Buenos Aires: CLACSO, 2008).

6. Piotr S. Wandycz, *The Price of Freedom: A History of East Central Europe from the Middle Ages to the Present*, 2nd ed. (London and New York: Routledge, 2001), 10.

7. Jiří Dienstbier, *From Dreams to Reality* (Prague: Nakladatelství Lidové Noviny, 1999), 21.

8. Dienstbier, *From Dreams to Reality*, 21.

9. Václav Havel, "Power of Powerless," in *Power of Powerless* (Armonk: Palach Press, 1985), 23–96; Czeslaw Milosz, *The Captive Mind* (New York: Vintage International, 1990); George Konrád, *Antipolitics* (New York: HBJ, 1984).

10. Jiří Dienstbier, *Snění o Evropě* (Prague: Nakladatelství Lidové Noviny, 1990), 20.

11. Václav Havel, "Děkovná řeč," in *Do různých stran* (Prague: Lidové Noviny, 1989), 97.

12. Dienstbier, *From Dreams to Reality*.

13. See Laurynas Jonavičius, *The Democracy Promotion Policies of Central and Eastern European States* (Madrid: FRIDE, 2008); and Tsveta Petrova, *The New Role of Eastern Europe in International Democracy Support* (Washington, D.C.: Carnegie Endowment for International Peace, 2011).

14. The Lisbon Treaty (effective since 2009) tried to address this issue and did so by Article 7, which stipulates that the EU may determine that there is a clear risk of a serious breach by a member state of the basic values (namely rule of law) of the EU. In fact, on January 3, the European Commission initiated first steps potentially leading to an unprecedented move of activating Article 7 with regard to the political development in Poland after the conservative government of Prime Minister Beata Szydło took office in late 2015.

15. See, for example, a special issue of *Journal of Democracy* (vol. 18, no. 4, October 2007) with the eloquent title, "Is East-Central Europe Backsliding?"

16. See the contribution by Jacque Rupnik in the special issue (see previous note): Jacque Rupnik, "From Democracy Fatigue to Populist Backlash," *Journal of Democracy* 18, no. 4 (2007).

17. Charles Gati, "Backsliding in Central and Eastern Europe," statement prepared for US House of Representatives, Foreign Affairs Committee Hearing, July 25, 2007.

18. See also F. Stephen Larrabee, "Danger and Opportunity in Eastern Europe," *Foreign Affairs* 85, no. 6 (November/December 2006).

19. Philip Levitz and Grigore Pop-Eleches, "Why No Backsliding? The European Union's Impact on Democracy and Governance before and after Accession," *Comparative Political Studies* 43, no. 4 (April 2010).

20. In March 2014, *The Economist* ran a special report titled "What's Gone Wrong with Democracy," which neatly summarizes all the anxieties related to the state of democracy.

21. Sylvana Habdank-Kołaczkowska, "Democracy on the Defensive in Europe and Eurasia," in Freedom House, *Nations in Transit 2015*, https://freedomhouse.org/report/nations-transit-2015/democracy-defensive-europe-and-eurasia.

22. In April 2015, the Jobbik party, which has been often (rightly) portrayed as a populist mix of anti-Semitism, antiminority sentiment, xenophobia, and extreme nationalism, won its first by-election over a FIDESZ candidate. Recent polls show almost constant growth in support for Jobbik.

23. "New Antiterrorism Legislation Risks Triggering Protests in Slovak Capital but Unlikely to Lower Ruling Party's Election Process." IHS Jane's Country Risk Daily Report, December 22, 2015, http://www.janes.com/article/56838/new-anti-terrorism-legislation-risks-triggering-protests-in-slovak-capital-but-unlikely-to-lower-ruling-party-s-election-prospects.

24. Full text of Viktor Orbán's speech at Baile Tusnad of July 26, 2014, archived at http://budapestbeacon.com/public-policy/full-text-of-viktor-orbans-speech-at-baile-tusnad-tusnad-furdo-of-26-july-2014/10592.

25. Michal Kořan, "Central Europe in the European Union: A Story of Hypocrisy," *Visegrád Insight "Border Anxiety"* 2, no. 8 (Online), December 7, 2015, http://visegradinsight.eu/central-europe-in-the-european-union/.

26. Reinicke, "Purpose Beyond Power."

27. Kořan, "Central Europe in the European Union."

28. "What's Gone Wrong with Democracy," *The Economist*, March 1, 2014, http://www.economist.com/news/essays/21596796-democracy-was-most-successful-political-idea-20th-century-why-has-it-run-trouble-and-what-can-be-do.

29. Pavol Demeš, *Twenty Years of Western Democracy Assistance in Central and Eastern Europe* (Stockholm: International Institute for Democracy and Electoral Assistance, 2010).

30. Valdas Adamkus et al., "An Open Letter to the Obama Administration from Central and Eastern Europe," *Gazeta Wyborcza*, August 15, 2009.

31. Rupnik, "From Democracy Fatigue to Populist Backlash," 24.

32. Scicluna, *European Union Constitutionalism in Crisis*, 131–32.

33. Peet and La Guardia, *Unhappy Union*, 123–24.

34. "Biden Asks Eastern Europe to Spread Democracy," *New York Times*, October 22, 2009, http://www.nytimes.com/2009/10/23/world/europe/23biden.html?_r=0.

35. Government-organized NGOs are organizations created by autocratic governments to maintain an illusion of a free civil society while retaining a tight control over it.

Chapter Eight

Reviving the Global Democratic Momentum

Larry Diamond

This book project comes at an important and volatile time for democracy in the world. Many people are questioning the viability of democracy, and the wisdom of trying to promote it. The fashionable mood these days is skepticism, if not downright pessimism, about the near-term prospects for democracy. The argument goes, we tried to do too much, and we should scale back our expectations. Or (in these neoisolationist times), it's not our business, we have too many problems at home. Or, we tried to support democratic movements in the Arab world, and look where it led: chaos, state disintegration, the advance of ISIS, and even harder forms of authoritarianism, as in Egypt.

It's still common to think that "those people" in the Arab world, Africa, or Russia and other parts of Asia weren't ready for democracy, don't value it culturally, and don't have the social conditions to make it work. Some believe democracy promotion was always a fool's errand. Others contend that we did what we could and should now pull back. Or that after thirty years of intensive democracy promotion, we still don't know how to do it effectively, except in places where democratic progress would have happened anyway. And finally (for now) there is the view that we have more important issues to deal with, like ISIS, Ebola, a rising China, a marauding Putin, a nuclear-weapons-chasing Iran, narco-trafficking in Latin America, child mortality among the bottom billion, and so on.

There is not enough space even in an entire chapter to rebut all these currents of pessimism, determinism, and despair. But there is a need to begin by setting the record straight on where we are and where we have come in terms of global democracy. The situation is not rosy, but nothing close to despair is warranted either. After assessing the current state of democracy globally, this chapter will consider some of the challenges, opportunities, and imperatives for democracy promotion, especially by the United States, at this critical juncture for democracy globally. My argument is that democracy and freedom have been mired in a prolonged period of stagnation, and in some respects recession, over the past decade, but if authoritarianism has been resurgent, it shows no sign of deep stability or global legitimacy. We live in politically fluid times when all forms of authority are challenged and vulnerable, and this heightens the imperative of a creative, focused, and multidimensional strategy to expand, deepen, reform, and consolidate democracy.

THE GLOBAL DEMOCRATIC RECESSION

This is a difficult and messy time for democracy and freedom around the world. We have been in a global democratic recession for something like a decade. In each one of the last nine years, as Freedom House has documented through January 2015, the number of countries declining in political rights or civil liberties has outpaced (by at least two to one) the number of countries gaining in freedom. And this has come after fifteen post–Cold War years when precisely the reverse was true. [1]

Since 2006, there has been no net expansion in the number of electoral democracies, which has oscillated between 114 and 119 (about 60 percent of the world's states). And there has also been stagnation in the number of liberal democracies—regimes which do a relatively good job of protecting not only political rights but also civil liberties and the rule of law. Over the past decade, that number has also held essentially flat, at seventy-nine (or about 40 percent of the world's states). [2] Since 2006, the average level of freedom in the world has also deteriorated slightly.

There have been a lot of democratic breakdowns in this new century. In fact, the rate of democratic breakdown in these last thirteen years has been 50 percent higher than in the preceding period. Since the third wave of global democratic expansion began forty years ago, nearly a third of the democratic regimes in the world have broken down. And roughly half of these failures have occurred since the year 2000.

Many of these breakdowns have come in big and strategically important states, like Russia, Nigeria, Pakistan, and Venezuela. In some cases, like the Philippines, and recently Sri Lanka and Nigeria following the dramatic opposition victories in national elections during 2015, democracy has been restored. In others, like Thailand, which in 2014 suffered its second military coup in a decade, democracy has broken down repeatedly. In others, like Pakistan, Kenya, and Turkey, the regime seems to occupy a gray zone somewhere between electoral democracy and electoral authoritarianism. But for countries like Turkey, the authoritarian drift has been so steady, so serious and so prolonged that an authoritarian threshold appears to have been crossed. This has long since happened in Nicaragua, and Ecuador also seems to have crossed the threshold as well. Moreover, instead of confronting or at least condemning the godfather regime of creeping authoritarianism in the Andes, Venezuela, most Latin American democracies have turned a blind eye toward its abuses, even rewarding it in 2014 with a seat on the UN Security Council.

Democracy has also eroded quite significantly in Africa, where many elected leaders believe that China's booming aid and investment gives them an alternative to Western conditionality, and that the expanding war on terror gives them additional political space to concentrate power, loot national resources, and abuse rights while the West looks the other way. The list of African elected presidents who have cavalierly manipulated the constitution to enable them to run for "third" terms keeps growing, with the recent additions of Burundi, Rwanda, and the Republic of Congo to such long-term personal autocracies as Uganda and Cameroon.[3] Deepening the sense of gloom for democrats globally have been: the implosion of the Arab Spring; the growing self-confidence, assertiveness, and cooperation of authoritarian states like China, Russia, and their club of fellow autocracies, the Shanghai Cooperation Organization; the mounting legal assaults and constraints on civil society; the sharing and development of tools of Internet censorship and suppression; and the poor performance of many of the most advanced democracies, beginning with the United States.

Two trends bear some brief elaboration here. First, the "authoritarian resurgence" has seen nondemocratic regimes moving much more skillfully and aggressively, and in more effective coordination with one another, to suppress human rights movements and other civil society organizations and independent media in their own countries, and to control flows of information and opinion more broadly on the Internet. As these autocracies have moved to criminalize flows of international financial and technical assistance to challenging organizations in their civil societies, they have made international efforts to promote democracy in their countries much more difficult and risky (which was precisely their aim).[4]

Second, the quality of democracy has been eroding in a few countries that we have come to take for granted as liberal and consolidated democracies, such as Hungary and South Africa. The classic U-turn toward illiberal rule has been navigated in Hungary, where Prime Minister Viktor Orbán has dramatically concentrated power in his own hands and that of his Fidesz party, while undermining judicial independence, open markets, press freedom, intellectual autonomy, minority rights, and other liberal values.[5] South African President Jacob Zuma has been increasingly contemptuous of the rule of law as his own corruption and that of his ruling party have become increasingly brazen, amid a steep general deterioration in the quality of governance. In fact, there is not a single country on the African continent where democracy is firmly consolidated and secure—the way it is, for example, in such third-wave democracies as Spain, South Korea, and Chile. Add new oil wealth to the mix, as in Ghana, and you have a major new challenge to the quality of governance. In the global democracy-promotion community, few actors are paying attention to the growing signs of fragility in the more liberal developing democracies, not to mention the more illiberal ones. For anyone who cares about democracy in the world, this is a troubling situation.

But this is not the whole story. We are in a prolonged political recession, not a depression. We have not yet seen the onset of "a third reverse wave." The extraordinary expansion in the number of democracies essentially halted around 2005. Since then, it has not significantly increased, but neither has it substantially diminished. Globally, average levels of freedom have ebbed a little bit, but not calamitously. Most importantly, there has not been significant erosion in public support for democracy. In fact, what the Afrobarometer has consistently showed is a gap—in some African countries, a chasm—between the popular demand for democracy and the regime supply of it.[6] And this is not just some shallow, vague notion that democracy is a good thing. Many Africans understand political accountability, transparency, the rule of law, and restraint of power. And they would like to see their government manifest these virtues.

Broadly, we know why democracy and freedom are slipping back. What Francis Fukuyama calls "neopatrimonial" tendencies are resurgent.[7] Leaders who think they can get away with it are eroding democratic checks and balances, hollowing out accountability institutions, overriding term limits and normative restraints, and accumulating power and wealth for themselves and their families, cronies, clients, and parties. Space for opposition parties, civil society, and the media is shrinking, and international support for them is drying up. Ethnic, religious, and other identity cleavages polarize many societies that lack well designed democratic institutions to manage those cleavages. State structures are too often weak and porous, unable to secure order, protect rights, meet the most basic social needs, or rise above corrupt, clientelistic and predatory impulses. Democratic institutions—parties and parliaments—are often poorly developed, and the bureaucracy lacks the policy expertise, and even more so the independence, neutrality, and authority, to effectively manage the economy. So weak economic performance, and certainly rising inequality, is added to the mix.

It isn't easy to develop democracy in poor countries and weak states. And there is a significant failure rate even in middle-income countries. If we don't become more focused, more creative, more determined, more resourceful, and less tentative in promoting democracy, the democratic recession will mutate into a wave of democratic regressions, a bleak period for freedom, political stability, and the American national interest.

OPPORTUNITIES AND IMPERATIVES FOR DEMOCRACY PROMOTION

So what is to be done? We need to begin by disaggregating the problem. The first imperative is to address the manifest ills of our own democracy in the United States, and in other Western democracies. Like many who travel widely, I have been increasingly alarmed by how pervasive and corrosive is the worldwide perception—in both autocracies and democracies—that American democracy has become dysfunctional and is no longer a model worth emulating. The accelerating trend toward hyperpolarization and institutional gridlock has not only damaged our own national strength but has challenged the appeal of democracy and the credibility of the United States in promoting it. And the surge of illiberal, nativist, anti-immigrant appeals in the electoral politics of the United States, France, Hungary, Poland, Switzerland, and other European democracies has done even more damage to the image of democracy as a universalistic value. The established democracies of the West will have neither the international credibility nor the domestic support to advance a robust agenda for promoting democracy and human rights unless these strains of political paranoia and hypocrisy are vigorously confronted and contained.

Within the United States, creative and plausible proposals for political reform are now being advanced—addressing, for example, electoral system incentives, campaign finance, lobbying, and the institutional capacity of the Congress and the federal bureaucracy—that can reduce the tendencies toward gridlock and state capture without having to scale the nearly impossible hurdle of a constitutional amendment.[8] If we do not mobilize institutional reforms and operational innovations to reduce partisan polarization, encourage moderation and compromise, energize executive functioning, and reduce the outsized influence of money and special interests in our own politics, how are we going to be effective in helping other countries to tackle these challenges?

Second, we need to be absolutely sure that we have harvested and preserved the low-hanging fruit. That is, we must truly help to consolidate incipient or assumed success stories. One of the biggest mistakes the global democracy promotion community has made over the last thirty years is to cross countries—a great many of them—off the list of democracy assistance recipients, because once the transition is completed and the new democracy lifts off in a middle-income country, we assume it can take care of itself. Or we believe that ten or twenty years of democratic assistance and engagement should be enough. This is all summed up in the term, "graduation." In my profession, we prefer the term "commencement" to "graduation."

Sometimes our graduates still need and deserve our help in certain areas. A strong and capable state; a genuine rule of law, buttressed by a neutral and capable judiciary; effective institutions of horizontal accountability; competent and honest local administration; a pluralistic and resourceful civil society; a culture of tolerance, vigilance, and civic responsibility—these and other foundations of a secure liberal democracy do not get constructed overnight. Many of them emerge gradually with economic development. In more mature economies, they can develop more quickly. But even many of the countries listed as "upper-middle income" by the World Bank remain well within the danger zone of democratic decay—as were Russia and Venezuela a decade and a half ago.

The list of upper-middle-income countries includes Argentina, which has been going through a profound economic and political crisis, but now has a new opportunity for democratic rejuvenation with the recent election of the opposition candidate, Mauricio Macri, to the presidency; Turkey, where the AKP has become a hegemonic party, the press functions in a state of fear, and the opposition parties are in disarray; Romania, an EU country where endemic corruption continues to undermine the health of democracy and governance; South Africa, where a corrupt leadership exhibits visibly declining commitment to the rule of law and liberal values; Thailand, which is now in the grip of the most repressive and domineering military dictatorship it has suffered in decades; Libya, which experienced a revolutionary uprising against Qadaffi, and then a state collapse; and Tunisia, which could become the one success story of the Arab Spring, but faces enormous political, economic, and security challenges.

A long-term strategic approach to promoting democracy would make the following resolution: Once a country (and especially a middle-income country) achieves or renews democracy, we will do everything possible to help lock it into place for the long run. That means that when a new, fragile Libyan transitional government appeals to us for security assistance (assistance, not occupying troops), we don't say, "sorry friends, we helped you get there, now let somebody else help you stay there." The failure to help the new Libyan transitional government secure itself after the fall of Qaddafi stands as one of the great blunders and missed opportunities of democracy assistance in recent years. A strategic approach also requires making a paramount priority of Tunisia, which is clearly indispensable to the future of democracy throughout the Arab world, despite its small size. What can we do to help revive the economy and rejuvenate flows of tourism and investment? Beyond our existing programs of party training, election observation, and other assistance, what can we do to support new civil society monitoring and training initiatives, to strengthen independent journalism and policy think tanks, to advance democratic civic education in the schools and the media, to support women's groups, student groups, human rights groups, and any other kind of social initiative to build a culture and civic infrastructure to sustain democracy? Only now is the United States beginning to respond to the scale of the challenge, but even the recent significant increases in assistance to Tunisia remain well short of the massive and urgent needs on all fronts—economic, political, and security.[9]

If we want to promote democracy in the Arab world for the long run, we should invest very heavily in Tunisia in every possible way, because what the Arab world most needs now is one example of a decent, functioning democracy that can serve as a lesson, an inspiration, and a point of diffusion for the region.

The same goes for Ukraine, though it is not as economically advanced. Ukraine is at a pivotal point in its history. It cannot afford another democratic regression, or an authoritarian, xenophobic Russia may swallow up the rest of it. It is struggling mightily with entrenched patterns of corruption, bad governance, and weak institutions. But it has some remarkable actors in the party system, the mass media, and civil society organizations. We need to invest heavily in these people and institutions, and in economic reform, revival, and integration with the West. It should be one of the major priorities for democracy assistance for the next decade or two. And we need to sustain these investments over an extended period in all three critical sectors: the state, the party and representative institutions, and civil society. Beyond political assistance, Ukraine will need even more far-reaching economic assistance.

The United States and its democratic allies in Europe (as well as Canada, Australia, and hopefully Japan) should offer Tunisia, Ukraine, and other pivotal transitional countries a far-reaching deal: massive, transformative levels of political, economic, and security assistance, but conditioned on serious efforts to control corruption, govern responsibly, and cooperate across party lines to enact the necessary reforms.

Thinking strategically means prioritizing countries where well-timed, adequately resourced, and carefully conceived flows of international democratic assistance could make a real difference to the fate of democracy. Some of these will be countries where democracy has been functioning for some time but has been slipping alarmingly, as in Turkey and South Africa. Others will be countries that have been underperforming in terms of democratic quality, but where new leadership provides new opportunities for democratic reform and consolidation, as in Argentina. Others will be countries where recent democratic breakthroughs provide new opportunities to develop effective institutions of governance and representation, and thereby help move the systems toward democratic consolidation. To the list of Tunisia and Ukraine, we can now add, following their historic and surprising electoral breakthroughs in 2015, Sri Lanka, Nigeria, and Burma (Myanmar). Having been a functioning democracy for many decades before it was decimated by civil war and abuse of power, Sri Lanka is in the best position to entrench its renewed democratic spirit. But it still faces steep challenges, including a deeply illiberal former president who lurks in the opposition. Nigeria must overcome decades of wanton abuse of power that has generated one of the most egregious cultures of corruption of any country in the world, but it has a new president who seems determined to control corruption and fight the terrorist challenge of Boko Haram more seriously, plus a vigorous independent press and civil society. Burma has a long way to go before it can even qualify as a democracy, given the numerous constitutional provisions that sustain a military veto over major political questions (in part, through the provision that gives the military 25 percent of the seats in parliament by appointment). But with the overwhelming victory of Aung San Suu Kyi's National League for Democracy in the November 2015 national elections, the popular hunger for democratic and accountable government, and the rapid growth of civil society, there is probably no country in the world where international engagement to develop democratic culture, institutions, and state capacity can do more good more quickly.

Finally, there are the countries where the authoritarian regime is in crisis and democratic parties and movements are gaining momentum. Today, no country is more primed for democratic change than Venezuela, where the ruling United Socialist Party of Venezuela (founded by the populist autocrat, Hugo Chavez) lost control of the National Assembly for the first time since 1999. With the stunning victory of the opposition coalition, the Democratic Unity Roundtable, Venezuela now has a chance to bring an end to the deeply corrupt Chavista autocracy, and renew the democracy it lost more than a decade ago. Democracy assistance efforts must tread carefully, because the regime, in its desperation, will seek any means possible of discrediting the opposition as a front for malevolent foreign interests. Opposition forces in Venezuela must be the ones to indicate what forms of assistance can make a difference at this crucial time. But nimble and creative diplomacy could help to ease the transition and even spare the country a bloodbath. Many of the leading figures in the Venezuelan military and political establishment fear prosecution for drug trafficking, massive corruption, and other crimes should their regime fall. At a crucial moment in the transition process, international diplomacy might be helpful by offering them an exit path to exile in another country, while ratcheting up targeted sanctions until they leave power.

THE PERILS OF TAKING DEMOCRACY FOR GRANTED

Taking democracy for granted can open the door to the kind of alarming backsliding that South African democracy is now experiencing. Here, the recent death of the historic democracy NGO in South Africa, Idasa, provides an instructive case of benign neglect. Idasa was one of the trailblazing organizations that came out of the white minority community to resist apartheid and help create the climate and culture for a peaceful, negotiated transition. And then it worked to promote democratic civic education and citizen monitoring of parliament and government. Some years after Nelson Mandela was elected president and South Africa seemed to have entrenched a liberal democracy with a remarkably rights-affirming constitution, the international democracy promotion community said, "Well, South Africa is a success story, and a relatively rich country. They don't really need much democracy help any more themselves, so we'll fund Idasa to help foster democracy, but only in other parts of Africa."

It's a very good thing to get the civil societies of emerging democracies involved in cross-border work to build democratic institutions and norms in the region, but it's a very bad thing to ignore the problems in their own societies. This is not the place to litigate all the accomplishments and challenges that Idasa faced organizationally, but it is important to ask: how is a civil society organization that is monitoring and sometimes challenging the incumbent government supposed to raise the resources from within its own society when most of those material resources lie in the hands of businessmen and corporations who feel extremely vulnerable to political punishment if they support "antigovernment" activity? The same problem exists today in Turkey, another middle-income country that is not on the strategic priority list of democracy assistance donors.

The dilemma is repeated over and over in countries that are seen as too rich, or too long in democratic experience, to justify continued flows of support to civil society organizations. These civil society organizations, critics say, need to be weaned off the mother's milk of international democracy funding. They need to develop their own sources of revenue. Typically, that is another way of saying they either need to go commercial, maybe by doing surveys or consulting, or they need to seek contracts from agencies of the same government they are supposed to be monitoring, or they need to seek grants to do more mainstream economic and social development work. None of these kinds of activities are intrinsically inappropriate, but they take the organization away from its original mission, which is to build and monitor democracy. If there are no organizations working mainly or exclusively for that, then democracy is in danger. This problem of a shrinking civil society is a big part of the story of democratic fragility or decay in key emerging democracies, and it is not adequately understood by democracy promoters.

The counter-argument is familiar: there is only so much money. How are we going to help people who have nothing—no financial resources, no protection for their human rights, and little or no democracy—if we dilute the available democracy assistance resources by devoting some of them to countries that are, comparatively, much better off? But this is the wrong way of viewing the challenge we face.

First, we need not accept that the pool of democracy promotion resources is fixed. It may be that total resources for international engagement or international development will not increase. But we need to rethink where the greatest leverage to advance and secure transformative development will lie. We need to set the clear goal of achieving and locking in development success stories. And that requires good governance, and ultimately democratic governance. Improving governance must be a paramount priority if we are serious about sustaining development progress.

Second, we need to take a fresh look at the allocation of democracy and governance assistance resources across our different instruments and organizations. Are some more cost-effective than others? What are the most effective instruments for developing state institutions, or, by contrast, civil society organizations? Do we have sufficient instruments to assist the birth of new independent media, which can often involve large start-up costs? What is the proper role of for-profit implementing partners?

Third, the issue is not just the countries we work in, but the constraints and mentalities we bring. We should always monitor and evaluate flows of assistance. But where democratic civil society organizations have accumulated a long track record of effective monitoring, civic education, issue analysis, policy reform, and civic advocacy, they should become candidates to receive new forms and levels of funding that are not tied to endless cycles of project grants. Many of them will be better served with block grants to cover their core operations as they set their own programmatic priorities in the quest to fight corruption and abuse of power and defend and improve democracy. Too many civil society organizations spend inordinate amounts of time constantly writing grant proposals for specific projects even when their work, their judgment, and their capacity to deliver are well known.

EXPANDING AND RESHAPING DEMOCRACY ASSISTANCE

Trying to influence the political trajectory of another nation is a risky and often murky endeavor. The quest (among donors of all kinds) for measurable outcomes is generally laudable. But it is intrinsically more difficult to specify a meaningful quantifiable impact on democracy that can be achieved (within a fixed time frame) by a grant to support human rights monitoring, as opposed to the impact that can be expected on child survival rates from the promotion of vaccinations or the distribution of malarial bed nets. We need to monitor democracy assistance grants, but we need more flexible notions of what constitutes a realistic metric in a meaningful time frame.

Many scholars who have examined the record of democracy assistance have recognized its potential to promote democratic change, under the right circumstances. Probably the most careful and thoughtful general assessment has been rendered by Thomas Carothers. He acknowledges that democracy assistance cannot substitute for the "courage, energy, skills, and legitimacy" of a country's own pro-democracy groups and leaders. These political forms of aid have the most visibly positive effects where there are already present at least moderately favorable conditions for democratic change, such as sincere and effective democrats, divided autocrats, and higher levels of economic and educational development. Nevertheless, where democracy assistance is "properly designed and implemented," by proceeding from sensitive knowledge of the local political terrain and then endeavoring to monitor grants carefully over time, it can "help broaden and deepen democratic reforms" in new democracies and sustain civic awareness, democratic hope, and independent information and organization in authoritarian regimes. [10]

Given this finding (and other quantitative and qualitative evidence), it makes sense to expand democracy assistance programming, while carefully targeting it on countries, organizations, and moments where it can make a difference. Fortunately, the Congress has recognized this in gradually increasing the budget of the National Endowment for Democracy (NED), the flagship organization providing assistance to democratic civil society organizations, independent media, political parties, election monitoring, as well as independent trade unions, business chambers, and think tanks dedicated to democracy and governance reform. Unfortunately, however, democracy and governance programming has not received the same budgetary priority within the US Agency for International Development (USAID), whose leadership under the Obama administration prioritized more traditional development sectors such as health and agriculture. For some observers and practitioners, this has reopened a longstanding question of whether the USAID is the logical agency to be delivering support to challenging organizations in civil society, or whether it would make more sense to establish a division of labor in which assistance to state agencies remained with the official US development agency while support for civil society was mainly channeled through nongovernmental organizations (such as NED and its core grantees).

OTHER STRATEGIC PRIORITIES FOR DEMOCRACY PROMOTION

I want to address in conclusion three other thematic priorities for reversing the democratic recession. One is the global struggle against corruption. The second is the global struggle to defend freedom. And the third is the need to promote universal liberal values.

It is hard to find an instance of the breakdown of democracy in which corruption did not play a leading or at least prominent role. To some extent, increased access to corruption is a natural concomitant of the early stages of democratization. The total amount of corruption may not increase, but more people get in on the game, and more cash is needed to fund the electoral contest for power. In fact, with democracy, the total amount of theft or diversion of public resources probably declines, but it may appear that corruption is increasing because it gets "democratized": it becomes more widely distributed (as opposed to a narrow kleptocracy at the top); it becomes more easily exposed by a press which has had the shackles of authoritarian control lifted; and rival parties have an incentive to denounce their opponents as corrupt. The resurrection of patron-client relations in the mobilization of support for political parties generates greatly expanded needs and opportunities for petty corruption. But the resources for petty corruption are never enough, and they can never be enough to make everyone feel included and better off. Moreover, corruption has no natural limiting point, and thus it becomes a grave danger to the legitimacy of democracy. As the competition intensifies in the context of weak institutions of accountability and rule of law, norms break down, and corruption then tends to escalate into predation.

Any long-term campaign to advance and consolidate global democratic progress must have as one of its key elements a war on corruption. This requires from democracy assistance programs bold, comprehensive initiatives addressed to every level of state and society: to transform public norms, consciousness, and capacities to monitor the conduct of government at all levels and expose wrongdoing; to help build a capable, well-paid, and meritocratic civil service and police; to help construct, train, and fund official accountability institutions to monitor and audit government expenditures and operations as well as the personal assets of public officials; and to diffuse the principles, digital tools, and best practices of open government, right to information, and budget transparency. All of this is to stress a more general point that democracy promotion efforts often fail to grasp: you cannot build an effective democracy without an effective state, and that requires a professional, neutral, impersonal bureaucracy.[11]

Improving governance—and in particular, combating the entrenched dynamics of corruption and clientelism—is notoriously difficult, because it runs up against deep structures of power and privilege that have developed over decades, if not centuries, and that represent the real underlying logic of how a society works. Thus, governance reform programs have learned that progress requires a highly contextualized analysis of these deep power relations and the economic interests underlying them. Thomas Carothers and Diane de Gramont argue that effective reform requires not the rigid application of some idealized "best practice" but rather a "best fit" approach that takes into consideration local factors and cultural mores and accepts that progress will be eclectic and incremental.[12] Donors, they find, are also learning other important insights: for example, that helping to generate informed citizen demand for better governance is as important as working on the "supply" side; that working at the local level and with informal institutions is crucial; and that "aiding governance effectively requires development agencies to rethink their own internal governance."[13]

Beyond this, the wealthy democracies need to do much more to track the locations and flows of assets by corrupt government officials; to set new standards of international banking practice; and to marginalize banks that eagerly offer themselves as havens for all sorts of dirty money, whether from corrupt politicians, drug traffickers, or terrorists. Much more vigorous and coordinated international efforts to shut down and criminally punish the movement and laundering of stolen assets across borders represent one of the best ways that the established democracies can help democracy grow in weak states, while undermining kleptocratic authoritarian regimes.

Second, we cannot win the struggle for democracy unless we also wage a vigorous struggle for liberty and human rights. Too many governments in the world—not just blatant autocracies but electoral authoritarian regimes, illiberal democracies, and even some democracies we think of as liberal—are moving backwards to constrain and punish freedom of speech, freedom online, freedom to organize and assemble, and freedom to receive funding from and form partnerships with international democratic actors. We need to use our tools of conventional diplomacy, public diplomacy, aid and trade relations, and other forms of leverage to call out and condemn these regressions, and to try to defend the individuals and organizations that are bravely working to make their societies freer and more accountable. This is not only a moral but a geopolitical imperative, if we are to keep the democratic recession from spiraling down into a depression. Autocrats must know that repression is not cost-free, that even while we pursue common interests, we are going to speak up for our values and take them into account as we weigh our bilateral relations.

It is a completely false and self-defeating notion to think that, in the era of China's rise and Russia's belligerence, we have no more leverage in the world. There is a lot of societal pushback in many countries against the growing presence on the ground of autocratic and corrupt foreign powers. And particularly in Asia, there is a great deal of anxiety about China's rise. There is no way to understand Burma's political opening except in this context. In Africa and Asia, we have a lot of scope to help civil societies and even governments balance off against a China that is coming on too strong, but we need to use this leverage to press for at least gradual democratic reform.

Finally, the democracies of the world should bear in mind one thing, above all else. We have the better set of ideas. Democracy may be receding in practice, but it is still ascendant in peoples' values and aspirations. Some people may accept authoritarian rule as a useful or necessary political order at a certain historical moment or phase of development. But aside from some self-serving rulers and ruling establishments, few people in the world today celebrate authoritarianism as a superior moral system, the ultimate destination, the best form of government.

Democracy remains the only broadly legitimate form of government in the world, and there is a growing hunger—including in authoritarian regimes like China, Iran, Cuba, and Vietnam—to understand what democracy is, and how it can be structured to operate effectively. We need to respond to and stimulate this appetite for democratic understanding. We need a comprehensive effort to translate into a number of critical languages a wide range of philosophical, historical and analytical works on the meaning and forms of democracy, democratic culture, democratic transitions, democratic constitutional designs, electoral systems, political parties, civil society, systems of horizontal accountability, civil-military relations, and so on. We should be arranging to distribute these translated works for free on the Internet, to develop different levels of instruction in democracy for citizens at different levels of knowledge and need, and to offer a wide range of massive, open online courses on various topics and issues related to democracy. We should be supporting initiatives to make the mobile phone a key platform for the distribution of this knowledge and exploring how we can make learning about democracy interesting and fun for young people in different cultures. And we need to prioritize the development of new technologies that can enable more people in authoritarian regimes, with greater ease and less risk, to circumvent Internet censorship to get at this knowledge.

We should bet heavily on this battle of information and ideas, because this is a battle we can win. The ultimate advantage that democracy promoters have is the diffuse global recognition that democracy is the ideal form of government, the only permanent basis of ruling legitimacy. This leaves authoritarian regimes in a dual dilemma. If they remain frozen in archaic institutions of centralized personal or one-party rule, they sit atop a fragile and brittle regime that could fall at any time. If they adopt the superficial outward form of democracy—multiple parties, elected parliaments and presidents, constitutions that in theory check and balance power—they have already conceded the point that democracy is the best system, and then some movement or event may show that they are a fraud. If they keep generating miraculous economic growth, they will produce—as China is now doing—a vibrant and pluralistic middle class that wants more freedom and self-determination. If they stop producing rapid economic growth, then the rising new classes will see their dreams shattered and will angrily demand more political voice.

A lot in global politics turns on perceptions of dynamism and momentum. This is part of what is meant by the term "zeitgeist," the spirit of the times. But the authoritarian spirit cannot speak to the fundamental human aspiration for freedom, autonomy, dignity, and self-determination. We need to find new ways, new energy, and new self-confidence to turn that to our advantage. Most of all, we need to promote the spirit of democracy.

NOTES

1. Freedom House, *Freedom in the World 2015*, Survey 2014, https://freedomhouse.org/report/freedom-world/freedom-world-2015#.VnXfTJMrKSM.

2. I count as liberal democracies all those regimes that receive a score of 1 or 2 (out of 7) on *both* political rights and civil liberties. This is a somewhat more demanding standard than the Freedom House category of "free" states, which includes countries with a score of 3 on one of the two scales, usually civil liberties. For documentation and further analysis of these trends, see Larry Diamond, "Facing Up to the Democratic Recession," *Journal of Democracy* 26, no. 1 (January 2015), http://www.journalofdemocracy.org/article/facing-democratic-recession, and also Larry Diamond, *In Search of Democracy* (London: Routledge, 2016), esp. chapter 4.

3. I place the number "third" in quotes because these African presidents have in fact been in power much longer than two terms, but the constitutional limit to two terms was activated only after they had already been in power for an extended period of time.

4. See the articles in the July 2015 (vol. 26, no. 3) and October 2015 (vol. 26, no. 4) issues of the *Journal of Democracy* under the title "Authoritarianism Goes Global" and the forthcoming book edited by Marc F. Plattner, Christopher Walker, and Larry Diamond, *Authoritarianism Goes Global* (Baltimore: Johns Hopkins University Press, 2016).

5. János Kornai, "Hungary's U-Turn: Retreating from Democracy,' *Journal of Democracy* 26, no. 3 (July 2015).

6. See the many analytic papers of the Afrobarometer project, for example, Michael Bratton and Richard Houessou, "Democracy for Democracy Is Rising in Africa, but Most Political Leaders Fail to Deliver," Policy Paper no. 11, Afrobarometer, April 23, 2014, http://afrobarometer.org/publications/pp11-demand-democracy-rising-africa-most-political-leaders-fail-deliver.

7. Francis Fukuyama, *Political Order and Political Decay* (New York: Farrar, Straus and Giroux, 2014).

8. See, for example, the essays by Francis Fukuyama, "Fuss Budgeting," Bruce Cain, "The Transparency Paradox," Didi Kuo, "Polarization and Partisanship," Nathaniel Persily, "The Campaign Revolution Will Not Be Televized," Larry Diamond, "De-Polarizing," and Stephen John Stedman, "Electoral Integrity," under the title "If It's Broke . . . Fixing American Democracy" in *The American Interest* 11, no. 2 (November/December 2015).

9. In December 2016 the US Congress adopted a budget that added $7.5 million to the Obama administration's request for $134.4 million in bilateral assistance for Tunisia (which was already a dramatic increase). The aid increase was explicitly intended, in the language of the Senate Appropriations Committee, "to expand economic growth, strengthen security services, support civil society and promote Tunisia's continued efforts to improve democratic processes and the rule of law." The appropriation was welcome news, but the $60 million in economic support is only a fraction of what the devastated Tunisian economy needs to get back on its feet.

10. Thomas Carothers, *Aiding Democracy Abroad: The Learning Curve* (Washington, D.C.: Carnegie Endowment for International Peace, December 1999), 307–308.

11. Francis Fukuyama, *Political Order and Political Decay,* and *State-Building: Governance and World Order in the 21st Century* (Ithaca, NY: Cornell University Press, 2004).

12. Thomas Carothers and Diane de Gramont, *Aiding Governance in Developing Countries: Progress Amid Uncertainties* (Washington, D.C.: Carnegie Endowment for International Peace, November 2011), 10–12.

13. Carothers and de Gramont, *Aiding Governance in Developing Countries*, 1.

Chapter Nine

Academic Conclusions, Working Hypotheses, and Areas for Further Research

Agnieszka Marczyk

In March 2014, Russia annexed the Crimean peninsula and started an undeclared war against Ukraine. Lilia Shevtsova, one of the most insightful analysts of the Kremlin, has argued that this crisis "may have more serious consequences than did the collapse of the Soviet Union in 1991. That earlier event brought to the fore a Russia that hoped to move toward the West. The 2014 Russo-Ukrainian war demonstrated Russia's ambition to challenge a West that has lost its vitality and struggles under the weight of its own dysfunctions."[1]

In Marc Plattner's view, Russia's regression into authoritarianism is one of the greatest setbacks for democracy in the last few decades.[2] And many would agree that this is true not just in the postcommunist region, but throughout the world. Today, Russia is only one of several authoritarian states—along with China, Iran, Venezuela, Saudi Arabia, and others—which are trying to reinforce their own autocracies, "contain" democracy and the West, and elevate their notion of sovereignty over the rule-based international order that emerged from the ashes of World War II. This—together with the failures of the Arab Spring, the global reach of ISIS, the migrant crisis facing the European Union (EU), and democratic backsliding in various countries—is causing serious concern among supporters of democracy around the world. And there is growing debate among scholars as to whether we are now facing a global authoritarian resurgence and democratic regression—from which the West is not exempt, and which it might not be able to counter.[3]

This chapter seeks to aid the policy community by highlighting a number of key academic findings and debates on post–Cold War democratization and authoritarian resurgence. I put these findings into dialogue with the work of FPRI's Project on Democratic Transitions, on the one hand, and the current global situation, on the other. The literature is vast, complex, and full of often spirited debates, and it is not my intention to create a falsely unified narrative that glosses over tensions and conflicting interpretations. Rather, I seek to identify areas of consensus, and point to persisting disagreements and crucial questions that remain unanswered.

The last decade, of course, is just one brief chapter in the much longer history of democracy's successes and travails since its initial upsurge in the seventeenth and eighteenth centuries. Samuel Huntington evocatively captured this ebb and flow of democratization in his notion of "waves" and "reverse waves" that took place over the last two hundred years. He identified the third and most extensive democratization wave with the changes that started in the mid-1970s and peaked in the 1990s, with the end of the Cold War.[4] The slowing of this upsurge arguably began around 2000—with Vladimir Putin's first presidency in Russia—and the broader trend of regression has been more clearly perceptible since around 2005.

If there is one thing we know when we take the centuries-long perspective into account, it is that there is no "historical necessity"—history is patterned but not determined. It remains open to the interplay of both individuals and broad economic, social, and political forces; neither success nor demise of democracy is guaranteed, and regime change need not be unidirectional. Thus rather than viewing the current authoritarian resurgence as a necessarily dominant tendency of the future, most of the contributors to this book regard it as an open historical moment. We take it as an occasion to assess what we know about democratization and authoritarianism, and use this knowledge in the service of policymaking capable of supporting democracy throughout the world—both in places where it is yet to be established, and in existing democracies that need to overcome internal problems and erosion of democratic practices.

Over the past two decades, trends in scholarship and policy debate have closely followed democracy's post-1989 global trajectory. The 1990s witnessed the emergence of the so-called transition paradigm, which assumed that there was a lasting, global movement away from authoritarianism and toward democracy. When Thomas Carothers diagnosed the end of this paradigm in 2002, he argued that it rested on five core assumptions: states moving away from authoritarianism were thought to be moving toward democracy; democratization was thought to unfold in a fixed sequence of stages; elections were regarded as instruments of democratization; structural factors and preconditions were largely relegated to the background; and finally, it was generally assumed that democratic transitions took place in the context of functioning states.[5] In this framework, the most important questions concerned identifying the causes and correlates of successful democratic transitions and consolidation processes. In the early 2000s, however, this paradigm began to appear too sanguine, and scholars shifted their attention toward the causes of democratic backsliding, and to new and persisting forms of authoritarianism. They also began examining and classifying regimes that mix elements of authoritarianism and democracy, and the study of hybrid regimes remains among the most important themes in scholarship today. There is also growing emphasis on investigating the relationship between democratization and governance, and the global threats posed by newly activist authoritarian states.[6]

Importantly, as Ambassadors Basora and Yalowitz point out in their introduction to this volume, there is currently no clear consensus on how to define democracy. Definitions vary from minimalist ones focused on elections to extensive ones that take socioeconomic factors, civil society, and individual rights and freedoms into account. And while some analysts use discrete definitions that juxtapose democracies against various forms of authoritarianism, others view political systems as existing on a continuum that stretches from democracy to dictatorship.[7]

Just as there are many approaches to defining democracy, there are many ways to thematize the existing literature. In this chapter, I use four broad aspects of democratization that form our analytic framework at the Project on Democratic Transitions: political factors; economic factors; civil society, media, and culture; and external influences.[8] Examining these factors together has the advantage of avoiding one-sided explanations while emphasizing the many complex dimensions of democratization.

Perhaps the single most important theme that emerges from scholarship is that many factors once thought to support democratization can actually strengthen either democracies or authoritarian governments. Elections and well-functioning states, for example, are crucial for liberal democracies, but they can also aid autocratic survival. Legislatures can check presidential powers, but autocrats can also informally control nominally democratic institutions and make them into a de facto part of their own support structures. These and other dilemmas are reflected in both recent investigations and emerging research agendas.

When it comes to economic factors, the major claim of modernization theory—the idea that economic development leads to democratization—has been deconstructed and replaced by several more limited and more specific claims. Scholars have found, for example, that while wealth does not drive democratization, it can serve to buffer democracies against backsliding. Conversely, however, it can also stabilize autocratic regimes. And both democracies and autocracies become vulnerable to change during times of economic turmoil. In addition, there is suggestive evidence that natural resource wealth can help impede democratization, and sudden growth in economic inequalities can be associated with democratic backsliding.

The literature on civil society, the media, and political culture is more fragmented, and there are fewer areas of consensus. Perhaps the single most important finding in this realm is that regime change initiated by broad-based mass movements is much more likely to lead to durable democratization than any other form of overthrowing an autocratic government. It is also relatively clear that civil society groups with local roots and funding are best at advancing lasting democratization, but precisely these groups—along with independent media and individual advocates of universal democratic values—are now increasingly targeted and repressed by authoritarian regimes throughout the world.

Finally, in the early 1990s there was much emphasis on the ways in which external players—both individual Western democracies and transnational organizations—can support emerging democratic movements by mechanisms like diffusion or multilateral conditionality; this was supplanted by the important concept of linkage and leverage in the early 2000s. The most recent trend in scholarship is to examine the limitations of these mechanisms, and to better understand how activist authoritarian powers are changing the international environment through their own leverage, linkage networks, and media offensives. We are also witnessing what some call "the return of geopolitics"—increasing attention to the political implications of geographic location, especially in authoritarian neighborhoods. In what follows, I examine these and other trends and debates, paying special attention to remaining questions and challenges.

POLITICAL FACTORS

Free, fair, and competitive elections are a hallmark of democracy, but their optimal form and significance remain highly contested. For decades, scholars have been exploring how political parties, electoral systems, and institutional design influence the stability and longevity of democracies. Although these debates continue today, there has been a perceptible shift in focus. As Jennifer Gandhi reminds us, great variations in the quality of democratic elections and the proliferation of authoritarian elections have led to "increasing skepticism about the use of solely electoral criteria to differentiate between democracies and dictatorships" and to "greater attention to elections under authoritarianism."[9] In fact, a transformation of the study of authoritarian elections is now underway, along with new explorations of how state capacity can influence both democracies and authoritarian regimes. These new analyses have not yet produced definitive findings, but they often explore a common theme:

political structures and mechanisms once thought to promote democratization can also be used by autocrats to strengthen their hold on power.

Democracies: Elections and Institutional Design

In the aftermath of the Cold War, two related debates became particularly salient—concerning institutional design and electoral systems. Today, it appears that neither electoral systems nor institutional design—in and of themselves—are ultimately responsible for the successes or failures of new democracies.[10] This, of course, does not mean that they are unimportant, but that they need to be analyzed within local configurations of social, political, and historical forces.

There is no simple answer as to whether parliamentary or presidential systems are best for new democracies since both can either strengthen or weaken democratic consolidation. In his now classic analysis, Juan Linz had argued that presidential regimes are more prone to abuse of power and political deadlock than parliamentary systems, which encourage compromise, and where unsatisfactory government can be changed through early elections.[11] A large following has built from his work, linking various forms of presidentialism to nondemocratic outcomes.[12] One of the most influential ideas in this context was Steven Fish's concept of super-presidentialism, which he coined in his work on post-Soviet Russia and defined as a "constitutional arrangement that invests greater power in the presidency and much less power in the legislature."[13] Against this line of thinking, a number of scholars have argued that parliamentary systems are no panacea either, as they can encourage partisan deadlock and procedural dysfunction, and they do not always guard against democratic backsliding or breakdown.[14] Moreover, large-scale comparative studies tend to suggest that the stability of new democracies does not appear to hinge on institutional design.[15] And in our own analysis at the Project on Democratic Transitions we emphasize the importance of vesting the legislative body with real powers, and balancing the competencies and responsibilities of the legislature and the executive.

Finally, Steven Levitsky and Lucan Way added two vital points to this debate. First, they stressed that we need to pay close attention to the direction of causality: super-presidentialist systems are often not the cause but the outcome of shifts toward authoritarianism (e.g., in Russia under Yeltsin, Belarus under Lukashenko, Romania under Illiescu, or Peru under Fujimori).[16] Similarly, strong legislatures can reflect rather than drive successful democratization. Equally important is the observation that all formal state institutions are subject to potential informal influences that can limit, undermine, or sabotage their functioning. Ultimately, Levitsky and Way did not argue that formal institutional arrangements do not matter, but rather that their importance varies greatly across regions and cases:

> Where formal institutions are regularly enforced and minimally stable, the causal power of institutional design may be considerable. In much of the developing world, however, formal institutions are weak: rather than constraining political elites, they are routinely circumvented and manipulated by them; rather than structuring the political game and determining winners and losers, they are repeatedly restructured by the winners at the expense of the losers. In such cases, the independent causal power of formal institutions is limited.[17]

Similarly, the debate about the merits of proportional representation and majoritarian electoral systems remains open, and it drew much attention, for example, in the early months of the Arab Spring.[18] A discussion of arguments advanced on both sides is beyond the scope of this chapter, but it is important to mention that many studies emphasize that decisions about electoral systems should be made on a case-by-case basis, with particular attention to social, ethnic, and religious cleavages in relevant societies.[19]

Autocracies and Hybrid Regimes: Elections, Parties, and Democratization

To help explain the proliferation of a wide range of nondemocratic regimes after the Cold War, Levitsky and Way focused on the interplay of domestic and international factors, and introduced the concept of "competitive authoritarianism." This category sought to distinguish consolidated authoritarian regimes, where elections might offer a patina of legitimacy without allowing for actual political turnover, from regimes where the electoral playing field is heavily skewed in favor of the incumbent, but where there is a realistic—even if very small—chance for opposition to gain political power. "Competitive authoritarianism," along with "hybrid regimes" and "electoral authoritarianism" were concepts developed in the early 2000s to classify and examine political systems that combine elements of authoritarianism and democracy.[20] Indeed, during the first decade of the new millennium, many scholars grappled with understanding new forms of autocracy, and key areas of research focus included the roles played by the elites, parties, and elections in various types of nondemocratic states.

One relatively clear finding is that in both hybrid and authoritarian regimes ruling elite cohesion is important for stability, whereas elite splits and defections can contribute to democratic breakthroughs. Adam Przeworski's classic model, for example, posits that transition can occur as elites split between hardliners and reformers, creating top-down liberalization within a regime.[21] Liberalization and simultaneous pressure from civil society movements can then work together to further influence the regime and highlight divisions and contradictions within it. This, in turn, can prompt reformers within the regime to ally with leaders of mass mobilization, resulting in transition. This model describes several 1989 transitions from communist governments, and, though it does not hold universally, it captures an important dynamic. Similar patterns have been noted in other cases, such as transitions out of military regimes in Latin America. Stephan Haggard and Robert Kaufman, for example, argue that economic crises may exacerbate existing divisions between hard- and soft-liners in authoritarian regimes, and thus help precipitate regime breakdown.[22] Moreover, as Jennifer Gandhi and Ellen Lust-Okar point out, a number of scholars have argued that dictators attempt to control elites (as well as party members and other social groups) by holding elections. For example, instead of simply appointing members of the elite to specific government posts, autocrats can stage elections to fill offices, ensuring "that the most 'popular' elites are associated with the regime and that they do not become complacent in serving the regime's goals."[23] Alternatively, a dictator's heavily manipulated and therefore decisive electoral victory can "serve as a signal to members of the regime elite that opposition is futile."[24]

These observations come from a much broader field of scholarship focused on authoritarian elections: their origins and functions; the behavior of voters, candidates, and incumbents; and the links between authoritarian elections and potential democratization.[25] In the present context, I focus only on the last of these—and the still open question whether authoritarian elections tend to strengthen or subvert the regimes that organize them. On the one hand, there is a substantial body of scholarship that argues that both single-party and multiparty elections in autocracies and hybrid regimes tend to stabilize and extend the life of these regimes.[26] Some argue that this happens primarily through the cooptation and consolidation of the ruling parties and elites, others focus on autocratic institutionalization in relation to the threats faced by the regime, while yet others explore how authoritarian elections convey information about the power and solidity of the autocrat.[27] On the other hand, many scholars argue the opposite: that authoritarian elections can help precipitate democratic breakthroughs.[28] In this vein, some propose that authoritarian elections, especially in multiparty systems, can encourage elite splits and subsequent regime breakdown; others focus on the social mobilization that can follow heavily manipulated or "stolen" elections.[29] In his recent work, Andreas Schedler, for example, reenvisions authoritarian elections as arenas of struggle endowed with enough ambiguity to provide new opportunities for contestation and social mobilization.[30] Meanwhile, several large quantitative studies suggest that democratic developments can be induced by elections in nondemocracies.[31] Based on a global sample of 163 countries, for example, Jan Teorell proposes that "authoritarian regimes with partial political openness, most important through multiparty electoral competition, are likeliest to grow even more democratic."[32] While some take this as indication that the democracy support community should welcome all forms of authoritarian elections in the hope of creating "voting muscle memory" for future democratization, others caution that this oversimplifies the picture.[33]

Rather than using existing data to arbitrate between those who view authoritarian elections as regime-supporting and those who regard them as creating openings for democratization, influential scholars in this field are calling for new empirical approaches and theoretical frameworks. Gandhi and Lust-Okar, for example, call for including more countries and caution that "scholars have tended to make universal claims based on a subset of cases. Research on Mexico, China, and Egypt, and to a lesser extent on Jordan, Taiwan, and Vietnam, drives our understanding of the politics of authoritarian elections."[34] In reviewing large quantitative studies, moreover, Gandhi points out that their often optimistic conclusions depend on using regime type as the independent variable. This is problematic because it often does not accurately reflect developments on the ground since regime types "may not be good proxies of regime and opposition strength."[35] To gain better insight into the democratizing potential of authoritarian elections, Gandhi suggests a turn toward more fine-grained analyses, and stresses the importance of also examining authoritarian electoral history before the Cold War. In this, she is in close agreement with Adam Przeworski, whose most recent work explores electoral turns away from authoritarianism in the period between 1788 and 2008.[36] Ultimately, Gandhi argues for a new research agenda that focuses on "detailed information on the actors, behavior, and events surrounding elections for as many contemporary and historical cases as possible." The goal is to understand "the iterative interactions between the government and the opposition," examine how these interactions change over time, what elite splits and new alliances they create, and how these can eventually lead to political change.[37]

State Capacity

Analysts are also reexamining other links between the state and democracy. As Francis Fukuyama noted in a recent debate, despite long-standing interest in the state-democracy nexus, it remains both understudied and undertheorized.[38] In the 1990s, studies explored ways in which strong states and good governance could aid democratization, but in recent years it has become clear that state capacity can stabilize both autocracies and democracies.[39] Scholars are therefore disaggregating state capacity into components—such as monopoly on violence, administrative effectiveness, or citizenship criteria—and relating these components to democratization.[40]

There is both a common sense expectation and evidence that coercive capacity—or the security and law enforcement apparatus—is important in sustaining autocracies, while administrative capacity—or the bureaucracy and infrastructure—can support democracies. Yet Fukuyama cautions that "either form of power can be used for good or bad purposes . . . [and] infrastructural power can be misused by being overused in clientelistic ways."[41] One of the crucial challenges before the scholarly community is therefore to better understand how exactly state capacity matters for new democracies, and to map out the full range of ways in which autocrats can use strong states to their advantage.

Already in the 1960s, many scholars argued that stable institutions and statehood are necessary prerequisites of successful democratization. According to this view, weak states struggle to govern through what can be chaotic transition periods, lacking the necessary experience to develop and maintain effective representative institutions. Huntington, for example, argued against modernization theorists who expected economic development to automatically lead to democracy. He cautioned that as societies modernize, increases in political participation must be carefully balanced by the development of political institutions that enhance the state's stability.[42] Juan Linz and Alfred Stepan, among many others, later developed and tested the notion that a sovereign state is required for democratization. They argued that without an organization with statelike attributes, "a government (even if 'democratically elected') could not effectively exercise its claim to the monopoly of the legitimate use of force in the territory, could not collect taxes (and thus provide any public services), and could not implement a judicial system."[43]

In contrast, scholars like Sebastian Mazzuca and Gerardo Munck argue that state capacity is not a prerequisite of democracy, but rather can be built up in the process of democratization.[44] Yet, as Fukuyama points out, we need not lock ourselves into a state-first or democracy-first dichotomy, remembering that there are degrees of institutionalization: "the possibility of a democratic community depends on the prior existence of a certain minimal degree of security; [but] higher levels of security require cooperation and buy-in from populations, and thus benefit from better democratic accountability."[45]

There is evidence to suggest that while state capacity can support and stabilize democracies, it can also enhance autocratic power. It is well known that weak states have been repeatedly associated with democratic failures in Africa.[46] In the postcommunist world, Jessica Fortin has shown that among states that transitioned to democracy, those with greater state capacity—defined as "the necessary means to maintain law and order and to protect the rights of citizens"—were better able to consolidate their democratic gains.[47] The situation is more complicated when it comes to Russia. In the 1990s and early 2000s, Stephen Holmes, Valerie Bunce and others identified various weaknesses in the Russian state and administration, and linked these to the failures of both market reforms and democratization.[48] Yet in his influential 2005 study of the failure of open politics in Russia, Steven Fish provided a compelling argument that it was the strong components of the Russian state and the resulting economic statism that proved particularly detrimental.[49]

And in their analysis of Russia and other authoritarian and hybrid regimes five years later, Levitsky and Way further explored how autocrats can use the state to prevent democratic openings. In their concept of the incumbent's "organizational power," they included control of party structures, access to economic resources, coercive state capacity, and ubiquitous informal institutions. All these, they argued, offer a range of means whereby autocrats can insulate themselves from pressure for change.[50] In addition, in his 2012 study of the "color revolutions" in Georgia, Ukraine, and Kyrgyzstan, Lincoln Mitchell pointed out that extensive American support offered to Georgia's President Mikheil Saakashvili helped him consolidate his hold on power and perpetuate repressive authoritarianism in the country.[51] Finally, Merete Seeberg has recently argued that autocrats presiding over strong states may abuse the bureaucracy to manipulate voters, while those presiding over weaker states are more likely to resort to coercion to prevent social opposition movements.[52] To illustrate this dynamic, she points to the examples of Malaysia, where a strong state helped secure one-party dominance, and the Philippines, where the state was weak and the Marcos dictatorship collapsed as it attempted to control the 1986 elections.

Rule of Law

The rule of law is an indispensable component of liberal democracy. It implies an impersonal system of justice that applies the law equally to all citizens, regardless of how much power they wield. And it functions best when embedded in a culture that values impartiality, compromise, and human rights.[53] Conventional wisdom suggests that instituting the rule of law is critically important in establishing democracies, and many studies argue that judicial independence may well be one of the most essential components of democratization.[54]

Yet mechanisms whereby the rule of law supports democracy remain poorly understood, quantitative studies are scarce, and evidence comes primarily from diverse, and often historically unique, case studies.[55] In addition, as Gibler and Randazzo remind us, scholars differ in how they understand the role of the judiciary: most see it as protecting minority rights, some as reflecting majority interests, and some as providing a consultative check on the executive and the legislature.[56] One claim that enjoys a good deal of consensus is that new court systems are unlikely to protect against democratic backsliding, since judiciaries need time to gain both power and legitimacy. Conversely, well-established court systems can protect democracies against regime reversal in the midst of economic or political crises.[57] In what follows, I give a very brief overview of how scholars approach the optimal and less than optimal functioning of the rule of law in democracies, and the role judiciaries can play in authoritarian and hybrid regimes—what Moustafa and Ginzburg call "rule by law" rather than "rule of law."[58]

At best, a strong and independent judicial system can strengthen a liberal democratic state in several important ways. First, courts can be the primary locus of articulating and protecting civil rights and liberties—including free speech, religious freedom, minority rights, and the freedom of assembly—all of which are critical to the democratic process. Second, independent courts can work to uphold economic reforms intended to create a fair playing field and prevent the emergence of oligarchs. And third, judiciaries can monitor the work of the government, ensuring constitutionality, transparency, and accountability, and limiting the reach of informal mechanisms of power.[59] Scholars often cite Poland and South Africa as examples of successful legal reforms that aided democratization. Conversely, Ukraine, Russia, Belarus, Mexico, and Nigeria, among others, are typically cited as cases where lack of sufficient legal reforms, judicial independence, and law-oriented political culture was associated with failures or delays of democratization.[60]

However, full judicial independence is very difficult to establish, and even the largely successful legal reforms in places like Poland or South Africa had many flaws and limitations. In fact, optimally functioning and independent court systems are rare even in established Western democracies. Thomas Carothers, for example, points out that "democracy often, in fact usually, co-exists with substantial shortcomings in the rule of law."[61] He cautions against the simple assumption that the rule of law automatically improves democracy, and argues that it is essential to understand what specific gains for democracy are offered by specific aspects of the rule of law. Other scholars observe that instead of protecting minority rights or mediating among conflicting social interests, in some circumstances courts can simply reflect elite interests. Or rather than giving full veto to either the executive or the legislature, members of the judiciary can influence the content of legislation through informal consultations.[62] On the positive side, there is evidence that long-established and independent courts can help prevent democracies from turning toward authoritarianism when economic or political crisis strikes. Gibler and Randazzo found this protective effect in a well-received study of a large global sample of countries examined between 1960 and 2000. They showed that the presence of established independent courts seems to protect against regime reversals (defined as a change of four or more points in Polity IV scores) in various types of states. While this is important for democracies, the obverse of this finding is that "established courts are also capable of thwarting regime collapses in non-democracies"— and they can thus contribute to the durability of autocratic regimes.[63]

It is well known that autocratic and hybrid regimes can use the judiciary to their advantage, and courts in authoritarian states are often associated with corruption, show trials, and harassment of civil society opposition. But recent literature shows that legal institutions can also have complex and varied functions in authoritarian states, with a potential to either sustain or subvert authoritarian regimes. For example, in a 2008 edited volume that brought together analyses of the legal systems in Latin America, Turkey, Iran, Singapore, and Egypt, Ginsburg and Moustafa showed that "[j]udicial politics in authoritarian regimes is often far more complex than we commonly assume."[64] Their cross-regional study shows that courts in autocracies share many functions with those in democracies, including oversight over the bureaucracy, support for the economy, and bolstering the regime's legitimacy. They also show that elected presidents can misuse courts to strengthen their position, while dictators can find themselves opposed by previously compliant courts and justices.

Finally, in the context of the current authoritarian resurgence, it is important to recall the obvious but important point that judiciaries and courts analyze and interpret laws and statutes—and these can themselves be repressive and devised to bolster autocratic rulers. As Javier Corrales has recently shown, for example, both under both Hugo Chavez and Nicolas Maduro, the Venezuelan legislature passed enabling laws that granted the president the right to rule by decree. And a special law concerning "Social Responsibility" was extended in 2010 to apply to the Internet, banning broadcasting of material that may "foment anxiety in the public," "incite disobedience to the current legal order," or "refuse to recognize legitimately constituted authority."[65] Such measures have numerous counterparts in Russia, China, and other autocratic states, and I will return to these in the discussion of civil society.

ECONOMIC FACTORS

The strong version of modernization theory—long a dominant approach to understanding democratic transitions—hypothesized a causal relationship between socioeconomic development and democratization. For several decades, scholars debated and sought to explain the claim—initially articulated by Martin Seymour Lipset in his classic 1959 study of Europe and Latin America—that "average wealth, degree of industrialization and urbanization, and level of education is much higher for the more democratic countries."[66] As Steven Fish put it in his 2005 study of Russia, analysts drew connections between "higher economic development [and] less social conflict, more sophisticated populations, larger middle classes, less desperate lower classes, and greater social pressure for popular rule, all of which may favor more open government."[67] In the course of investigating these links, however, it became clear that there is nothing automatic about the relationship between a country's overall wealth and democratization, and there are important examples of states—such as China and Saudi Arabia—where overall wealth has not led to democracy. Specialists found that both "wealth" (most often measured by per capita GDP) and "economic development" need to be disaggregated into narrower components that can be related to sociopolitical realities. In recent years, the broad association between economic development and democratization has therefore been replaced by several more limited and more specific claims.

Protection against Backsliding

There is a relatively broad consensus about the claim that while economic development does not necessarily trigger democratization, it can support democratic consolidation once a transition occurs.[68] This finding holds regardless of how the transition took place, and it is supported by both quantitative and qualitative studies of diverse countries around the world.[69] One of the most compelling works to initially suggest this effect was Adam Przeworski and his colleagues' examination of a large global sample of states over a forty-year period between 1950 and 1990.[70] Among other things, they found that

> [t]he probability that a dictatorship will die and a democracy will be established is pretty much random with regard to per capita incomes, about 2 percent each year. But the probability that, once established, a democracy will survive increases steeply and monotonically as per capita incomes get larger. Indeed, democracy is almost certain to survive in countries with per capita incomes above $4,000.[71]

More recent quantitative studies confirm this protective effect of wealth, even though we can no longer talk about democratic survival in middle-income democracies as "almost certain"—witness the current backsliding processes in Hungary, Turkey, Venezuela, Thailand, and other countries.[72] In fact, Larry Diamond is among those who caution about the premature withdrawal of financial support from newly consolidating middle-income democracies.[73]

Even though the protective effect of wealth against backsliding is robust, the causal mechanisms remain unresolved. It is unclear whether what matters is the size of the national economy, its structure, the extent and type of urbanization, rising literacy levels, or other factors.[74] One key element that does seem to matter is the existence of a large and diverse middle class, which is more likely to emerge in wealthier states. Analysts have argued that it is more difficult for autocrats to resort to repression in societies that have a strong middle class, and that ultimately "[t]he conditions necessary for a lasting democracy are the same [as those] necessary for the security of property and contract rights that generates economic growth."[75] This is in line with our own work at the Project on Democratic Transitions, which suggests that the growth of the middle class—a group of citizens who want predictable and profitable economic exchange—goes along with the need for a consistent legal system that secures property rights. And—both historically and currently—members of the middle class are often the ones to press for and achieve political representation. [76]

Economic Crises

Just as wealth tends to stabilize all types of regimes, economic shocks can have disruptive effects on both autocracies and democracies. As Isobel Coleman and Terra Lawson-Remer emphasize,

> [o]ver the past three decades, many democratic transitions have been precipitated by serious economic shocks that inflicted unacceptable costs on citizens, rupturing the authoritarian bargain. . . . The relationship between economic growth, economic crisis, and political transition is by no means automatic, but the evidence is clear that shocks make regimes of all types vulnerable, whereas prosperity makes regimes of all types more stable. Statistical findings suggest, however, that democracies are less vulnerable to economic crises than are autocracies, though the reason for this is unclear. [77]

Haggard and Kaufman, for example, point out that in Argentina, Bolivia, Brazil, Peru, Uruguay, and the Philippines, democratic transitions took place in the context of profound economic downturns; they argue that widespread economic difficulties resulted in loss of social support for the regime and deepened existing cleavages among ruling elites. [78]

Likewise, a number of studies report that economic recessions can lead to democratic backsliding or breakdown, which results—at least in part—from citizens' dissatisfaction with the performance of elected officials. [79] In this context, some have argued that crises tend to radicalize the masses and make them more inclined toward extremist political solutions—hollowing out the political center and undermining democratic stability. Others, however, critique this logic and suggest that the elites—rather than the general population—are more likely to radicalize in times of economic trouble. [80]

These measured scholarly debates stand in sharp contrast to the often alarmist tone of various media outlets that have linked recent right-wing extremism in Europe to images of post–2008 "Weimar Europe" or "Weimar Greece." While we should recognize that economic shocks—especially those that are both deep and widespread, like the Great Depression of the 1930s or the Great Recession of 2008—pose real challenges to democracy, we also need to guard against accepting exaggerated rhetoric. Comparative analyses show that the upsurge of populist extremism throughout Europe is only partly related to the 2008 financial crisis, and right-wing extremist tendencies have been on the rise since at least the mid-1980s.[81] It is essential to investigate the negative impact of extremist groups and parties on European democracy, but this requires skepticism about oversimplified historical analogies and one-sided linkages between economic crises and democratic breakdown. We know, for example, that a number of far-right European parties (most famously France's Front National) are actively supported by Russia in an effort to undermine European unity. Europe is facing an unprecedented migrant crisis, and many other factors—including cultural and demographic anxieties, as well as racial prejudice—are feeding the growth of xenophobic, anti-immigrant tendencies throughout the continent today.[82] One of the key challenges facing scholars is to continue refining our understanding of this wider configuration of factors and to calibrate the impact of economic downturns within it.

Socioeconomic Inequalities and Wealth Redistribution

In addition to showing the protective effect of wealth in new democracies, in 2000, Przeworski and his colleagues also drew the scholarly community's attention to the importance of economic inequalities in democratization. The effect they found was admittedly small, and it was secondary to changes in countries' overall income, but it nonetheless provided suggestive evidence that economic inequalities can be a factor undercutting democratic consolidation. Specifically, they found that both autocracies and democracies

> are slightly less stable when the share of the top 20 percent increases. Democracies, and only democracies, are somewhat less stable when the income share of the bottom 40 percent declines. Thus, with all the caveats, it appears that both regimes are threatened when the rich get relatively richer, but only democracy is vulnerable when the poor get relatively poorer.[83]

The other key work to explore links between socioeconomic inequalities and democratization was Acemoglu and Robinson's 2006 study of the political economy of dictatorships and democracies.[84] They envisioned society as consisting of elites and the rest of the population—two broad groups with conflicting policy preferences, especially regarding income and wealth distribution. In autocracies with high levels of economic inequality, they argued, the majority of the population has a strong incentive to revolt and win both power and wealth redistribution, but the ruling elite is also more willing to resort to repression to maintain their hold on power and resources. Conversely, in autocracies with low income disparities there is less of an incentive for regime change. Acemoglu and Robinson therefore posited that democratic transitions are most likely in states with medium levels of inequality. And they argued that the reduction of socioeconomic inequalities in the aftermath of a democratic transition increases the odds of successful consolidation.[85]

While this interpretive framework has been influential, Jan Teorell reminds us that despite strong theoretical expectations, there is only weak quantitative support for a link between socioeconomic inequality and democratization.[86] And a number of other scholars argue other factors often take precedence over economic inequalities in explaining democratization pathways.[87]

Even with these caveats, our own judgment at the Project on Democratic Transitions is that it is important to address socioeconomic inequalities early in the consolidation process. The negative effects of quickly growing inequalities in the post-Soviet and postcommunist region have clearly contributed to public dissatisfaction—creating fertile ground for the appeals of anti-democratic populist leaders. We therefore view adequate investment in social needs as critical to lasting democratic change. Similarly, Coleman and Lawson-Remer advise that insofar as possible, socioeconomic inequalities should be addressed as soon as possible in the consolidation phase:

> The trajectory of emerging democracies depends fundamentally on whether political democratization can also deliver shared opportunity and inclusive growth to materially improve people's lives. The mere procedural freedoms of ballot box and marketplace participation are not enough to sustain nascent democracies over the longer term. Citizens—especially the poor—must also begin to realize the substantive social and economic freedoms that generate the capability to live full and meaningful lives. When they do enjoy such social inclusion and rising living standards, they reward the politicians who provide them, creating a powerful feedback loop that helps consolidate democracy. On the other hand, a return to autocracy, perhaps under a populist authoritarian, becomes more likely if the transition fails to deliver material benefits.[88]

Natural Resource Wealth

No one has done more than Michael Ross to alert the scholarly community to the so-called oil curse—or the negative impact of natural resource wealth on democratization.[89] Based on a global sample of many states, studied over several decades starting in the 1960s, he proposed that oil hurts democracy, and the damage is greater in poor states than in rich ones. This, he argued, is ultimately traceable to "the most important political fact about oil . . . that the revenues it bestows on governments are unusually large, do not come from taxes, fluctuate unpredictably, and can be easily hidden."[90] Oil wealth—or other abundant mineral wealth easily controlled by the state—he argued, can prevent democratic breakthroughs in at least three ways. First, authoritarians with access to oil can assuage or preempt the population's demands for democracy by offering low taxes and high public spending (the rentier effect). Second, they can resort to repression by a security apparatus financed by secretive oil income. And third, oil wealth tends to prevent economic diversification and thus the emergence of alternate centers of economic power and a social class that would likely demand democracy ("impeded modernization"). To counteract these effects, Ross argued, external actors should encourage developing states to establish diversified economies and introduce transparency into their political and economic systems. Finally, although Ross's main argument focused on the how oil wealth can impede democratic transitions, he also linked oil wealth to democratic backsliding: "oil helps empower incumbents, regardless of whether the country is authoritarian or democratic . . . at the case-study level, there are indications that oil has strengthened the hand of democratically elected incumbents, and enabled them to roll back democratic constraints."[91]

Although awareness of the "oil curse" is now nearly ubiquitous, the debate remains open as to how robust and consistent this effect is. While a number of scholars have found evidence supporting Ross's claims, others have modified and questioned them.[92] And quantitative evidence remains suggestive rather than decisive.[93] One key study that should be mentioned in this context is Steven Fish's exploration of the failure of democracy in post-Soviet Russia, where he confirmed Ross's finding of negative effects of natural resource wealth in Russia, but provided a different explanatory framework.[94] He tested Ross's tripartite model and found no clear statistical support for either the rentier effect or the impeded modernization effect; he only found some weak support for the repression effect. Instead, he found that in Russia reliance on raw materials fueled corruption and encouraged extensive economic statism.[95]

Economic Liberalization and Diversification

In exploring links between mineral wealth and economic statism, Fish engaged the much broader—and still open—debate about whether economic liberalization and diversification have a salutary effect on emerging democracies. As he points out, many scholars view economic liberalism as a threat to democracy and claim that "neoliberal economic policies depress popular living standards and undercut the legitimacy of open government . . . [while] [e]conomic liberalization requires state officials to ignore popular demands, contain popular participation, deceive the electorate, and generally act undemocratically."[96] Those who view the free market as supportive of democratization, on the other hand, tend to present the "expansive realm of autonomous economic activity as a bulwark against despotism."[97] One particularly important dimension of this debate consists of arguments about whether gradual reforms or "shock therapy" is better for democratic consolidation, but as Mitchell Orenstein has shown, the final verdict on this question—at least in the post-Soviet and postcommunist regions—is yet to be reached.[98]

Our own work at the Project on Democratic Transitions emphasizes local variations in democratization, and we therefore do not advocate either gradualism or shock therapy as universally superior—in each specific case, it is essential to consider local history, political culture, and the dynamics of the transition itself when making decisions about how to transform the market. This analysis is broadly in agreement with studies that regard the free market—subject to government regulation—as a key factor that supports democracy's durability. Importantly, we view both state regulation that protects the poorest citizens and economic diversification as key safeguards against oligarchical control, which is often tied to authoritarian tendencies (Ukraine under Viktor Yanukovych is one of the best examples). We share this approach with a number of scholars, but our thinking is particularly close to Juan Linz and Alfred Stepan's notion of "economic society," which they use to advocate post-transition economic reforms and state regulation.[99] They stress that

> there has never been and there cannot be a non-wartime consolidated democracy in a command economy. Second, there has never been and almost certainly there never will be a modern consolidated democracy in a pure market economy. If both of these claims are demonstrated to be sound, modern consolidated democracies require a set of socio-politically crafted and socio-politically accepted norms, institutions, and regulations, which we call economic society, that mediates between state and market.[100]

CIVIL SOCIETY, POLITICAL CULTURE, AND INDEPENDENT MEDIA

Civil Society

At least since de Tocqueville's *Democracy in America*, a vibrant civil society has been regarded as a symbol of liberal democracy. Civil society actors, groups, and independent media were crucially important in many post–Cold War democratic transitions, and they continue to figure prominently in new democratization efforts throughout the world today. Importantly, however, while recent literature recognizes the great practical and symbolic importance of civil society, scholars do not view it as an exclusive driver of democratization. Rather, attempts are made to situate civil society's impact in relation to other social, political, and economic factors that either support or undermine democracy's potential success.[101] And today's thinking about civil society and independent media is increasingly mindful of the newly sophisticated tools deployed by autocrats intent on suppressing citizen initiatives and the free flow of information. As Adam Przeworski once noted:

> What is threatening to authoritarian regimes is not the breakdown of legitimacy but the organization of counter-hegemony: collective projects for an alternative future. Only when collective alternatives are available does political

choice become available to isolated individuals. This is why authoritarian regimes abhor independent organizations; they either incorporate them under centralized control or repress them by force. [102]

While some definitions of civil society focus primarily on the presence and functioning of NGOs, the most useful ones emphasize the breadth and diversity of associational life. Juan Linz and Alfred Stepan, for example, define civil society as "that arena of the polity where self-organizing groups, movements, and individuals, relatively autonomous from the state, attempt to articulate values, create associations and solidarities, and advance their interests." [103] Similarly, Thomas Carothers points out that it is a mistake to equate civil society solely with NGOs. He emphasizes that it encompasses all organizations and associations that exist outside the state and the market—including religious organizations, labor unions, and other groups, which often have a genuine base in the population and secure domestic sources of funding. [104]

The most important finding regarding civil society—and one that holds throughout the world—is that democratic change initiated by broad-based, nonviolent mass movements is much more likely to result in lasting, durable democratization than change resulting from violent revolutions, coups, or any other form of overthrowing autocracy. [105] This is borne out by both large-scale quantitative analyses and individual case studies. Whether through labor organizing, mass mobilization in response to poor economic performance, or electoral revolutions—nonviolent civic movements tend to lay the most durable foundations for democracy. [106] As Isobel Coleman and Terra Lawson-Remer emphasize,

> [p]roponents of nonviolence, from Mohandas Gandhi and Martin Luther King to Gene Sharp, have noted that sustained peaceful protests lead to a more engaged citizenry and a better-organized civil society with a deep stake in the outcome of the transition. This sustained engagement often proves critical for staying the course during the inevitable challenges of democratic transitions. [107]

Beyond this, findings are less definitive, but two aspects of civic groups tend to be seen as particularly important for democratization: their local roots and funding, on the one hand, and their internal democratic structure, on the other. Based on cases from the post-Soviet and postcommunist space, our work at the Project on Democratic Transitions emphasizes that civil society groups are most likely to aid democratization when they build strong and independent roots within their own societies. Conversely, Peter Lewis and his colleagues point to Nigeria to argue that when funding comes almost exclusively from abroad, it is all too easy for corrupt leaders and intermediaries to divert money from its intended uses. [108] Regarding the need for democracy within civil society groups, Robert Putnam cites a variety of cases from

Italian history to argue that egalitarianism within civic associations can help bolster democratic governance. And, based on East Central European case studies, Umut Korkut argues that a vertically organized civil society can be detrimental to democracy. What matters, he proposes, is not the mere presence of civic associations, but rather their democratic structures and practices, which give their members hands-on experience with collective participation.[109] Finally, Thomas Carothers observes that sometimes the mere existence of civil society groups is not necessarily indicative of democratic health since in some cases civil society groups "can actually reflect dangerous political weaknesses . . . [and] the proliferation of interest groups in immature democracies could choke the workings of representative institutions."[110] In this vein, scholars have suggested that when civil society fails to mature and take deep roots within society, democratic backsliding becomes more likely—witness Ukraine before Maidan or Hungary under Prime Minister Viktor Orbán.[111]

Part of civil society's maturing is the diversification of its interactions with the government and other political actors. While opposition against an oppressive regime is the defining function of civil society before and during a democratic breakthrough, consolidation requires the establishment of both opposition and complementarity between civil society and centers of power. Martin Seymour Lipset and Jason Lakin, for example, emphasize that constructive interplay between civil society and political parties is crucial for democracy's functioning. They argue that civic associations can mediate between the government, parties, and society; they can also give rise to new parties and movements.[112] Similarly, Juan Linz and Alfred Stepan situate civil society in relation to both "political society" (comprised by political parties, institutions, and the state) and "economic society" (comprised by both public and private actors who shape the market).

Finally, more and more scholars are drawing attention to authoritarian governments' growing offensive against civil society groups—both within and outside their borders.[113] As Lilia Shevtsova recently made clear, since 2012 the Duma not only stripped Russian NGOs of financial aid from the West, but also passed laws that recriminalize libel, limit the right to free assembly, and expand the notion of "treason" to include involvement in international human rights work.[114] And the twenty-year prison sentence meted out to the Ukrainian filmmaker Oleg Sentsov in August 2015 signals the Kremlin's willingness to resort to brutal, unapologetic repression. China has also intensified repressions against civil society actors, augmenting its regular police force with the paramilitary People's Armed Police, and creating a special bureau (the *guobao*) within the Ministry of Public Security to target dissidents, scholars, journalists, and other activists. Chinese cyberespionage attacks target not only businesses and governments, but also international NGOs.[115]

Alexander Cooley reminds us that the turning point in the authoritarian offensive against NGOs came in the mid-2000s, in the wake of the "color revolutions" in Ukraine, Georgia, and Kyrgyzstan.[116] This was a crucial moment when NGOs receiving Western funding came to be regarded as agents of "foreign-sponsored regime change." Legal restrictions—ranging from outright bans to severe limits—were then put in place to "limit NGOs' access to foreign funds and even stigmatize groups as Trojan horses that covertly serve the West. In addition to the best-known cases in Eurasia and the Middle East, countries including Ecuador, Ethiopia, Hungary, India, Mexico, Pakistan, Sudan, Venezuela, Vietnam, and even Canada have moved over the last ten years to put a squeeze on the activities of foreign-funded NGOs within their borders."[117] At the same time, "governments have been promoting pseudo-NGOs and fake democracy monitors that emulate the form but not the substance of true civil society groups."[118] Better understanding of the full spectrum of ways in which authoritarian regimes are attempting to control civil society is thus likely to remain a priority on the academic research agenda in the coming years.

Political Culture

The working assumption of many pro-democracy initiatives is that democracy benefits from strong independent media embedded in a political culture that favors pluralism, compromise, and active citizen involvement in politics. These basic claims, however, have proven very difficult to investigate empirically, and scholarly literature on political culture remains relatively fragmented. From an initial focus on survey research, the field has expanded to include a variety of methodological and theoretical approaches (interpretive, social learning, and cognitive epistemological, just to name a few). It is now widely accepted that political culture is not reducible to public opinion—it evolves slowly and reflects attitudes and behavior patterns that take generations to form. Investigating political culture therefore requires interdisciplinary work that draws on history, anthropology, sociology, and other disciplines. Yet none of the currently available studies offer a broadly accepted conceptual approach for investigating how political culture affects democratization.[119]

Within our own analytic framework at the Project on Democratic Transitions, we see a supportive political culture as essential to the consolidation of a democratic polity. We understand political culture as consisting of both societal expectations and attitudes toward the political process, and behaviors that either perpetuate or transform these beliefs. We therefore value approaches that acknowledge both that political culture has the power to influence politics, and that political culture itself is subject to change and evolution. Two studies are illustrative here. Mayer Zald, for example, defines political culture as a broad set of attitudes, values, and expectations that shape the horizon of possible concepts and actions in a society. He therefore argues that "repertoires of contention" and ways in which problems are framed and solved are culturally constructed. These frames are influenced by mass media, and, in turn, they suggest how to protest, solve problems, and organize civil society.[120] In contrast, Jeffrey Goldfarb has recently analyzed examples from the former Soviet Union, the Middle East, and the United States to draw attention to the ways in which political cultures themselves can be reinvented and molded by social actors, thereby offering new resources and opportunities for democratization.[121]

Because political culture always has a long-term, historical component, in understanding the post-Soviet context, for example, it is essential to analyze not just the legacy of communism, but also Russia's longer social and political history. And in exploring the role of culture in democratization in places like Russia, China, or states which are home to large Muslim populations, we must be careful not to perpetuate deterministic stereotypes, which posit that the legacy of the tsars, "Asian values," or Islam are insurmountable obstacles to democratization. It is worth recalling that not too many decades ago Latin America was widely considered to be a poor candidate for democratization on the premise that Catholicism was antithetical to democracy. And, as Lilia Shevtsova often points out, there are large and resilient pro-democratic segments within Russian society today, despite the often overtly antidemocratic weight of Orthodox Christianity. Examples of successful democratization in Asia belie the notion that "Asian values" preclude democracy. And, despite ISIS and the failures of the Arab Spring, there are examples of successful coexistence of Islam and democracy, such as the increasingly vibrant democracy of predominantly Muslim Indonesia. It is thus essential to keep exploring the many difficult questions concerning realms of compatibility and conflict between various interpretations of Islam, on the one hand, and democracy and human rights, on the other. This vitally important process is taking place today both within and outside Muslim communities.[122]

A nondeterministic approach to culture is also supported by studies that examine how prior democratic experience influenced the global patterns of post–Cold War democratization. In the immediate aftermath of 1989, some posited that democratization should be severely disadvantaged in postcommunist states (given their Leninist and Stalinist legacies) and advantaged in former British colonies (which experienced British schooling and administration).[123] With time, however, it became clear that while prior democratic experience is helpful for new democracies, it is not an absolute prerequisite for democratization, and other factors—such as committed democratic leaders and social elites—can compensate.[124]

Finally, nondeterministic thinking about culture is especially important in the present context, when several authoritarian regimes are promulgating allegedly culture-specific antidemocratic counter-norms. China, for example, uses the language of "civilizational diversity" and the concomitant principle of sovereignty and noninterference, while Russia presents itself as a defender of "traditional values"—such as national culture, heritage, and religion. Both states are devoting massive resources and a global media presence to popularize these alternatives to democracy's universal concepts of liberty, human rights, and equality before the law.[125] It is important to remember that this is largely a false and ideologically deployed dichotomy—democracy does not have to be an alternative to either diversity or tradition, democracy's power consists in its potential to maintain respect for the local and the specific, while championing universal rights that protect human dignity and the right of citizens to determine their own futures. When the otherwise important concepts of diversity and tradition are used by autocrats in their informational war, they become inflammatory ideological weapons.

Independent Media

Much like a supportive political culture, a free and diverse media environment is widely acknowledged as a key element of consolidated democracies. Journalists often hold elected officials accountable and expose corruption and human rights violations. As Krishna Kumar emphasizes, independent media are the "lifeblood of democracy"; their presence helps improve the functioning of public institutions and encourages pro-democratic culture. Economic liberalization and media liberalization are mutually reinforcing, and NGOs and the media often have a positive, mutually supportive relationship.[126] Yet despite the media's crucial importance for democracy, systematic investigations of exactly how independent media affect democratization are still not very numerous, and much of the evidence remains suggestive rather than conclusive.[127]

Part of the difficulty comes from the fact that independent media in specific countries function within a broader global media environment, which can have both positive and detrimental effects on people's political involvement. First, there is a longstanding debate about whether contemporary media are more likely to lead to political mobilization or passivity and malaise. In 1999, for example, Kenneth Newton argued that general television programming is weakly tied to disengagement and malaise, while news tends to inform and mobilize viewers.[128] It would be worth probing whether this still holds today, when our lives are oversaturated with digital flows of information, lines between news and entertainment get blurred, and we are subject to the twenty-four-hour news cycle. In addition, the effects of the media are often "weak" in the sense that they can be diluted, deflected, or even destroyed by other, more salient, factors such as audience members' class, religion, age, education, gender, social networks, or personal values, knowledge and experience.[129]

Even with such caveats, existing literature suggests at least two important things about the relationship between the media and democratization. First, social media have become the most visible aspect of recent pro-democracy movements. As Eva Anduiza and her colleagues have shown, by 2012 internet usage appeared to have a positive impact on political involvement in most countries. This effect was clear across fifteen EU states and in Latin America, the Middle East and China, where younger organizers are increasingly Internet-savvy, and their campaigns rely heavily on new technologies. In addition, in Saudi Arabia, Egypt, Indonesia, and Pakistan, Internet usage tends to increase the consumption and production of political information, supports independent public opinion and civil society, and increases women's political participation.[130]

Secondly, while media proliferation is in itself insufficient to trigger a democratic transition, both proliferation and diversification of media outlets are important safeguards against backsliding, and hence a key factor in consolidation.[131] Jan Teorell, for example, points out that diverse media channels contribute to preempting antidemocratic coups by making information widely available. Since this effect is only possible when basic press freedoms are already guaranteed, it is unlikely before a transition to democracy.[132]

Finally, the important pro-democratic role of the media is sharply underscored by the lengths to which authoritarian governments go to deploy, coopt, and control media outlets. One of the first objectives in military coups is often to seize control of radio and television broadcasting centers, and both traditional and digital media are emerging as crucially important tools in the current authoritarian antidemocracy offensive.[133] As Ron Deibert points out, when it comes to cyberspace,

> authoritarians have developed an arsenal that extends from technical measures, laws, policies, and regulations, to more covert and offensive techniques such as targeted malware attacks and campaigns to coopt social media. Subtler and thus more likely to be effective than blunt-force tactics such as shutdowns, these measures reveal a considerable degree of learning.[134]

For example, many chat applications in China have built-in censorship and surveillance capabilities, and Russia's surveillance system collects copies of all electronic communications. Authoritarian rulers in countries including Venezuela, Egypt, Syria, Russia, Kenya, Saudi Arabia, and China deploy pro-government e-warriors and bloggers who seek to discredit and undermine democratic activists and initiatives.[135] As a result, bloggers and other e-activists have been arrested and subjected to repressions, and social media are no longer an unproblematic "tool of liberation." Activists and the democracy promotion community will need to find new ways to overcome this aspect of the authoritarian offensive. And, as Deibert persuasively argues, the undeniably important discussion initiated by Edward Snowden's revelations about NSA surveillance—the debate about how to strike a balance between liberty and security in the United States and the West—needs to be situated within this broader global context.[136]

Finally, traditional media have played an important role in the current information warfare, which seeks to present the West as defunct, hypocritical, and ready to threaten the sovereignty of states that do not share democracy's universal norms. As Alexander Cooley and others document, in 2013 the China Central Television (CCTV) had up to seventy international bureaus, Russia Today recently rebranded as RT and expanded its global reach, and in November 2014 a Russian state-run multimedia outlet called Sputnik was launched in thirty-four countries across the globe. These efforts, along with Iran's Press TV, Venezuela's Telesur media consortium, and a number of Gulf broadcasters, "pose a serious, amply funded challenge across large swaths of the world in covering news, setting journalistic standards, and editorializing about political events."[137]

GLOBAL NEIGHBORHOODS AND "UNDEMOCRATIC DIFFUSION"

In addition to promulgating antidemocratic counter-norms through a vast media offensive, a number of authoritarian states are also attempting to change international rules and reshape global institutions from within. In the UN, for instance, a group of authoritarians led by China, Russia, and Iran routinely blocks democracy-friendly initiatives and deemphasizes the importance of human rights. A Russian-led effort resulted in the UN Human Rights Council resolution of September 28, 2012, which sought to undermine the universality of human rights by calling for "better understanding and appreciation of traditional values" in human rights work.[138] During the 2014 Universal Periodic Review of Iran's compliance with human rights standards, states like Russia, China, Syria, and Cuba refrained from serious investigation.[139] Russia, together with other authoritarian Eurasian regimes, has worked to weaken the election-monitoring work of the Council of Europe and the OSCE. And major authoritarian powers now increasingly rely on regional organizations and networks (most importantly the SCO, the EEU, and the CSTO) to share security information, exchange surveillance tactics, and foster economic cooperation that seek to bypass Europe and the United States. Meanwhile, both China and some key Gulf countries have increased international lending and development aid which is not tied to democratic or good-governance conditionality.[140] These and other measures are attended by the rhetoric of "containing" the West, and the willingness to undermine democratic gains by both soft-power tactics and, in most extreme cases, military intervention—such as Russia's recent aggression against Ukraine.

It is important to keep these developments in perspective and remember that democratic norms and rules still command the allegiance of many states and citizens throughout the world. And the Community of Democracies and other intergovernmental and international organizations are working hard to keep universal, democratic norms at the forefront of global discussions and initiatives.[141] But we must recognize that the present activities of authoritarian states have far-reaching implications for both democracy and democratization. While in the early 1990s and 2000s scholars tended to focus on how external actors can strengthen democratization, it is now clear that external influences can either support or undermine new democracies. Some findings still hold: we know, for example, that support for democracy can be effective when it is tailored to local conditions, and that foreign-imposed regimes are unlikely to lead to democratization. But scholars are revisiting other earlier findings with an emphasis on the potentially damaging influence of activist autocratic regimes.

Perhaps the most widely used conceptual tool in analyzing external influences is Steven Levitsky and Lucan Way's idea of linkage and leverage. They defined leverage as "governments' vulnerability to external democratizing pressure," including both their "bargaining power vis-à-vis the West . . . and the potential impact . . . of Western punitive action."[142] Linkage, Levitsky and Way proposed, "encompasses the myriad networks of interdependence that connect individual polities, economies, and societies to Western democratic communities."[143] Linkage thus includes the full spectrum of economic, intergovernmental, technocratic, social, informational, and civil-society ties. The most important source of linkage, Levitsky and Way argued, is geographic proximity, but it is also created by historical connections and capitalist development. As we saw earlier, Levitsky and Way combined linkage and leverage with the incumbent's "organizational power" to explain when hybrid regimes democratize. They found linkage to be a more powerful predictor of democratization than leverage, and argued that its influence is especially important when the autocrat has low organizational capacity. Importantly, while they focused on the effects of Western linkage, they also observed that significant non-Western linkage (to Russia, China, or the international Islamic community) tended to blunt and counter the effects of Western democratizing pressure.[144]

Levitsky and Way sought to synthesize and go beyond earlier approaches to external influences on democratization, which posited five broad mechanisms: direct democracy promotion by the United States and Europe, governmental and nongovernmental democracy assistance, transnational advocacy networks, multilateral conditionality, and democratic diffusion.[145] It is worth recalling that—like linkage—the concept of "diffusion" was initially developed to examine the relationship between social, political, and geographical aspects of democratization. It, too, emphasized the effects of geographical proximity to democratic states. Unlike linkage, however, it referred to the relatively passive spread of democratic ideas and practices.[146] In 2000, for example, Jeffrey Kopstein and David Reilly found that within the postcommunist space, proximity to Western Europe was by itself a powerful predictor of democratic success. Like Levitsky and Way, they also made the important point that poor location could have detrimental effects on a country's "structure of interest, institutional reform, state behavior, and political discourse."[147] Similarly, working with a larger global sample in 2006, Daniel Brinks and Michael Coppedge found that proximity to either the EU or the United States increased the likelihood of democratization, while proximity to Russia was associated with greater likelihood of nondemocratic outcomes.[148]

Thus even before the current authoritarian pushback, scholars pointed to the limits of Western linkage, leverage, and other mechanisms of supporting democracy. Take the EU-accession process as one key example. In the early years of EU expansion, it seemed that accession conditionality would provide lasting pro-democratic incentives for aspiring members from the postcommunist and post-Soviet space. With time, however, it became clear that—despite a dense linkage network—the EU may be able to hold countries to democratic standards as conditions for membership, but it has only limited power in enforcing these standards after accession, whether via sanctions or political pressure.[149] Hungary's backsliding and Prime Minister Orbán's assault on the country's constitutional order dramatically exemplify this point. And, in light of the current Polish government's actions, we have yet to see what role the EU will be able to play in safeguarding democratic gains in Poland.

It is thus essential to further explore what one might call "undemocratic diffusion"—the many ways in which linkage with activist authoritarian players can support autocrats in smaller states. Precisely this focus on geography is at the heart of the recent "return of geopolitics." In January 2015, for example, Alina Mungiu-Pippidi stressed the importance of location in the increasingly divergent outcomes in East Central European and Central Asian post-Soviet states.[150] And Robert Kagan recently proposed that in the current environment democracy may falter if it does not get active support from the United States, as several key regions are now poised to follow in the footsteps of neighboring authoritarian powers.[151] Geopolitical analysis is clearly indispensable, not least because it reminds us that the neutral international conditions needed for either Western linkage or democratic diffusion are simply no longer there in many parts of the world. Yet it is crucial to do geopolitical thinking without succumbing to either determinism or resignation (e.g., the implicit or explicit claims that since Ukraine is within Russia's supposed "sphere of influence" its path to democracy is necessarily blocked.)

Finally, as a number of authors in this volume emphasize, any new thinking about the current state of Western leverage and multilateral conditionality has to recognize the crisis of democracy in democracy's historic heartland in Europe and the United States. A few facts should suffice to point to the scope of the problem. In the United States, the 114th Congress was elected in 2014 by 36.6 percent of eligible voters—the lowest turnout since World War II; and since it convened in January 2015, its approval ratings have hovered around 15 percent.[152] Meanwhile, the EU is witnessing undemocratic tendencies in both older and newer member states: throughout the continent, populist politicians are capitalizing on economic difficulties, xenophobia, and anti-immigrant sentiment, and far-right parties (sometimes with ties to Russia) exert direct and indirect influence on European politics.[153] Globally, the West is broadly perceived as divided and in crisis, especially since the 2008 financial meltdown. Against this background, and in the face of global cyberauthoritarianism, information warfare, and the sustained assault on universal democratic norms, scholars need to help identify what remains of the prodemocratic power of Western linkage, leverage, and ability to support democracy at home and abroad.

CONCLUSIONS

This chapter has sought to show that there are some important areas of scholarly consensus on democratization that can be useful to both policymakers and democratic activists. The key new theme perceptible in scholarship is that many political factors once thought to promote democratization can prove beneficial for either democrats or autocrats. This is true of elections and state capacity, as well as judiciaries and party institutions. One of the crucial challenges facing the scholarly community is therefore to carry out more fine-grained and historically attuned investigations of the precise circumstances and configurations when political factors play regime-sustaining or regime-supporting roles in authoritarian and hybrid regimes. As Jennifer Gandhi, Andreas Schedler and others argue, new approaches to the study of authoritarian elections are urgently needed. Likewise, as Francis Fukuyama and other analysts observe, much remains to be done in investigating the relationship between democratization and state capacity. Scholars have started to disaggregate this larger construct into components and examinine how these affect both democratization and autocratic survival. This area of research is especially important since much development-based democracy support rests on the notion that good governance and state capacity support democratization. In addition, more detailed knowledge of the relationship between judiciaries and both democratic and autocratic governments is in demand. And there is much we still need to learn about the causes and mechanisms of democratic backsliding—especially how to recognize its early stages in time to enact concrete preventative or countervailing measures.

In addition to the renewed efforts to understand what remains of Western pro-democracy linkage and leverage, there is a clearly growing need to better understand the ongoing authoritarian resurgence. The *Journal of Democracy* and the National Endowment for Democracy together produced a series of invaluable articles on this topic throughout 2015, starting what is likely to be a longer investigation that will be joined by wider circles of scholars. We need to continue researching the mechanisms whereby autocrats consolidate their power and prestige, and to better understand how they promulgate antidemocratic propaganda. Concurrently, it is essential to investigate factors that can protect civil society groups and individual democratic activists in the face of the challenges they face. It will also be necessary to contextualize today's authoritarian resurgence, so that scholars and policymakers alike can appreciate the significance of what is going on, but without exaggerating it, in order to keep adapting democracy support to the currently evolving conditions. And finally, it will be essential to continue identifying and addressing the causes of dysfunction within established democracies—both old and new—such as the workings of electoral systems, undue influence of money in politics, lack of transparency, citizen disillusionment, lack of adherence to international democratic norms, and myriad other factors. As we ask and seek to answer new questions about democracy and democratization, it is essential to remain open to interdisciplinary collaboration and new connections between macro-level findings and historical and sociological investigations of democracy's unique trajectories in diverse contexts around the world.

NOTES

1. Lilia Shevtsova, "Russia's Political System: Imperialism and Decay," *Journal of Democracy* 26, no. 1 (January 2015): 174.

2. Denis Volkov, "Marc Plattner: 'If Russia Had Become Democratic, the World Would Look Very Different Now,'" *Institute of Modern Russia*, April 2, 2015, http://imrussia.org/en/analysis/politics/2220-marc-plattner-if-russia-had-become-democratic-the-world-would-look-very-different-now.

3. Marc F. Plattner, "Is Democracy in Decline?" *Journal of Democracy* 26, no. 1 (January 2015); Francis Fukuyama, "Why Is Democracy Performing So Poorly?" *Journal of Democracy* 26, no. 1 (January 2015); Steven Levitsky and Lucan A. Way, "The Myth of Democratic Recession," *Journal of Democracy* 26, no. 1 (January 2015); Larry Diamond, "Facing Up to the Democratic Recession," *Journal of Democracy* 26, no. 1 (January 2015).

4. Samuel P. Huntington, *The Third Wave: Democratization in the Late Twentieth Century* (Norman: University of Oklahoma Press, 1991); Samuel P. Huntington, "Democracy's Third Wave," *Journal of Democracy* 2, no. 2 (Spring 1991).

5. Thomas Carothers, "The End of the Transition Paradigm," *Journal of Democracy* 13, no. 1 (January 2002): 6–9. This article generated much debate, which goes beyond the scope of this chapter. Since the "transition paradigm" came into question, some scholars choose to stay away from terms like democratic "transition" and "consolidation." In this chapter, I use these terms without assuming that they are part of a predictable or necessary sequence.

6. See, for example, a recent discussion of the "transition paradigm" in the aftermath of the Arab Spring: Larry Diamond, Francis Fukuyama, Donald L. Horowitz, and Marc F. Plattner, "Reconsidering the 'Transition Paradigm,'" *Journal of Democracy* 25, no. 1 (January 2014). See also Larry Diamond, "Elections Without Democracy: Thinking About Hybrid Regimes," *Journal of Democracy* 13, no. 2 (April 2002); Andreas Schedler, "Elections Without Democracy: The Menu of Manipulation," *Journal of Democracy* 13, no. 2 (April 2002); Steven Levitsky and Lucan A. Way, "Elections Without Democracy: The Rise of Competitive Authoritarianism," *Journal of Democracy* 13, no. 2 (April 2002); Nicolas Van de Walle, "Elections Without Democracy: Africa's Range of Regimes," *Journal of Democracy* 13, no. 2 (April 2002); Daron Acemoglu and James A. Robinson, *Economic Origins of Dictatorship and Democracy* (Cambridge: Cambridge University Press, 2005); M. Steven Fish, *Democracy Derailed in Russia* (Cambridge: Cambridge University Press, 2005); Steven Levitsky and Lucan A. Way, "Linkage versus Leverage: Rethinking the International Dimension of Regime Change," *Comparative Politics* 38, no. 4 (2006); Andreas Schedler, *Electoral Authoritarianism: The Dynamics of Unfree Competition* (Boulder: Lynne Rienner Publishers, 2006); and Lucan A. Way, "Authoritarian State Building and the Sources of Regime Competitiveness in the Fourth Wave: The Cases of Belarus, Moldova, Russia, and Ukraine," *World Politics* 57, no. 2 (January 2005). For a summary of how authoritarianism was brought back to the research agenda, see Jason Brownlee, "Authoritarianism after 1989: From Regime Types to Transnational Processes," *Harvard International Review* (Winter 2010); and Isobel Coleman and Terra Lawson-Remer, eds., *Pathways to Freedom: Political and Economic Lessons from Democratic Transitions* (New York: Council on Foreign Relations Press, 2013). And see the following thematic discussions: *Democratization* 21, no. 7, "The State-Democracy Nexus (August 2014); *Journal of Democracy* 26, no. 1, "Is Democracy in Decline?" (January 2015); *Journal of Democracy* 26, no. 2, "The Authoritarian Resurgence" (April 2015); *Journal of Democracy* 26, no. 3, "Authoritarianism Goes Global" (July 2015); *Journal of Democracy* 26, no. 4, "Authoritarianism Goes Global (II)" (October 2015); *Journal of Democracy* 27, no. 1, "The Authoritarian Threat" (January 2016).

7. For a discussion of the variety of definitions of democracy, see Jason Brownlee, "Authoritarianism after 1989: From Regime Types to Transnational Processes," *Harvard International Review* (Winter 2010).

8. For alternative thematizations, see, for example, Jan Teorell, *Determinants of Democratization* (Cambridge: Cambridge University Press, 2010); Coleman and Lawson-Remer, *Pathways to Freedom*; and Sergio Bitar and Abraham F. Lowenthal, eds., *Democratic Transitions* (Baltimore: Johns Hopkins University Press, 2015).

9. Jennifer Gandhi, "Elections and Political Regimes," *Government and Opposition* 50, no. 3 (July 2015): 446.

10. See, especially, Jan Teorell, "Statistical Evidence," in *Pathways to Freedom: Political and Economic Lessons from Democratic Transitions*, ed. Isobel Coleman and Terra Lawson-Remer (New York: Council on Foreign Relations Press, 2013), Kindle edition, 27–29; and Steven Levitsky and Lucan A. Way, *Competitive Authoritarianism* (Cambridge: Cambridge University Press, 2010), Kindle edition, 80–81.

11. Juan J. Linz, "The Perils of Presidentialism," *Journal of Democracy* 1, no. 1 (Winter 1990); Juan J. Linz, "Presidential or Parliamentary Democracy: Does It Make a Difference?" in *The Failure of Presidential Democracy: The Case of Latin America*, ed. Juan J. Linz and Arturo Valenzuela (Baltimore: Johns Hopkins University Press, 1994).

12. Scott Mainwaring and Matthew S. Shugart, "Juan Linz, Presidentialism, and Democracy: A Critical Appraisal," *Comparative Politics* 29, no. 4 (July 1997); Alfred Stepan and Cindy Skach, "Constitutional Frameworks and Democratic Consolidation: Parliamentarism versus Presidentialism," *World Politics* 46, no. 1 (1993); Timothy Colton and Cindy Skach, "The Russian Predicament," *Journal of Democracy* 16, no. 3 (2005).

13. Fish, *Democracy Derailed in Russia*, 248.

14. For a counterargument to the claim that presidential systems have negative consequences see, for example, Matthew Longo, "The HDZ's Embattled Mandate: Divergent Leadership, Divided Electorate, 2003," *Problems of Post-Communism* 53, no. 3 (2006). For an analysis of potential problems of parliamentary systems see Donald L. Horowitz, "Comparing Democratic Systems," *Journal of Democracy* 1, no. 4 (Fall 1990).

15. See, for example, Teorell, "Statistical Evidence," 21; and Jose Antonio Cheibub, *Presidentialism, Parliamentarism, and Democracy* (Cambridge: Cambridge University Press, 2006).

16. Levitsky and Way, *Competitive Authoritarianism*, 80–81.

17. Levitsky and Way, *Competitive Authoritarianism*, 81.

18. For a debate that provides a particularly useful summary of arguments on both sides, see Timothy M. Meisburger, "Getting Majoritarianism Right," *Journal of Democracy* 23, no. 1 (January 2012); and Andrew Reynolds and John M. Carey, "Getting Elections Wrong," *Journal of Democracy* 23, no. 1 (January 2012).

19. Martin Lipset and Jason M. Lakin, *The Democratic Century* (Norman: University of Oklahoma Press, 2004), argue that PR with presidentialism promotes fragmentation of political parties, and encourages the emergence of authoritarian executives; on the other hand Valerie Bunce, "Democracy and Diversity in the Developing World: The American Experience with Democracy Promotion," *The National Council for Eurasian and East European Research* (August 2005), argues that PR is needed in highly divided societies; Valerie Bunce and Sharon Wolchik, "Defining and Domesticating the Electoral Model: A Comparison of Slovakia and Serbia," in *Democracy and Authoritarianism in the Postcommunist World*, ed. Valerie Bunce, Michael McFaul, and Kathryn Stoner-Weiss, 134–154 (Cambridge: Cambridge University Press, 2009), argue for electoral systems that encourage inter-party cooperation. See also Arend Lijphart, "Democracies: Forms, Performance, and Constitutional Engineering," *European Journal of Political Research* 25, no. 1 (1994); Frank S. Cohen, "Proportional Versus Majoritarian Ethnic Conflict Management in Democracies," *Comparative Political Studies* 30, no. 5 (October 1997); Pippa Norris, "Choosing Electoral Systems: Proportional, Majoritarian and Mixed Systems," *International Political Science Review* 18, no. 3 (July 1997); G. Bingham Powell, *Elections as Instruments of Democracy: Majoritarian and Proportional Visions* (New Haven, CT: Yale University Press, 2000); and Joanne McEvoy and Brendan O'Leary, eds., *Power-Sharing in Deeply Divided Places* (Philadelphia: University of Pennsylvania Press, 2013).

20. An important moment in this debate was the 2002 *Journal of Democracy* forum titled "Elections Without Democracy," including Diamond, "Thinking about Hybrid Regimes"; Schedler, "The Menu of Manipulation"; Levitsky and Way, "The Rise of Competitive Authoritarianism"; and Van de Walle, "Africa's Range of Regimes." Also, Gandhi, "Elections and Political Regimes," 446, makes the important point that elections in authoritarian regimes are not solely a post–Cold War phenomenon; their relative paucity during the Cold War seems to have been an exception in a much longer historical trend.

21. Adam Przeworski, *Democracy and the Market: Political and Economic Reforms in Eastern Europe and Latin America* (Cambridge: Cambridge University Press, 1991).

22. Stephan Haggard and Robert Kaufman, *The Political Economy of Democratic Transitions* (Princeton, NJ: Princeton University Press, 1995).

23. Jennifer Gandhi and Ellen Lust-Okar, "Elections under Authoritarianism," *Annual Review of Political Science* 12 (June 2009): 405.

24. Gandhi and Lust-Okar, "Elections under Authoritarianism," 405.

25. Gandhi and Lust-Okar, "Elections under Authoritarianism," 405.

26. See, for example, Gandhi and Lust-Okar, "Elections under Authoritarianism"; Andreas Schedler, *The Politics of Uncertainty: Sustaining and Subverting Electoral Authoritarianism* (Oxford: Oxford University Press, 2013); and Gandhi, "Elections and Political Regimes." On single-party regimes, see Barbara Geddes, "What Do We Know about Democratization after Twenty Years?" *Annual Review of Political Science* 2 (June 1999); Benjamin B. Smith, "Life of the Party: The Origins of Regime Breakdown and Persistence under Single-Party Rule," *World Politics* 57, no. 3 (April 2005); and Kenneth F. Greene, *Why Dominant Parties Lose: Mexico's Democratization in Comparative Perspective* (Cambridge: Cambridge University

Press, 2007). On multiparty regimes, see Ellen Lust-Okar, "Elections under Authoritarianism: Preliminary Lessons from Jordan," *Democratization* 13, no. 3 (2006); Jason Brownlee, *Authoritarianism in an Age of Democratization* (Cambridge: Cambridge University Press, 2007); Jennifer Gandhi and Adam Przeworski, "Authoritarian Institutions and the Survival of Autocrats," *Comparative Political Studies* 40, no. 11 (November 2007); Jennifer Gandhi, *Political Institutions under Dictatorship* (Cambridge: Cambridge University Press, 2008); and Beatriz Magaloni, "Credible Power-Sharing and the Longevity of Authoritarian Rule," *Comparative Political Studies* 41, no. 4–5 (April 2008).

27. See, especially, Geddes, "What Do We Know about Democratization after Twenty Years?"; Greene, *Why Dominant Parties Lose*; Gandhi, *Political Institutions under Dictatorship*; Beatriz Magaloni, *Voting for Autocracy* (Cambridge: Cambridge University Press, 2006); Brownlee, *Authoritarianism in an Age of Democratization*; and Alberto Simpser, *Why Governments and Parties Manipulate Elections: Theory, Practice, and Implications* (Cambridge: Cambridge University Press, 2013).

28. See, especially, Gandhi and Lust-Okar, "Elections under Authoritarianism"; and Schedler, *The Politics of Uncertainty*, tables on pages 149–60.

29. Gandhi and Lust-Okar, "Elections under Authoritarianism," 415; Brownlee, *Authoritarianism in an Age of Democratization*; Valerie Bunce and Sharon L. Wolchick, "Favorable Conditions and Electoral Revolutions," *Journal of Democracy* 17, no. 4 (October 2006).

30. Schedler, *The Politics of Uncertainty*, 6–13.

31. Gandhi, "Elections and Political Regimes," 455, cites Marc Morjé Howard and Philip G. Roessler, "Liberalizing Electoral Outcomes in Competitive Authoritarian Regimes," *American Journal of Political Science* 50, no. 2 (April 2006); Daniela Donno, "Elections and Democratization in Authoritarian Regimes," *American Journal of Political Science* 57, no. 3 (July 2013); Jason Brownlee, "Portents of Pluralism: How Hybrid Regimes Affect Democratic Transitions," *American Journal of Political Science* 53, no. 3 (July 2009); and Michael K. Miller, "Electoral Authoritarianism and Democracy: A Formal Model of Regime Transitions," *Journal of Theoretical Politics* 25, no. 2 (April 2013).

32. Teorell, "Statistical Evidence," 21–22; Teorell, *Determinants of Democratization*. See also Coleman and Lawson-Remer, *Pathways to Freedom*.

33. The notion of "voting muscle memory" is from Coleman and Lawson-Remer, *Pathways to Freedom*, 5–6. For cautionary notes, see Gandhi, "Elections and Political Regimes"; Simpser, *Why Governments and Parties Manipulate Elections*. Adam Przeworski, "Acquiring the Habit of Changing Governments through Elections," *Comparative Political Studies* 48, no. 1 (January 2015), shows both sides of the coin: how difficult it is to get the first electoral turnover of power, and how much easier it is to get the next ones.

34. Gandhi and Lust-Okar, "Elections under Authoritarianism," 406.

35. Gandhi, "Elections and Political Regimes," 455–57, 462.

36. Przeworski, "Acquiring the Habit of Changing Governments through Elections."

37. Gandhi, "Elections and Political Regimes," 455–57, 463.

38. Francis Fukuyama, "States and Democracy," *Democratization* 21, no. 7 (2014): 1326.

39. See, for example, David Andersen, Jørgen Møller, and Svend-Erik Skaaning, "The State-Democracy Nexus: Conceptual Distinctions, Theoretical Perspectives, and Comparative Approaches," *Democratization* 21, no. 7 (2014); and David Andersen, Jørgen Møller, Lasse Lykke Rørbæk and Svend-Erik Skaaning, "State Capacity and Political Regime Stability," *Democratization* 21, no. 7 (2014).

40. Andersen et al., "The State-Democracy Nexus."

41. Fukuyama, "States and Democracy," 1328.

42. Samuel P. Huntington, *Political Order in Changing Societies* (New Haven, CT: Yale University Press, 1968), 397–98.

43. Juan J. Linz and Alfred Stepan, *Problems of Democratic Transition and Consolidation: Southern Europe, South America, and Post-Communist Europe* (Baltimore: Johns Hopkins University Press, 1996), Kindle edition, 579–82.

44. Sebastián L. Mazzuca and Gerardo L. Munck, "State or Democracy First? Alternative Perspectives on the State-Democracy Nexus," *Democratization* 21, no. 7 (2014): 1221–43.

45. Fukuyama, "States and Democracy," 1337.

46. See, for example, Michael Bratton, "Building Democracy in Africa's Weak States," *Democracy at Large* 1, no. 3 (2005): 12–15; Michael Bratton and Eric C. C. Chang, "State-Building and Democratization in Sub-Saharan Africa: Forwards, Backwards, or Together," *Comparative Political Studies* 39, no. 9 (2006).

47. Jessica Fortin, "Is There a Necessary Condition for Democracy? The Role of State Capacity in Postcommunist Countries," *Comparative Politics* 45, no. 7 (2012). In a more recent article, Fortin focuses on the distinction between administrative and coercive aspects of state capacity, Jessica Fortin-Rittberger, "Exploring the Relationship between Infrastructural and Coercive State Capacity," *Democratization* 22, no. 7 (2014).

48. On Russia, see especially Stephen Holmes, "What Russia Teaches Us Now: How Weak States Threaten Freedom," *American Prospect* 8 (July–August 1997); Stephen Holmes, "Simulations of Power in Putin's Russia," *Russia after the Fall*, ed. Andrew C. Kuchins (Washington, D.C.: Carnegie Endowment for International Peace, 2002); Valerie Sperling, ed., *Building the Russian State: Institutional Crisis and the Quest for Democratic Governance* (Boulder: Westview Press, 2000); Valerie Bunce, "Rethinking Recent Democratization: Lessons from the Post-Communist Experience," *World Politics* 55, no. 2 (2003).

49. Fish, *Democracy Derailed in Russia*, see especially "The Policy Problem: Economic Statism," 139–92.

50. Levitsky and Way, *Competitive Authoritarianism*, Kindle edition, 366–70, and "Measuring Organizational Power," 376–80.

51. Lincoln A. Mitchell, *The Color Revolutions* (Philadelphia: University of Pennsylvania Press, 2012).

52. Merete Bech Seeberg, "State Capacity and the Paradox of Authoritarian Elections," *Democratization* 21, no. 7 (2014).

53. See, for example, Rachel Kleinfeld Belton, "Competing Definitions of the Rule of Law, Implications for Practitioners," *Carnegie Papers, Rule of Law Series* (Washington, D.C.: Carnegie Endowment for International Peace, 2005).

54. See, for example, Theodore L. Becker, *Comparative Judicial Politics: The Political Functioning of Courts* (Chicago: University Press of America, 1987); Christopher M. Larkins, "Judicial Independence and Democratization: A Theoretical and Conceptual Analysis," *American Journal of Comparative Law* 44, no. 4 (Fall 1996); Albert P. Melone, "The Struggle for Judicial Independence and the Transition toward Democracy in Bulgaria," *Communist and Post-Communist Studies* 29, no 2. (1996); Stacia L. Haynie, "Courts and Revolution: Independence and Legitimacy in the New Republic of South Africa," *Justice System Journal* 19, no. 2 (1997); Shannon Ishiyama Smithey and John Ishiyama, "Judicious Choices: Designing Courts in Post-Communist Politics," *Communist and Post-Communist Studies* 33, no. 2 (2000); Ran Hirschl, "The Political Origins of Judicial Empowerment through Constitutionalization: Lessons from Israel's Constitutional Revolution," *Comparative Politics* 33, no. 3 (April 2001); Jennifer Widner, *Building the Rule of Law: Francis Nyalali and the Road to Judicial Independence in Africa* (New York: W.W. Norton, 2001); Gretchen Helmke and Frances Rosenbluth, "Regimes and the Rule of Law: Judicial Independence in Comparative Perspective," *Annual Review of Political Science* 12 (June 2009); Matias Iaryczower, Pablo T. Spiller, and Mariano Tommasi, "Judicial Independence in Unstable Environments, Argentina 1935–1998," *American Journal of Political Science* 46, no. 4 (October 2002); and Erik S. Herron and Kirk A. Randazzo, "The Relationship Between Independence and Judicial Review in Post-Communist Courts," *Journal of Politics* 65, no. 2 (May 2003).

55. Thomas Carothers, ed., *Promoting the Rule of Law Abroad: In Search of Knowledge 2006* (Washington, D.C.: Carnegie Endowment for International Peace, 2006); Gibler and Randazzo, "Testing the Effects of Independent Judiciaries on the Likelihood of Democratic Backsliding"; Coleman and Lawson-Remer, *Pathways to Freedom*, 26–27.

56. Gibler and Randazzo, "Testing the Effects of Independent Judiciaries on the Likelihood of Democratic Backsliding," 697.

57. Gibler and Randazzo, "Testing the Effects of Independent Judiciaries on the Likelihood of Democratic Backsliding," 697. See also James L. Gibson, Gregory A. Caldeira, and Vanessa A. Baird, "On the Legitimacy of National High Courts," *American Political Science Review* 92 (1998).

58. Tom Ginsburg and Tamir Moustafa, eds., *Rule by Law: The Politics of Courts in Authoritarian Regimes* (Cambridge: Cambridge University Press, 2008).

59. For more on the optimal benefits of independent courts for democracy, see Coleman and Lawson-Remer, *Pathways to Freedom*, 14, 26; and Linz and Stepan, *Problems of Democratic Transition and Consolidation*.

60. See, for example, the relevant country case studies in Coleman and Lawson-Remer, *Pathways to Freedom*.

61. Carothers, *Promoting the Rule of Law Abroad*, 7.

62. Gibler and Randazzo, "Testing the Effects of Independent Judiciaries on the Likelihood of Democratic Backsliding," 698. See also Lee Epstein, Jack Knight, and Olga Shvetsova, "The Role of Constitutional Courts in the Establishment and Maintenance of Democratic Systems of Government," *Law and Society Review* 35, no. 1 (January 2001): 117; Stephen B. Burbank, Barry Friedman, and Deborah Goldberg, *Judicial Independence at the Crossroads: An Interdisciplinary Approach* (London: Sage, 2002); George Tsebelis, *Veto Players: How Political Institutions Work* (Princeton, NJ: Princeton University Press, 2002).

63. Gibler and Randazzo, "Testing the Effects of Independent Judiciaries on the Likelihood of Democratic Backsliding," 706; Julio Rios-Figueroa, "Judicial Institutions," in *Routledge Handbook of Comparative Political Institutions*, ed. Jennifer Gandhi and Rubén Ruiz-Rufino (London: Routledge, 2015); Christopher Reenock, Jeffrey Staton and Marius Radean. "Legal Institutions and Democratic Survival." *Journal of Politics* 75, no. 2 (2013); and Joseph Wright, Simone Dietrich, and Molly Ariotti, "Foreign Aid and Judicial Independence," *Aid Data*, April 6, 2015.

64. Ginsburg and Moustafa, *Rule by Law*, 21.

65. Corrales, "The Authoritarian Resurgence: Autocratic Legalism in Venezuela," 39.

66. Martin Seymour Lipset, "Some Social Requisites of Democracy," *American Political Science Review* 53, no. 1 (1959): 75.

67. Fish, *Democracy Derailed in Russia*, 83. He mentions some of the key literature on this topic: Carles Boix and Susan C. Stokes, "Endogenous Democratization," *World Politics* 55, no. 4 (2003): 517–49; Valerie Bunce, "Comparative Democratization: Big and Bounded Generalizations," *Comparative Political Studies* 33 (September 2000): 703–34; Andrew C. Janos, *East Central Europe in the Modern World: The Politics of the Borderlands from Pre- to Postcommunism* (Stanford, CA: Stanford University Press, 2000); Martin Lipset, *Political Man: The Social Bases of Politics* (New York: Doubleday,1960); and Andreas Schedler, "Measuring Democratic Consolidation," *Studies in Comparative International Development* 36, no. 1 (Spring 2001): 66–92.

68. See, for example, Adam Przeworski, John Alvarez, Jose Antonio Cheibub, and Fernando Limongi, "What Makes Democracies Endure?" *Journal of Democracy* 7, no. 1 (1996): 39–55; Adam Przeworski and Fernando Limongi, "Modernization: Theories and Facts," *World Politics* 49, no. 2 (1997): 155–83; Adam Przeworski, Michael E. Alvarez, Jose Antonio Cheibub, and Fernando Limongi, *Democracy and Development: Political Institutions and Well-Being in the World, 1950–1990* (New York: Cambridge University Press, 2000); Torsten Persson and Guido Tabellini, "Democratic Capital: The Nexus of Political and Economic Change," *American Economic Journal: Macroeconomics* 1, no. 2 (2009): 88–126; Teorell, *Determinants of Democratization*; and Teorell, "Statistical Evidence." For an analysis that examines both domestic economic development and the international political system, see Carles Boix, "Democracy, Development, and the International System," *American Political Science Review* 105, no. 4 (2011): 809–28. The role of wealth in establishing democracy is questioned by Carles Boix, *Democracy and Redistribution* (Cambridge: Cambridge University Press, 2002); Boix and Stokes, "Endogenous Democratization"; and David L. Epstein, Robert Bates, Jack Goldstone, Ida Kristensen, and Sharyn O'Halloran, "Democratic Transitions," *American Journal of Political Science* 50, no. 3 (2006): 551–69.

69. Teorell, "Statistical Evidence," 22.

70. Przeworski et al., *Democracy and Development*.

71. Przeworski et al., *Democracy and Development*, 273.

72. See, for example, Teorell, "Introduction," in *Determinants of Democratization*, 1–15; and Gibler and Randazzo, "Testing the Effects of Independent Judiciaries on the Likelihood of Democratic Backsliding."

73. See, for example, Larry Diamond's chapter in this volume.

74. Teorell, "Statistical Evidence," 24.

75. On repression, see Barrington Moore, *Social Origins of Dictatorship and Democracy* (Boston: Beacon Press, 1966); Dietrich Rueschemeyer, Evelyne Huber Stephens, and John D. Stephens, *Capitalist Development and Democracy* (Chicago: University of Chicago Press, 1992). Quote from Mancur Olson, "Dictatorship, Democracy, and Development," *American Political Science Review* 87, no. 3 (1993): 567.

76. A closely related discussion concerns the role of rising literacy levels and education in protecting democratic gains, but evidence remains mixed. For further discussion, see Teorell, "Statistical Evidence," 28–29.

77. Isobel Coleman and Terra Lawson-Remer, "Political and Economic Lessons from Democratic Transitions," in *Pathways to Freedom*, ed. Isobel Coleman and Terra Lawson-Remer (New York: Council on Foreign Relations Press, 2013), Kindle edition, 3, 5.

78. Stephan Haggard and Robert Kaufman, "Economic Crisis and Withdrawal," in *The Political Economy of Democratic Transitions* (Princeton, NJ: Princeton University Press, 1995).

79. See, for example, Adam Przeworski et al., *Democracy and Development*; Rueschemeyer et al., *Capitalist Development and Democracy*; and Milan W. Svolik, "Authoritarian Reversals and Democratic Consolidation," *American Political Science Review* 102, no. 2 (2008).

80. For a key example of this debate, see Giovanni Sartori, *Parties and Party Systems: A Framework for Analysis, Vol. 1* (Cambridge: Cambridge University Press, 1976); and Nancy Bermeo, *Ordinary People in Extraordinary Times: The Citizenry and the Breakdown of Democracy* (Princeton, NJ: Princeton University Press, 2003).

81. See, for example, Matthew Goodwin, "Europe and the Ongoing Challenge of Right-Wing Extremism," *World Politics Review*, January 22, 2013, http://www.worldpoliticsreview.com/articles/12654/europe-and-the-ongoing-challenge-of-right-wing-extremism.

82. For more on the alarmist tendencies in the media and the need to return to sober comparative analyses, see Cas Mudde, "The Myth of Weimar Europe," *Open Democracy*, August 20, 2013, https://www.opendemocracy.net/can-europe-make-it/cas-mudde/myth-of-weimar-europe; Cas Mudde, "Russia's Trojan Horse," *Open Democracy*, December 8, 2014, https://www.opendemocracy.net/od-russia/cas-mudde/russia's-trojan-horse; and Cas Mudde, "'Weimar Greece' and the Future of Europe," *Huffington Post*, March 16, 2015, http://www.huffingtonpost.com/cas-mudde/weimar-greece-and-the-future-of-europe_b_6876944.html. See also Mitchell A. Orenstein, "Putin's Western Allies: Why Europe's Far Right Is on the Kremlin's Side," *Foreign Affairs*, March 25, 2014, https://www.foreignaffairs.com/articles/russia-fsu/2014-03-25/putins-western-allies; and Andrew Monaghan, "A 'New Cold War'? Abusing History, Misunderstanding Russia," *Chatham House*, May 22, 2015, https://www.chathamhouse.org/publication/new-cold-war-abusing-history-misunderstanding-russia.

83. Przeworski et al., *Democracy and Development*, 121.

84. Acemoglu and Robinson, *Economic Origins of Dictatorship and Democracy*.

85. Acemoglu and Robinson, "Our Argument," in *Economic Origins of Dictatorship and Democracy*, 15–47. For another argument emphasizing the importance of economic inequalities in democratization, see Boix, *Democracy and Redistribution*.

86. Teorell, "Statistical Evidence," 22.

87. See, for example, John R Freeman and Dennis P. Quinn, "The Economic Origins of Democracy Reconsidered," *American Political Science Review* 106, no. 1 (2012); and Stephan Haggard and Robert R. Kaufman, "Inequality and Regime Change: Democratic Transitions and the Stability of Democratic Rule," *American Political Science Review* 106, no. 3 (2012).

88. Coleman and Lawson-Remer, *Pathways to Freedom*, 11.

89. See especially Michael Ross, "Does Oil Hinder Democracy?" *World Politics* 53, no. 3 (2001); and Michael Ross, *The Oil Curse* (Princeton, NJ: Princeton University Press, 2012).

Other key works on the oil curse include Pauline Jones Luong and Erica Weinthal, "Prelude to the Resource Curse: Explaining Oil and Gas Development Strategies in the Soviet Successor States and Beyond," *Comparative Political Studies* 34, no. 4 (May 2001); and Jefferey Sachs, "The Curse of Natural Resources," *European Economic Review* 45 (2001).

90. Ross, *The Oil Curse*, 6.

91. Ross, *The Oil Curse*, 86–90.

92. For examples of supportive scholarship, see Fish, *Democracy Derailed in Russia*; Adrian A Basora, "Understanding Democratic Transitions," *The Best of FPRI's Essays on Democratic Transitions*, originally published October 2006 (July 2015): 1–6; and Lucan A. Way, "Authoritarian State Building and the Sources of Regime Competitiveness in the Fourth Wave: The Cases of Belarus, Moldova, Russia, and Ukraine," *World Politics* 57, no. 2 (January 2005). For examples of studies that question Ross's findings, see Daniel Treisman. "Rethinking Russia: Is Russia Cursed by Oil?" *Journal of International Affairs* 63, no. 2 (Spring-Summer 2010); and Stephen Haber and Victor A. Menaldo, "Natural Resources in Latin America: Neither Curse nor Blessing," *Social Science Research Network Working Paper,* June 15, 2010 (Oxford: Oxford Handbook of Latin American Political Economy, 2012).

93. Teorell, "Statistical Evidence," 25.

94. Fish, *Democracy Derailed in Russia.*

95. Fish, *Democracy Derailed in Russia*, 118–38.

96. Fish, *Democracy Derailed in Russia*, 140.

97. Fish, *Democracy Derailed in Russia*, 141.

98. See especially Mitchell A. Orenstein, "What Happened in East European (Political) Economies? A Balance Sheet for Neoliberal Reform," *East European Politics and Societies* 23, no. 4 (Fall 2009); Mitchell A. Orenstein, "Recovering from Transition in Eastern Europe: Neoliberal Reform in Retrospect," in *Developments in Central and East European Politics*, ed. Stephen White, Paul G. Lewis, and Judy Batt (London: Palgrave Macmillan, 2013); and David R. Cameron and Mitchell A. Orenstein, "Russia's Influence on Democratization in Post-Communist Europe and Eurasia," *APSA 2010 Annual Meeting Paper* (Rochester: Social Science Research Network, July–August 2010).

99. Linz and Stepan, *Problems of Democratic Transition and Consolidation*. For an argument about the importance of regulation that protects the poor, see Coleman and Lawson-Remer, *Pathways to Freedom*, 18, 228.

100. Linz and Stepan, *Problems of Democratic Transition and Consolidation*, 11.

101. See, for example, Linz and Stepan, *Problems of Democratic Transition and Consolidation*; Levitsky and Way, *Competitive Authoritarianism*; and Coleman and Lawson-Remer, *Pathways to Freedom*.

102. Przeworski, *Democracy and the Market*, 54–55.

103. Linz and Stepan, *Problems of Democratic Transition and Consolidation*, 414–17.

104. Thomas Carothers, *Critical Mission: Essays on Democracy Promotion* (Washington, D.C.: Carnegie Endowment for International Peace, 2004).

105. See, for example, Freedom House, *Study: Nonviolent Civic Resistance Key Factor in Building Stable Democracies* (New York: Freedom House, 2005); Adrian Karatnycky and Peter Ackerman, *How Freedom Is Won* (New York: Freedom House, 2005); Teorell, *Determinants of Democratization*; and Coleman and Lawson-Remer, *Pathways to Freedom*.

106. Stephan Haggard and Robert Kaufman, *The Political Economy of Democratic Transitions* (Princeton, NJ: Princeton University Press, 1995); Ruth Berins Collier, *Paths toward Democracy: The Working Class and Elites in Western Europe and South America* (Cambridge: Cambridge University Press, 1999); Bunce and Wolchik, "Defining and Domesticating the Electoral Model"; and Bunce and Wolchick, "Favorable Conditions and Electoral Revolutions."

107. Coleman and Lawson-Remer, *Pathways to Freedom*, 7.

108. Peter M. Lewis, Pearl T. Robinson, and Barnett R. Rubin, *Stabilizing Nigeria: Sanctions, Incentives, and Support for Civil Society* (New York: Council on Foreign Relation Center for Preventative Action and the Century Foundation, 1998).

109. Robert D. Putnam, *Making Democracy Work: Civic Traditions in Modern Italy* (Princeton, NJ: Princeton University Press, 1993); Umut Korkut, "The Position of Interest Groups in

Eastern European Democracies: Maturing Servicemen or Trojan Horses?" (presentation at the ECPR Joint Sessions of Workshops, Turin, Italy, March 2002).

110. Thomas Carothers, "Think Again: Civil Society," *Foreign Policy* 117 (Winter 1999–2000).

111. See, for example, Sharon L. Wolchik, "Can There Be a Color Revolution?" *Journal of Democracy* 23, no. 3 (2012); Bela Greskovits, *The Hollowing and Backsliding of Democracy in East Central Europe* (Budapest: Central European University Press, 2015); and Marc Morjé Howard, *The Weakness of Civil Society in Post-Communist Europe* (New York: Cambridge University Press, 2003).

112. Lipset and Lakin, *The Democratic Century*.

113. See, for example, Anne Applebaum, "Authoritarianism Goes Global (II): The Leninist Roots of Civil Society Repression," *Journal of Democracy* 26, no. 4 (October 2015); Douglas Rutzen, "Authoritarianism Goes Global (II): Civil Society under Assault," *Journal of Democracy* 26, no. 4 (October 2015); and Christopher Walker, "The Authoritarian Threat: The Hijacking of 'Soft Power,'" *Journal of Democracy* 27, no. 1 (January 2016).

114. Lilia Shevtsova, "The Authoritarian Resurgence: Forward to the Past in Russia," *Journal of Democracy* 26, no. 2 (April 2015).

115. Andrew J. Nathan, "China's Challenge," *Journal of Democracy* 26, no. 2 (January 2015).

116. Alexander Cooley, "Countering Democratic Norms," *Journal of Democracy* 26, no. 3 (July 2015).

117. Cooley, "Countering Democratic Norms," 53–55.

118. Cooley, "Countering Democratic Norms," 53–55.

119. See, for example, Gabriel A. Almond and Sidney Verba, *The Civic Culture* (Boston: Little, Brown, 1965); Putnam, *Making Democracy Work*; John A. Ferejohn and James H. Kuklinski, *Information and Democratic Processes* (Champaign: University of Illinois Press, 1990); and Richard Wilson, "The Many Voices of Political Culture: Assessing Different Approaches," *World Politics* 52, no. 2 (January 2000).

120. Mayer N. Zald, "Culture, Ideology, and Strategic Framing," in *Comparative Perspectives on Social Movements: Political Opportunities, Mobilizing Structures, and Cultural Framings*, ed. Doug McAdam, John D. McCarthy, and Mayer N. Zald (Cambridge: Cambridge University Press, 1996).

121. Jeffrey C. Goldfarb, *Reinventing Political Culture* (Cambridge: Polity Press, 2012).

122. See especially Larry Diamond, *The Spirit of Democracy* (New York: Macmillan, 2008); Larry Diamond, ed., *Political Culture and Democracy in Developing Countries* (Boulder: Lynne Rienner Publishers, 1994); Lilia Shevtsova, "Humiliation as a Tool of Blackmail," *American Interest*, June 2, 2015; Lilia Shevtsova, "Russia's Political System: Imperialism and Decay," *Journal of Democracy* 26, no 1. (January 2015); and Shevtsova, "The Authoritarian Resurgence." On Islam and democracy see, for example, John Donohue and John Esposito, ed., *Islam in Transition: Muslim Perspectives* (Oxford: Oxford University Press, 2007).

123. For a summary of this debate, see Fish, *Democracy Derailed in Russia*, 94–95. See also Ken Jowitt, *New World Disorder* (Berkeley: University of California Press, 1992); Jon Elster, "Constitution-Making in Eastern Europe: Rebuilding the Boat in the Open Sea," *Public Administration* 71, no. 1–2 (March 1993); Petr Kopecky and Cas Mudde, "Explaining Different Paths of Democratization: The Czech and Slovak Republics," *Journal of Communist Studies and Transition Politics* 16, no. 3 (2000); and Ken Jowitt, *New World Disorder* (Berkeley: University of California Press, 1992).

124. Fish, *Democracy Derailed in Russia*; Valerie Bunce, "Comparative Democratization: Big and Bounded Generalizations," *Comparative Political Studies* 33 (September 2000); Kopecky and Mudde, "Explaining Different Paths of Democratization."

125. Cooley, "Countering Democratic Norms."

126. Krishna Kumar, *Promoting Independent Media: Strategies for Democracy Assistance* (Boulder: Lynne Rienner Publishers, 2006).

127. On the shortcomings of earlier studies see, for example, Larry M. Bartels, "Messages Received: The Political Impact of Media Exposure," *American Political Science Review* 87, no. 2 (1993). See also Denis McQuail, *Media Performance: Mass Communication and the Public*

Interest (London: Sage Publications, 1992); and Katrin Voltmer, *Mass Media and Political Communication in New Democracies* (London: Routledge, 2006).

128. Kenneth Newton, "Mass Media Effects: Mobilization or Media Malaise?" *British Journal of Political Science* 29, no. 4 (1999).

129. Kenneth Newton, "May the Weak Force Be with You: The Power of the Mass Media in Modern Politics," *European Journal of Political Research* 45, no. 2 (2006): 225.

130. Eva Anduiza, Michael James Jensen, and Laia Jorba, eds., *Digital Media and Political Engagement Worldwide: A Comparative Study* (Cambridge, Cambridge University Press, 2012).

131. Teorell, *Determinants of Democratization*, 5–6, 67–69; Teorell, "Statistical Evidence." See also Pippa Norris, *Driving Democracy: Do Power-Sharing Institutions Work?* (Cambridge: Cambridge University Press, 2008); and Woodrow Wilson International Center for Scholars, *The Role of the Media in the Consolidation of Democracy* (Washington, D.C.: Inter-American Commission on Human Rights and the Organization of American States, 2005).

132. Teorell, *Determinants of Democratization*; and Teorell, "Statistical Evidence."

133. See, for example, Eric A. Nordlinger, *Soldiers in Politics: Military Coups and Governments* (Upper Saddle River, NJ: Prentice-Hall, 1977); and Ron Deibert, "Cyberspace under Siege," *Journal of Democracy* 26, no. 3 (July 2015).

134. Deibert, "Cyberspace under Siege," 65.

135. Deibert, "Cyberspace under Siege," 69–71.

136. Deibert, "Cyberspace under Siege," 74–77.

137. Cooley, "Countering Democratic Norms," 60. For more about the media offensives of various authoritarian regimes, see Andrew J. Nathan, "China's Challenge," *Journal of Democracy* 26, no. 1 (January 2015); Lilia Shevtsova, "Russia's Political System: Imperialism and Decay," *Journal of Democracy* 26, no. 1 (January 2015); Lilia Shevtsova, "The Authoritarian Resurgence: Forward to the Past in Russia," *Journal of Democracy* 26, no. 2 (April 2015); Abbas Milani, "The Authoritarian Resurgence: Iran's Paradoxical Regime," *Journal of Democracy* 26, no. 2 (April 2015); Alex Vatanka, "The Authoritarian Resurgence: Iran Abroad," *Journal of Democracy* 26, no. 2 (April 2015); Javier Corrales, "The Authoritarian Resurgence: Autocratic Legalism in Venezuela," *Journal of Democracy* 26, no. 2 (April 2015); Frederic Wehrey, "The Authoritarian Resurgence: Saudi Arabia's Anxious Autocrats," *Journal of Democracy* 26, no. 2 (April 2015); Peter Pomerantsev, "Authoritarianism Goes Global (II): The Kremlin's Information War," *Journal of Democracy* 26, no. 4 (October 2015); and Anne-Marie Brady, "Authoritarianism Goes Global (II): China's Foreign Propaganda Machine," *Journal of Democracy* 26, no. 4 (October 2015).

138. Cooley, "Countering Democratic Norms," 52.

139. Christopher Walker, "Authoritarian Regimes Are Changing How the World Defines Democracy," *Washington Post*, June 13, 2014; and Vatanka, "The Authoritarian Resurgence: Iran Abroad."

140. Cooley, "Countering Democratic Norms"; and Andrew J. Nathan, "China's Challenge," *Journal of Democracy* 26, no. 1 (January 2015).

141. See especially "The Warsaw Declaration" of the Community of Democracies, https://www.community-democracies.org/Visioning-Democracy/To-be-a-Democracy-The-Warsaw-Declaration.

142. Levitsky and Way, *Competitive Authoritarianism*, 40–41.

143. Levitsky and Way, *Competitive Authoritarianism*, 43.

144. Levitsky and Way, *Competitive Authoritarianism*, 50. For more on this point in the post-Soviet space, see David R. Cameron and Mitchell A. Orenstein, "Post-Soviet Authoritarianism: The Influence of Russia in Its 'Near Abroad,'" *Post-Soviet Affairs* 28, no. 1 (January–March 2012).

145. Levitsky and Way, *Competitive Authoritarianism*, 38–39. For a somewhat different classification of democracy promotion mechanisms, see Peter J. Schraeder, "The State of the Art in International Democracy Promotion: Result of a Joint European–North American Research Network." *Democratization* 10, no. 2 (2003): 23–24.

146. For an early definition of diffusion, see Everett M. Rogers, *Diffusion of Innovations*, 4th ed. (New York: Free Press, 1995), 10: "A process by which [1] an innovation is [2] communi-

cated through certain channels [3] over time among the members of [4] a social system," as cited by Daniel Brinks and Michael Coppedge, "Diffusion Is No Illusion: Neighbor Emulation in the Third Wave of Democracy," *Comparative Politics Studies* 39, no. 4 (May 2006): 468.

147. Jeffrey Kopstein and David A. Reilly, "Geographic Diffusion and the Transformation of the Postcommunist World," *World Politics* 53, no. 1 (October 2000): 25.

148. Brinks and Coppedge, "Diffusion Is No Illusion."

149. See especially Milada Anna Vachudova, *Europe Undivided: Democracy, Leverage, and Integration after Communism* (Oxford: Oxford University Press, 2005); and Milada Anna Vachudova, "Tempered by the EU? Political Parties and Party Systems Before and After Accession," *Journal of European Public Policy* 15, no. 6 (2008).

150. Alina Mungiu-Pippidi, "The Splintering of Postcommunist Europe," *Journal of Democracy* 26, no. 1 (January 2015).

151. Robert Kagan, "The Weight of Geopolitics," *Journal of Democracy* 26, no. 1 (January 2015). For similar arguments, see Carl Gershman's and Richard Kraemer's chapters in this volume.

152. Real Clear Politics, "Congressional Job Approval," *Real Clear Politics Polls*, http://www.realclearpolitics.com/epolls/other/congressional_job_approval-903.html; and Elizabeth Drew, "Why the Republicans Won," *New York Review of Books*, November 8, 2014, http://www.nybooks.com/blogs/nyrblog/2014/nov/08/midterms-why-republicans-won/.

153. See especially Cas Mudde, "Three Decades of Populist Radical Right Parties in Western Europe: So What?" *European Journal of Political Research* 52, no. 1 (2013).

Chapter Ten

Policy Conclusions and Recommendations

Adrian A. Basora and Kenneth Yalowitz

We entered this project from the perspective of foreign policy practitioners who had helped to formulate and carry out democracy support policies and programs in four different postcommunist states after the fall of the Berlin Wall and the dissolution of the Soviet Union. This experience was subsequently enhanced by more than a decade of retrospective study from our vantage points in the think tank and academic worlds.

The views expressed in this chapter are our own and do not purport to be those of our fellow chapter authors, nor of the Foreign Policy Research Institute (FPRI) or the Woodrow Wilson Center. Nevertheless, our conclusions have been greatly enriched by our interactions with these colleagues and with other participants in the FPRI Project on Democratic Transitions and in our joint Wilson Center conference.

Broadly stated, our conclusions are the following:

1. American foreign policy *should* continue to assign a high priority to supporting the spread and consolidation of democracy abroad—while recognizing that this objective remains only one among several major national security goals.
2. The implementation of such a strategy currently faces challenges that are far more difficult than those of the 1990s, principally a resurgence of authoritarianism and decline in influence of the liberal democratic model of political and economic development.
3. Given these adverse international circumstances, significant changes are needed in where and how we promote democracy. We argue for a policy of explicit balancing of our democratization goals with our

other national security goals. This should also include careful "triage" among potential target countries, so as to ensure that our various democracy support tools are used to optimal effect and do not prove counterproductive.
4. Our conclusions underscore the need for further academic research and public policy discussion, as we seek to design and implement new approaches tailored to these new circumstances.

THE NEW GLOBAL CONTEXT

As mentioned by several of our fellow authors, the past decade has been a much less auspicious period for the spread of democracy abroad than were the 1990s. Many would argue that the trend had already begun to shift well before 2006, starting with Vladimir Putin's gradual consolidation of autocratic power in Russia from 1999 onward, and accelerated by his strong negative reactions to the "color revolutions" in Georgia (2003) and Ukraine (2004). Certainly by 2006, Putin and other autocratically oriented leaders in the post-Soviet space had begun to develop active countermeasures against what they saw as an existential threat to their own regimes—a threat that they depicted as being aided and abetted by the United States and NATO, and by European Union (EU) expansion.

The autocrats' success in consolidating their own dictatorial rule, and in undercutting earlier democratization progress in a number of former communist countries, has been facilitated by the West's self-inflicted wounds and by other adverse developments. Negative fallout from the US intervention in Iraq, the failures of the Arab Spring, the Great Recession of 2008–2009, and the subsequent "Euro-crisis" and immigration flood are prime examples. These and other setbacks have fed into and strengthened a Putin-led counter-narrative that stresses national sovereignty, noninterference in internal affairs, and economic and social distinctiveness—as against what is depicted as the Western democracies' dissolute and chaotic societies. Conversely, the West's triumphalist democratic rhetoric of the 1990s began to lose much of its appeal as American and allied forces became bogged down in Afghanistan and then Iraq in 2001 and 2003. Not only did viable democracies fail to emerge in these two nations, but instability, civil war and extreme jihadist terrorism developed in both and have now spread to the broader region.

Furthermore, the 2008–2009 financial crisis and its Euro sequel took a significant economic toll, not only in the postcommunist region, but also within the EU, which had previously served as an economic and political Mecca for nearby countries in transition. This prolonged economic distress, compounded by the current refugee crisis, helped to foster democratic disillusionment in many transitional countries and to provide fodder for autocratically inclined leaders such as Viktor Orbán in Hungary and the Kaczinski brothers in Poland. It is also clear that both the image and the operational effectiveness of American and other democracies have diminished in comparison with the 1990s and earlier decades. One obvious consequence is that the US and European democratic "models" are currently seen by some as less attractive than in the past.

It is thus from a more challenged position that the Western democracies now face a very active and determined push by Putin and other autocrats to establish at home, and to propagate abroad, a carefully buffed "authoritarian counter-model." This model is based on autocratic leadership, xenophobic nationalism, stifling of dissent and free media, corrupt linkages of political and economic power, and rigged elections engineered to lend a veneer of legitimacy.

The current situation contrasts sharply with that of the early years after the fall of the Berlin Wall, when the West was riding high and memories of the East's deeply discredited communist predecessor regimes and their economic failings were fresh. Those autocrats who survived the tectonic shifts of 1989–1991 and were either in disarray or not yet in positions of dominance at the time have now had a full generation to remake their images, redesign their tactics, and consolidate their instruments of state control.

This current antidemocratic offensive may not be as systematic or as ideologically based as it had been during the Cold War, but it is nevertheless having a marked impact in Europe/Eurasia, as well as farther afield. One example is Russia's cooperation with and support of extreme right nationalist parties which oppose the EU in Western Europe and echo some of the anti-liberal themes coming from Moscow and other autocratic capitals. Further enhancing the appeal of the Eurasian authoritarian model is the dramatic rise of China's market-based prosperity and its seemingly stable political system. This, contrasted with the economic and political problems of the United States and of democratic Europe, contributes to an overall context that is significantly less auspicious for the spread of democracy globally. China's recent economic problems, however, could diminish this advantage.

To this new global dynamic must be added the Internet and the telecommunications revolution, which some authoritarians have learned to use for their own purposes. In fact, Moscow under Putin has transformed the use of these technologies and combined them with covert action measures to create a formidable new level of "information warfare" that is having an impact in many European countries and elsewhere.

The combination of all of these factors has not only slowed down the democratic diffusion effect that was so powerful in the 1990s, but it has also helped to undermine earlier democratic gains in certain postcommunist countries that had previously seemed well on their way towards democratic consolidation.

In sum, the conditions under which the West currently seeks to encourage democratization are less favorable and sharply different from those of the 1990s—the period when many of our current democracy support policies and programs were initially designed.

DEMOCRACY PROMOTION: NEW THINKING URGENTLY REQUIRED

The Western liberal democractic model is now more challenged than at any time since the fall of the Soviet Union. Not only does the West have to deal with the counterdemocratic models of Russia and China, but also with international terrorism, multiple Middle Eastern crises, an aggressive Iran, massive refugee flows, and prolonged economic malaise. We therefore believe that new policy thinking about democracy promotion and new operational approaches are urgently required.

With many of the most promising opportunities to build democracy already exploited, and with authoritarians consolidating their own grip and attempting to undermine democracy elsewhere, opportunities for spreading democracy abroad are now fewer and more challenging.

Furthermore, US efforts will remain somewhat handicapped until we can more fully live up to our own political ideals and economic potential at home, and thus regain the ability to project a more attractive international image. The same can be said of the EU as it struggles with its serious economic and refugee crises, handicapped by the weakness of its own supranational institutions.

Does this mean that America and Europe should focus only on democratic reform at home and give up on promoting democracy abroad? On the contrary, we have no doubt about the long-term superiority of liberal values and of the ability of our democratic and market institutions to self-correct. We also believe that this self-correction can be synergistic with strategically conceived and carefully targeted support for democracy abroad.

One approach to framing this core question inevitably takes us into the classic *realpolitik versus idealism* debate discussed in chapter 2. In this perspective, we incline toward the *realism* end of the spectrum. Precisely because we favor a foreign policy based on clear-eyed self-interest rather than moral imperatives, however, we see every reason for *not* abandoning democracy support. On the contrary, the time has come to up our game so as to ensure that what Larry Diamond describes in chapter 8 as our current "democratic recession" does not become a prolonged global democratic depression. Such an outcome would obviously have the potential to damage our own prosperity and national security—and potentially the quality of our own democracy.

Our central conclusion, therefore, is that *the consolidation and further spread of democracy abroad is in itself a major national interest for the United States, as well as for the EU countries and the world's other democracies.* Increased democratization abroad improves prospects for peace and stability, facilitates freer trade and stronger economic growth, and enhances the dignity and human rights of individual citizens. The greater the number of consolidated and effectively functioning democracies there are in the world, the more support there will be for a liberal and rules-based international order—an order that China, Russia, and other autocracies have been working to undermine. The spread of democracy is thus an integral part of our leadership role in the world, it strengthens our physical and economic security, and it ultimately enhances our own democracy and prosperity.

It is nevertheless true that poorly conceived interventions or attempts at premature or excessively rapid democratic transformation can produce results that may work against US interests, as Nikolas Gvosdev points out in chapter 2. Libya provides a good recent example. A more considered intervention, one that included a realistic postconflict stabilization strategy, might have produced a less damaging outcome. The Palestinian elections that gave Hamas control of Gaza may be another example of poorly timed or counterproductive interventions.

Nonetheless, we are convinced that carefully conceived and selectively targeted policies of democracy support, combined with well-executed assistance programs, will pay solid dividends over the longer term. But support for democracy should not be pursued either as a moral crusade or as a dominant theme that supersedes or attempts to ignore all other foreign policy considerations. Properly understood and carefully balanced within the overall cluster of interests that are invariably at stake in any bilateral relationship and multilaterally, the defense and encouragement of democracy abroad remains an essential part of any American policy that is based on realistic self-interest. The democracy goal should be factored into all major foreign policy decisions, even though at a given moment democratization may not be the primary objective in our dealings with a particular country or region.

We have so far not returned to an all-out Cold War in which the competition between democracy and totalitarianism presents ultimate existential questions. Logically, therefore, our need to make common cause with dictators who are "the enemy of our enemy" has diminished. Nevertheless, there are situations in which urgent military, nonproliferation, counterterrorism, or other strategic goals require transactional cooperation with entrenched authoritarian regimes whose domestic policies and political philosophy we oppose. Our dealings with Russia and China in the Iran nuclear negotiations, and with China regarding climate change, are recent cases in point. But these examples also make it clear that we do not need to give up on our overall support for democratization in order to achieve agreements that are based solidly on pragmatic mutual interest.

What is required instead is a more tailored democracy promotion approach. The need to deal realistically with powerful and newly aggressive autocracies such as Russia means that we may need to focus less on bilateral persuasion or assistance programs and more on international public diplomacy, on the use of international organizations to promote human rights and the rule of law, and on economic, educational and cultural exchanges. Many authoritarian regimes now place severe restrictions on foreign nongovernmental organizations (NGOs) working in-country, but whatever openings do exist should be used. In such cases, we will thus be sowing the seeds of democracy more indirectly, in the hope that they will ultimately germinate even in the least fertile ground.

In the case of highly consolidated dictatorships such as Azerbaijan, Kazakhstan, and Uzbekistan, clever autocrats can also try to box in Western democracy promotion programs to render them ineffective, to manipulate them in ways that help them strengthen their own domininance, or at least to maintain a veneer of legitimacy for their regimes. Having an in-country presence in such countries entails programmatic compromise. Operating online, however, or through NGOs without field-based offices in authoritarian countries can guard against guileless programming, as argued by Melinda Haring in chapter 5. When, inevitably, severe human rights violations occur in these autocratic countries they must be condemned publicly, rather than muting our criticism so as not to antagonize the regime—and this is hard to do if we are committed to maintaining in-country programs at all cost.

Furthermore, the United States need not always take the lead. In some cases, European or other established democracies may have more access or influence than does Washington, and these countries should be encouraged to take the lead. In chapter 6, Tsveta Petrova discussed the value added by the democracy promotion programs of some of the former communist countries themselves. In other cases, it may be best to rely on the influence and leverage of international organizations such as the World Bank, the UN or the Organization for Security and Cooperation in Europe (OSCE), and on global NGOs.

IMPROVING CURRENT APPROACHES: THE IMPORTANCE OF TRIAGE AND OF DIFFERENTIATED TACTICS

Building on the more subtle and differentiated approach with authoritarian countries outlined above, we believe that the "triage" concept outlined by Nikolas Gvosdev in chapter 2 merits further analysis and discussion. Following below is a preliminary outline for the design of such a system. The first category is the seemingly "lost causes." This group would include the deeply entrenched authoritarian states such as those just mentioned, along with certain other countries defined by one or more of the following characteristics:

- The effort in the particular country would be futile, waste resources and/or discredit democracy promotion by seeming to validate regime propaganda that equates these programs with aggressive intrusion into a country's internal affairs. Russia is a prime example.
- The effort would be counterproductive because of potential misuse by the regime to create a veneer of respectability. The example of Azerbaijan is discussed in chapter 5.
- The country and regime in question is so critical to other major and more immediately pressing national security concerns that we cannot afford to alienate the regime. Saudi Arabia is often cited as an example.

In these cases, the West should endeavor to plant seeds for the future as suggested previously, in the hope that some of them will eventually germinate and begin to create a more favorable environment for a future transition to democracy. We should also take advantage of ad hoc openings, such as the need of even the most deeply autocratic regimes to hold an occasional election with some semblance of competition, or to release political prisoners, so as to burnish its image internally or to gain greater international acceptance. On these occasions, we should take the fullest possible advantage of the opportunity to consolidate any possible increase in the degree of pluralism or freedom in that country. Any efforts, however, by these states to posit that they are in fact democratic should be vigorously countered and their human rights violations publicly condemned.

These approaches of ad hoc opportunism and of "scattering of seeds" for the long term were a successful component of what the United States and the Western European democracies accomplished during the Cold War with respect to the Soviet Union and Eastern Europe. These policies were particularly productive after the conclusion of the Helsinki Agreements in the mid-1970s, which opened the door to expanded initiatives in educational, scientific, and cultural exchanges, trade and investment openings, and other forms of exposure to the West. Arguably, the increasingly dense interactions that resulted helped to lay the groundwork for successful transitions to democracy in many of the postcommunist states two decades later. The number of eventual democratic leaders from countries such as Poland, Czechoslovakia, the Baltic States, Georgia and Ukraine who had studied or resided for periods in the United States provides one example of the potential for "delayed germination."

In addition to the hardened autocracies and a few other special cases, the remaining triage "baskets" can usefully be divided into three additional groups of countries. One consists of already-emerging democracies and of a few "hybrid" regimes that have already experienced substantial liberalization. A second group involves what had once seemed well-established democracies in which existing freedoms have more recently been imperiled, such as Hungary and potentially Poland. And a third group consists of what Steven Levitsky and Lucan Way call "competitive authoritarian regimes."

Our triage categories would thus look something like the following:

Group I: Lost causes. This is the category in which we do the least democracy promotion bilaterally and use the indirect methods sketched out above.

Group II: Investing in the most promising new cases. The most fertile ground for encouraging democracy may well be found in countries where autocratic regimes have recently fallen or have evolved into a "negotiated" transition (e.g., Tunisia, Ukraine, Myanmar and Indonesia), or where semi-autocratic governments are already visibly weak and opposed by broad-based indigenous movements that seek to create a more liberal form of government (e.g., Poland in 1989 and Venezuela currently).

Group III: Defending earlier gains. The problems of regression during the past decade also underline a renewed challenge for American and allied foreign policies in support of democracy—a challenge that had been largely absent in the 1990s. In view of the aggressive tactics and the partial successes of the authoritarian counteroffensive, we now need to help protect existing or emerging democracies such as Poland and Hungary from sliding backward, and from foreign attempts to weaken or subvert them such as we have seen in Ukraine, Moldova, and Georgia. The EU should take the lead in many of these cases via EU partnership programs or free trade agreements, and by more rigorously holding member countries such as Hungary and Poland to their professed democratic commitments. US technical assistance and political and security support should also be a major component.

Group IV: Dealing opportunistically with competitive authoritarian regimes. There is another large and quite important category of nondemocratic regimes in the political space that lies in between consolidated dictatorships in Group I and emerging democracies or the more promising hybrid regimes along the Freedom House spectrum that we would place in Groups II and III. This category includes difficult cases such as Armenia, Thailand, and Belarus—states that are currently run by strongly autocratic regimes, but that have felt obliged to retain enough of the trappings of democracy so that there is also a modicum of political competition or openness to the outside in order to maintain a degree of domestic or international legitimacy. These competitive authoritarian regimes provide difficult, but not totally infertile, ground for democratization. For example, they may conduct elections with at least some semblance of competition; permit a modicum of international travel and educational exchanges; and leave some space for private economic initiative, media openness, and other forms of pluralism. These openings can often be used to help lay some of the groundwork for eventual democratization through carefully calibrated and targeted democracy promotion programs.

CRITICAL RESEARCH AREAS AND POLICY ISSUES

The triage concept sketched out above clearly needs further research and fuller analysis and elaboration. Although much of our foreign policy focus is currently directed at urgent problems such as international terrorism and ongoing wars in the Middle East and South Asia, we need to pay more attention to creating successful democratic transitions in the current complex environment, to deciding where our main democracy promotion efforts should be focused, and to learning how to better use the tools presented by international media and information technology. The potential for far more effective use of the Internet and social media needs to be thoroughly vetted by the policy analysis and academic research communities, and discussed among the leaders of the United States, the EU countries, and other allied democracies.

Next, we need to study what does and does *not* work in existing US and European democracy assistance programs. Research on democracy promotion has blossomed in recent years, but, as Sarah Bush noted in chapter 4, there is still much to learn about where, why, and how democracy promotion is most effective. Studies that disaggregate the concepts of democracy and democracy promotion into more fine-grained indicators and measures are likely to be particularly valuable in this regard.

Research agendas in the academic and think tank communities also need to focus on the dynamics of democratization in the face of assertive authoritarianism. The *Journal of Democracy* in 2015 published a series of articles on the ongoing authoritarian resurgence, which should be followed by further investigation into how Russia, China, and other authoritarian regimes control their own societies and work to alter the rules-based international order. Aware that we are facing the proliferation of global cyber-authoritarianism, information warfare, and an increasingly systematic attack on universal democratic norms and human rights, it is essential to identify the best Western tools to promote democratic trends.

Finally, the alarming democratic deterioration in Hungary and the more recent problems in Poland are just two of many examples that suggest that we still have much to learn about the causes and mechanisms of democratic backsliding. We need to find ways to identify its earliest stages in time to prevent the deterioration of liberal democratic norms and institutions. And since much recent research suggests that many factors once believed to promote democratization—such as elections or state capacity—can be used to benefit either democrats or authoritarians, there is a clear need for detailed and historically informed studies of what sustains and what subverts various kinds of hybrid and authoritarian regimes.

FINAL THOUGHTS

We have tried to lay out a rationale and a schema for a more realistic and balanced approach to democracy promotion in keeping with our national values and core interests, and in the face of daunting new challenges. This task is an essential part of America's leadership role in maintaining the liberal world order. It is from that order that much of our prosperity and security derive, and which thus contributes to the preservation of our own democracy. It is our hope that the present volume will help provide the basis for a fuller debate on these issues not only in academia and the think tank world, but also in Congress, in the executive branch, in the media, and in the broader public discourse.

The hopes for a smooth, wholesale, rapid and continuous unfolding of transitions to democracy after the collapse of Soviet and Eastern European communism have proven overly optimistic. It is clear that political cultures change far more slowly than many had assumed during the ebullient 1990s, and autocrats have proven considerably more resourceful than expected in maintaining or reconstituting their monopolies of power. Nevertheless, based on a longer perspective on the impressive worldwide wave of democratization of the past three decades, we remain confident that democratization can be successfully nurtured through the pursuit of realistic policies.

Looking back at the Soviet model's legacy, it is evident that the atomization of the individual; the stifling of popular expression, political parties and interest groups; and the resilience of autocratic leaders after an initial period of state weakness have left us with formidable challenges today in most of the former USSR as well as in China, Cuba, and Vietnam. For these and similarly entrenched autocracies, strategic patience and the sowing of seeds for the long term are essential.

As for the rest of the world, a more nuanced and differentiated approach is called for in light of the new global context. Traditional approaches of institution-building and promotion of the rule of law must be accompanied by placing more stress on local democratic forces; extending multiyear block grants to local NGOs to ensure their sustainability; devoting more resources to educational and professional exchanges; transforming Western-sponsored NGOs into local organizations headed by local nationals; and talking less of democracy and more of human rights and basic freedoms. In sum, we will need to be more subtle and more indirect in much of what we do in support of democracy.

All of this will take time to show results, and thus patience and a long-term perspective will also be essential. Furthermore, the West's ability to promote broad-based economic growth and to refurbish and better demonstrate the effective functioning of its own political systems will also be highly important for promoting democratic growth.

Democratization progress in the coming years is likely to be more complicated and more gradual than it was in the 1990s. For Americans, however, democracy is who we are as a nation, and an essential part of how the United States became a leader among nations. And, for the five hundred million citizens of the EU, democracy is what has brought peace and prosperity to a continent previously torn by struggles among warring states and competing ideologies.

Democracy is also a system of government that, despite all its imperfections and oft-repeated prophesies of doom, has demonstrated an ability to take root in every single region of the world—despite repeated predictions that certain cultures and religions were totally incompatible with democratic values and institutions.

In conclusion, we restate our conviction that the United States and its democratic allies can and should continue to support the consolidation and spread of democracy abroad—albeit with new approaches based on a realistic assessment of what will work best in each specific situation. This is not only in keeping with our own fundamental values and aspirations, but also compatible with a careful longer-term reading of history. Let us therefore approach the recalibration of our policies in support of democracy not only with a cold eye, but also with renewed optimism and conviction.

Glossary

CEPPS: Consortium for Elections and Political Processes Strengthening

CIPE: Center for International Private Enterprise (one of the core institutes of the National Endowment for Democracy)

Consolidated Authoritarian Regimes (6.00–7.00) are countries that are closed societies in which dictators prevent political competition and pluralism and are responsible for widespread violations of basic political, civil, and human rights.

Consolidated Democracies (1.00–1.99) are countries that closely embody the best policies and practices of liberal democracy. Countries receiving a Democracy Score of 2.00–2.99 closely embody the best policies and practices of liberal democracy. However, challenges largely associated with corruption contribute to a slightly lower score.

Field-based organization: Nonprofit or for-profit organization with local offices that deliver programs; most organizations implementing democracy and governance programs are field-based. Also called implementers.

NDI: National Democratic Institute, one of the NED's core institutes

IFES: International Foundation for Electoral Systems

NED: National Endowment for Democracy, an independent grant-making organization that does not maintain field offices and distributes grants directly to indigenous NGOs

Semi-Consolidated Authoritarian Regimes (5.00–5.99) are countries that attempt to mask authoritarianism or rely on external power structures with limited respect for the institutions and practices of democracy. They typically fail to meet even the minimum standards of self-governing, electoral democracy.

Semi-Consolidated Democracies (3.00–3.99) are countries that meet relatively high standards for the selection of national leaders but exhibit some weaknesses in their defense of political rights and civil liberties.

Solidarity Center: one of the NED's core institutes

Transitional or Hybrid Regimes (4.00–4.90) are countries that are typically electoral democracies that meet only minimum standards for the selection of national leaders. Democratic institutions are fragile and substantial challenges to the protection of political rights and civil liberties exist. The potential for sustainable, liberal democracy is unclear.

USAID: United States Agency for International Development (government agency that distributes the bulk of US democracy dollars)

Index

About the Editors and Contributors

EDITORS

Adrian A. Basora is a former US ambassador to Prague and a Foreign Policy Research Institute (FPRI) senior fellow. He served as director of the Foreign Policy Research Institute's Project on Democratic Transitions and is currently codirector of the FPRI Eurasia Program.

Agnieszka Marczyk is a fellow at the FPRI Eurasia Program. She holds a PhD in intellectual history from the University of Pennsylvania.

Maia Otarashvili is a research fellow at the FPRI and manager of its Eurasia Program (previously the Project on Democratic Transitions). She holds an MA in globalization, development, and transition from the University of Westminster in London, with emphasis on postauthoritarian transitions.

CONTRIBUTORS

Sarah Sunn Bush is an assistant professor of political science at Temple University and a senior fellow at the FPRI.

Larry Diamond is a senior fellow at the Hoover Institution, Stanford University, and founding coeditor of the *Journal of Democracy*.

Carl Gershman is the president of the National Endowment for Democracy.

Nikolas K. Gvosdev is a professor of national security studies at the US Naval War College. He is a senior editor at *The National Interest* and a senior fellow of the FPRI Eurasia Program. The views expressed in this chapter are the personal ones of the author.

Melinda Haring is the editor of *Ukraine Alert*, a biweekly publication of the Atlantic Council. She is a fellow at the FPRI Eurasia Program.

Michal Kořan is the deputy director of Prague Institute of International Affairs. He is an assistant professor at the Masaryk University in Brno.

Richard Kraemer is a senior program officer for Afghanistan, Iran, and Turkey at the National Endowment for Democracy. He is a fellow at the FPRI Eurasia Program.

Tsveta Petrova is a senior analyst at the Eurasia Group. She holds a PhD in political science from Cornell University.

Kenneth Yalowitz is a former US Ambassador to Belarus and Georgia, a global fellow at the Woodrow Wilson Center, and the director of the MA Conflict Resolution Program at Georgetown University.